SYMBOLICALLY SPEAKING

VOLUME

AFRICAN LODGE #1

THE CONTEXT

JEFF MENZISE, PH.D.
with a brief history by P.M. Alton Roundtree

Symbolically Speaking, Vol. 1: African Lodge #1 - The Context.
Copyright ©2015 by Jeffery Menzise. All rights reserved. Printed in the United States of America. No part of this book may be used or reproduced in any manner without written permission from the author except in the case of brief quotations embodied in critical articles and reviews.
For information address Mind on the Matter Publishing, Post Office Box 755, College Park, Maryland 20741.

10 9 8 7 6 5 4 3

Cover Design by Jeffery Menzise, Ph.D.

Library of Congress Cataloging-in-Publication Data
Menzise, Jeffery,
    Symbolically Speaking, Vol. 1: African Lodge #1 - The Context/ by Jeffery Menzise, Ph.D.
Includes Cover Artwork & Design, and Foreword by Alton Roundtree

ISBN 978-0-9856657-7-7 (Hardcover)
ISBN 978-0-9856657-4-6 (Paperback)

Published in 2015 by
Mind on the Matter Publishing,
P.O. Box 755, College Park, MD 20741
Website: www.mindonthematter.com
Email: drjeff@mindonthematter.com
240-988-9639 office

Acknowledgements

I would like to thank the Most High and my Ancestors for their continued support and guidance as I strive to live on purpose. I'd like to extend special thanks to the Brothers of the Masonic Fraternity for doing their part, in their own unique way, so that our fraternity continues to shine. I am also grateful to my home Lodge St. John's #3 in Cincinnati, OH (MWPHGLOH), the David A. McWilliams, Sr. Research and Education Lodge (MWPHGLDC), and the Phylaxis Society, for the endless amounts of Masonic resources provided both directly and indirectly. Honorable mention also goes to Past Master Alton Roundtree for his contribution and encouragement, and to Brother John Hairston for sharing the original records of African Lodge with me. Appreciation is also extended to Brother Durrell Hodge for helping to silence some of the noise by sharing a document demonstrating the African orientation of those in the early African Lodge, and to Brothers A. Tehuti Evans and James Morgan, III for the many conversations and for your dedication to Masonic research and scholarship. Thanks also goes to the many people who have read my manuscript and have given me their honest feedback (whether I directly incorporated it or not, it was valuable to me). I also want to thank Morgan State University and the Institute for Urban Research for their support while completing this project. Saving the best for last, I would like to thank my wife, children and the rest of my family for their unlimited support and encouragement. I am thankful that you all were as excited as I, when it came to traveling to distant lodges and learning more about the African presence in Freemasonry.

Dedication

This book is dedicated to those Ancient souls who have ensured that their message of initiation and spiritual cultivation would live on forever; To those who were insightful enough to preserve the Ancient Mysteries in modern times; To those who labor tirelessly, to maintain these mysteries with integrity; Lastly, this book is dedicated to Prince Hall and his fourteen co-founders (which I collectively call the "Founding 15"), for having enough courage, insight, and perseverance to reclaim the birthright of African descendants, to freely travel and earn wages. Thank you for stepping up and not backing down.

Table of Contents

Foreword: A Brief History of African Lodge #1 and the Founding of Prince Hall Freemasonry..................p. vii

Preface..................p. xiii

Chapter 1: Introduction - African Lodge #1..................p. 21

Chapter 2: Ritual..................p. 43

Chapter 3: African Spiritual Systems..................p. 67

Image Gallery..................p. 99

Chapter 4: Reclaiming Our Stolen Legacy..................p. 111

Appendix A: African Lodge #459 Charter..................p. 157

Appendix B: Prince Hall Speech 1792..................p. 159

Appendix C: Prince Hall Speech 1797..................p. 167

Appendix D: John Marrant Sermon 1789..................p. 169

Appendix E: Martin R. Delany - The Origin and Objects of Ancient Freemasonry Its Introduction into the United States, and Legitimacy Among Colored Men..................p. 185

Appendix F: The African Lodge, an Oration: Delivered Before the Grand Master, Wardens, and Brethren of the Most Ancient and Venerable Lodge of African Masons..................p. 207

Index..................p. 211

Symbolically Speaking: African Lodge #1

Foreword

A Brief History of African Lodge #1 and the Founding of Prince Hall Freemasonry

Remarkably, it was in 1775 on the eve of the Revolutionary War that African Lodge No. 1 was established under the harsh conditions of slavery in Boston, Massachusetts. Massachusetts was the first colony in New England to establish and sanction slave ownership, and was a center for the slave trade throughout the 17th and 18th centuries.

Black Freemasonry began when Prince Hall, and fourteen other free Black men, were initiated into Lodge No. 441, Irish Constitution, attached to the 38th Regiment of Foot, British Army Garrisoned at Castle William (now Fort Independence), Boston Harbor on March 6, 1775. The Master of the Lodge was Sergeant John Batt. Along with Prince Hall, the other newly made Masons were: Cyrus Jonbus, Bueston Slinger, Prince Rees, John Canton, Peter Freeman, Benjamin Tiber, Duff Bufform, Thomas Sanderson, Prince Rayden, Cato Speain, Boston Smith, Peter Best, Fortin Howard, and Richard Tilley.

When the British Army left Boston in 1776, this Lodge granted Prince Hall and his brethren the Masonic authority to meet as African Lodge No. 1 (Under Dispensation), to march in procession on St. John's Day, and as a Lodge to bury their dead. However, the additional limitation was that they could not confer degrees nor perform any other Masonic "work", important privileges and authority given to regular Lodges. African Lodge No. 1 was organized on July 3, 1775, with Prince Hall as Worshipful Master. Official acknowledgment of the legitimacy of African Lodge No. 1 was made immediately by John Rowe of Boston, a Provincial Grand Master for North America holding authority from the premier Grand Lodge of Freemasons, the Grand Lodge of England. He, too, issued a permit authorizing African Lodge No. 1 to appear publicly in procession as a Masonic body for the purpose of celebrating the Feast of St. John and to bury its dead.

By the end of the Revolutionary War, in 1781, American White Lodges had begun declaring independence from the English Grand Lodge. They were strongly opposed to granting a charter to Prince Hall. Although the members of African Lodge No. 1 were free men, Black men were automatically assumed by the Masonic colonists to have "obligations" to masters. Thus, early colonial White Lodges in America, were not interested in interacting with or having Black members and they certainly were resistant to the idea of recognition of an African Lodge coming under their umbrella. Unable to receive a charter from the Grand Lodge of Massachusetts, African Lodge No. 1 applied to the Grand Lodge of England for a Charter. This application is demonstrated in an address delivered before the African Grand Lodge of Boston, Massachusetts No. 459, June 24, 1828, by John T. Hilton, on the Annual Festival of St. John the Baptist. Some extracts follow:

> In making this selection, you will permit me, first, to direct your attention to the origin of the Lodge to which you stand so dearly connected, and which this present year completes the forty-fourth Anniversary.
> It appears to be literal fact from the information which I have been able to obtain concerning this Institution, that the first petition for a Charter was presented by our beloved brother Prince Hall, Boston Smith, and Thomas Sanderson, to the Grand Lodge of Massachusetts, and although their petition appeared in proper form, it was rejected. The cause of which sprang from that difference which colour has established. But this refusal I can with pleasure state, did not dishearten them from their laudable purpose, but rather served as a stimulant to make further trial. And here let us, brethren, indulge in pleasing reflection, (which their actions fully justify) that the Founders and Patrons of our beloved Institution, after being thus denied the means of establishing the object nearest to their hearts, and while consulting on the subject, did exclaim, with all their enthusiasm and vigor of thought so peculiar to them, this shall never discourage nor move us from our objective; we have undertaken, and we will accomplish; our purpose are known the end of which we will see; we will

Foreword: A Brief History

therefore petition to foreigners, for that which is denied us at home; we will make our appeal to men, whose philosophic minds will not allow them to refuse any class of people the means of obtaining those blessings which the precepts taught by Free Masonry is capable of imparting on account of the colour of their skin. Accordingly their petition was sent to the Most Worshipful Grand Lodge of Scotland and Lord Howard, Earl of Effingham, then acting as Grand Master, under his Royal Highness; and Henry Frederick, Duke of Cumberland, not deeming it beneath his dignity to claim coloured men as brothers, as soon as it was convenient, transmitted to them a Charter, bearing the Grand Seal of London, accompanied with an elegant book of Constitutional Rules. On its arrival, their hearts throbbed with inexpressible joy and gratitude. With joy to see the fulfillment of their prophecy, and with gratitude, to witness the philanthropic spirit and benevolent kindness of their English friends.

For nine years the brothers of African Lodge No. 1, together with others who had received their degrees elsewhere, assembled and enjoyed their limited privileges as Masons. On March 2, 1784 and June 30, 1784, African Lodge No. 1 petitioned the Grand Lodge of England for a warrant (or charter) to organize a regular Masonic Lodge, with all the rights and privileges thereunto prescribed. Prince Hall petitioned the Grand Lodge of England through Worshipful Master William Moody of Brotherly Love Lodge No. 55 (London, England) for this warrant or charter. The charter was prepared and issued on September 29, 1784, although for reasons still unknown, it would be three years (1787) before African Lodge actually received it. The Grand Lodge of England assigned number 459 to African Lodge No. 1. Captain James Scott delivered the charter on April 29, 1787. James Scott was Captain of the sea vessel Neptune, and had also worked for John Hancock, who was one of the signers of the Declaration of Independence. By virtue of the authority of this charter, African Lodge No. 459 was organized one week later and began work as a regular Masonic Body on May 6, 1787. The warrant to African Lodge No. 459 of Boston is the most significant and highly prized document known to the Prince Hall Masonic Fraternity. The document is considered by Black masons

Symbolically Speaking: African Lodge #1

to be a national treasure[1].

Under the authority of the charter of African Lodge No. 459, Prince Hall established African Lodge No. 459 of Philadelphia on March 22, 1797 and Hiram Lodge No. 3 in Providence, Rhode Island on June 25, 1797. African Lodge of Boston became the "Mother Lodge" of the Prince Hall Family. It was typical for new lodges to be established in this manner in those days.

Shortly after establishing African Lodge No. 459 of Philadelphia, African Lodge No. 459 of Massachusetts chartered Union Lodge No. 3 and Laurel Lodge No. 4 of Pennsylvania. These Lodges remained subordinate to the Mother Lodge in Massachusetts until December 27, 1815, at which time the three Pennsylvania Lodges met in general assembly and organized First Independent African Grand Lodge of North America with jurisdiction over the State of Pennsylvania and the South.

African Lodge No. 459 was stricken from the rolls of the Grand Lodge of England before the 1813 merger of the Ancients (Grand Lodge of 1751) and the Moderns (Grand Lodge of 1717) (two rival Grand Lodges of England), along with many other North American Lodges (there were over 70 Lodges stricken from the roles of the Ancients and Moderns along with African Lodge No. 459). The Lodges were stricken from the roles because there had been no contact with the English Grand Lodges for many years.

From 1784 to 1813, African Lodge No. 459 was not deemed to be a Prince Hall Lodge. It was considered to be a regular Lodge that had not been accepted by predominately White American Lodges. Since they came from the same source and had the same authorization, African Lodge No. 459 did not seek recognition from other American Grand Lodges since there was no need to. There is no indication that African Lodge considered itself to be anything other than a regular Lodge until its Declaration of Independence in 1827. African Lodge likely did not know that it had been removed from the rolls of the Grand Lodge of England in 1813 and that the Lodge had been renumbered to 370 in 1792. It is likely that no Mason in America knew of the removal of African Lodge and other American Lodges until the 1860s when inquiries were being made to England about the status of African Lodge No.

[1] See Appendix A for a complete transcription of the Charter.

Foreword: A Brief History

459. From the time of the Revolutionary War until the late 1840s there was no contact between American Grand Lodges and European Grand Lodges, except by African Lodge #459. This was noted when the mainstream Grand Lodges held the 1845 Baltimore, Maryland Convention.

Prince Hall, the first Worshipful Master of African Lodge No. 459, died on December 4, 1807. His successors were Nero Prince (1808), George Middleton (1809-1810), Peter Lew (1811-1816), Sampton H. Moody (1817-1825), John T. Hilton (1826-1827), C.A. Deredomie (1828), Walker Lewis (1829-1830), Thomas Dalton (1831-1832), George Gaul (1833-1834), James H. Howe (1835-1836), and John T. Hilton (re-elected) (1836-1847). It was John T. Hilton who recommended adopting a Declaration of Independence from the English Grand Lodge in 1827—as the Grand Lodge of Massachusetts had done in 1772—thereby assuming the power and prerogatives of an independent Grand Lodge.

In 1827, African Lodge No. 459 followed the recommendation of WM Hilton and declared its independence from the Grand Lodge of England. It also stated its independence from all of the White Grand Lodges in the United States.

Newspaper clippings from 1775 to 1848 show that African Lodge No. 459 was engaged in performance of work germane to Lodges. Also, the Lodge members were active in endeavors to uplift the plight of Black people. Prince Hall and the brethren of African Lodge No. 459 submitted a number of petitions to the Massachusetts Legislature. An article in the May 12, 1831 Rhode Island American Newspaper (Providence, RI), Volume II, Issue 103, Page 2, is an example of newspaper coverage of the African Grand Lodge:

> Tuesday, The brethren of the African Grand Lodge assembled at their Lodge room in Cambridge Street, and opened on the entered apprentice step. Then the procession was formed, composed of brethren of St. John's African Lodge, St. John's Royal Arch Chapter, and of the Grand Encampment and Council of Sir Knights and Knights of Malta, and of the holy order of Knights of St. John of Jerusalem, with some visiting brethren, among whom, was the Most Worshipful Master of Harmony Lodge, Providence, R.I. under the jurisdiction of

Symbolically Speaking: African Lodge #1

this Grand Lodge, who honored the brethren on this joyful anniversary. The brethren, dressed and decorated in their appropriate Masonic insignia, bearing the regalia of the order, moved in solemn procession, bearing the banner of the order, up Cambridge Street, proceeded by the music from the excellent New York African Band, which is now on a visit in this city, then through Hancock Street, Myrtle Street, Belknap Street to the Meeting House, and followed by a discourse illustrating and ably enforcing the duty of masons…

African Lodge No. 459 ceased to exist in 1848 when the Lodge was split into three Lodges (Union Lodge No. 2, Rising Sons of St. Johns Lodge No. 3 and Celestial Lodge No. 4) to form the Prince Hall Grand Lodge (formerly African Grand Lodge) of Massachusetts.

The role that African Lodge No. 459 played in the development and legitimacy of Prince Hall Freemasonry is still relevant today. Any study or check on the history, regularity, or legitimacy of Prince Hall Freemasonry leads to African Lodge No. 459 and the charter that the Lodge received from the Grand Lodge of England in 1787. The original charter of African Lodge No. 459 is still in the possession of the Most Worshipful Prince Hall Grand Lodge of Massachusetts. The charter is displayed periodically on special occasions.

Alton G. Roundtree, 33°
Past Master Redemption Lodge No. 24
Author "Out of the Shadows: The Emergence of Prince Hall Freemasonry in America (Over 225 Years of Endurance)" and "The National Grand Lodge and Prince Hall Freemasonry: The Untold Truth"

Preface

Symbolically Speaking: African Lodge #1 is a presentation of theory. A theory designed to explore the early use of the word African when describing the "first" Masonic lodges constructed by those of African descent, in the Western world. First is in quotations because some argue that Masonic lodges, constructed by Africans, had long existed in the West, citing the temples and pyramids continually found in North, South, and Central America. These are seen as extensions of the temples and pyramids found in the Nile Valley[2]. Others may argue that there was no African "Freemasonry" in any hemisphere prior to the founding of the European Lodges. Those that maintain the latter perspective, often depend heavily on the non-existence of the actual words "Freemasonry" or "Masonry" or "Masonic" in the language of the cultures in question. Or they cite the unique nature of the obligations, signs, etc. of modern Freemasonry to distinguish it from anything found in ancient times. One will tell you that it is our "obligations" that make us Freemasons; dismissing when they were first made a Mason (which has nothing to do with an obligation or becoming a member of a Lodge). In reality, such arguments are as incorrect as saying ancient Africans didn't have a system of "yoga" simply because you don't find the word "yoga" in their texts or monuments; or the argument that there was no knowledge of geometry just because you don't find the word geometry written anywhere.

    The truth in each of these cases is evidenced by the symbolism left hidden in plain sight. The problem for many is they have not been trained to truly recognize and interpret the signs and symbols that have been left. They are perhaps even unaware of their existence. To exasperate this problem, many are overly dependent upon their "intellectual" training and their ability to regurgitate information and "facts" ad infinitum, at the expense of the true ac-

---

2   See Appendix E for Martin R. Delany's perspective of the African origins of Freemasonry. And "When Rocks Cry Out" by Horace Butler.

quisition of knowledge and understanding. Otherwise, they would be comfortable with admitting that the facts are themselves but a symbolical representation of a truth, that itself, extends well beyond the discoverable facts.

One recent example of this type of quandary occurred during a discussion of whether or not there appeared to be a "Black" man on the back of the two dollar bill. Based on all the information made available, it seems that there is no "Black" man on the two dollar bill. However, if one simply examines the two dollar bill, with their own two eyes, they will see that the argument is idiotic. Why? Because there is CLEARLY a representation of what appears to be a "Black" man sitting right there at the table (See Image 1). Now the information says, based on the original painting, Robert Morris occupied that position (See Image 2). In the original painting, the artist's rendition is consistent with other images of the wealthy former Senator and financier of the Revolutionary War; however, on the back of the two dollar bill, it couldn't possibly be him. Why? Because he did not have dark skin. Others try to explain this away as an ink smear, while others say that his "dark" face is due to how small his face is and that it may be due to a shadow. For the record, there are several people on the bill that are literally standing in the shadows and their faces are not dark. If it was an ink smear, the smear would not perfectly fit within the boundaries of the face (respecting his wig-line and collar). If it were an error, don't you think the Bureau of Engraving would have made the correction by now? Once these irrefutable points are made, then people will "move the goal line" by shifting the argument to focus on the question: "If it is a Black man, then who is it?" That we don't know. It may be no one in particular; it could simply be a symbolic representation of the Africans with whom the colonialists and some founding fathers had relationships and agreements[3]. Remember, the scene painted is fictitious. There was never a time when everyone represented actually sat in the same room together. In fact, some of the images are based on relatives of the actual people featured because they were not available for the artist to draw from life.

Again this is simply an example of how the over depen-

---

3   See The Barbary Treaties 1786-1816 and Treaty with Morocco June 28 and July 15, 1786.

Preface

dence on intellectualism and so-called information-based facts, and the strengthening of Rhetoric and Logic at the expense of thinking and seeking Knowledge and Truth, can cripple. It can make you deny what is plainly in front of your eyes. In this Western paradigm, bound within the limits of the Western worldview, information and intellectualism rules. The ability to be witty, argumentative, and slick while presenting the information you have acquired and memorized, is sadly mistaken for being wise, knowledgeable and truthful. The high position of such a lowly (as in basic) function, creates a state of arrogance, egoism and pridefulness, fueled by enough insecurities, that the wise should simply let burn itself out, rather than continue to engage in the dance of futility.

On the other hand, a symbolist sees this very same image, complete with the position that this "dark-faced" person occupies (that of Robert Morris), and begins to wonder what could the symbolism of the name have to do with the symbolism of the image? Naturally, and obviously, there is a sign hidden in plain sight; the name Morris etymologically traces back to the word commonly used by Europeans for dark skinned people, moor. As a symbolist, there is no need to deny the obvious to uphold certain "facts" and positions; there is only a desire to seek the truth hidden behind the veil. As Freemasons, that is what we are taught, or at least told, to do. As a Speculative Craft, we take the operative and more concrete tools and apply them towards more glorious and noble purposes; in this case, we take the obvious and apparent "facts" and transmute them to higher truths and understandings. All too often, we crawl out of darkness into the intellectual light, and find comfort there. By doing so we neglect the next task that we are charged with and actually were supposed to accomplish as part of our Passing: "to come out of ignorance into knowledge"; and at our Raising: "to seek diligently to find that the illustration of our symbolic teachings has infinite meaning." Sadly, when this approach is taken, some will try to dismiss it as being "speculative," as if it's a bad thing[4].

Specific to the notion that the term "African" had deep and symbolic meaning at the outset of what is currently referred to as Prince Hall Freemasonry, I present the following thesis:

---

[4] The irony is that we will also boast of being a speculative craft...go figure.

Symbolically Speaking: African Lodge #1

The founders of the African Lodge used the word African in the name of their first Lodges and first Grand Lodge as a symbolic cue indicating the true way to return to Light; the ways of our direct Ancestors. This Light that we are seeking as we trod the eastern path is encoded in the symbolism of Africa, her civilizations and cultures.

This is not *instead* of the modern symbols our Craft has adopted, but is in *addition too*. For in all actuality, many of these very symbols can be found in the operative crafts of our ancient African ancestors (this will be explored in greater detail in volume 2)[5]. To embrace and study the symbolism of African culture, as a descendant of the original African Lodge, is to further follow the nudge we received during our Raising to go from general knowledge to embracing self-knowledge, which is more than a notion. Immediately my fact-driven Bredren will ask "where is the evidence for that notion?" They will claim that "MWGM[6] Prince Hall and his co-founders named their initial Lodge "African Lodge #1" for the same reason why the A.M.E. Church[7] included African in their name… it's how we were identified at that time." I agree with this notion and reply, "the evidence to support my thesis is hidden in plain sight."

How often have you encountered references to Ancient Egypt while participating in Masonic ritual, study or discourse? All throughout the Scottish Rite, we find strong reference to the Hebrew culture and languages, which, itself is directly traceable to an Ancient African origin and/or influence[8]. As illustrated by the mythology surrounding the origins of the Scottish people, Scota who is considered the original "Queen of the Scots" was an Egyptian princess thought to have been exiled from her home and eventually settled in what is now Scotland[9]. Even our Sisters in the Order

---

5   See Images 17 - 20.
6   It is STRICTLY out of honor and respect for Prince Hall that I acknowledge him as MWGM. Even though he was never "officially" the Grand Master of any Grand Lodge, and thus NEVER officially a MWGM, he was acknowledged as such during his time. Additionally, he performed the duties of a Grand Master by granting dispensations and by giving permission to open other Lodges under his existing Charter for the African Lodge. He was also acknowledged as GM in several documents by others in his time.
7   Founded by African Lodge Masons Richard Allen, Abasalom Jones, etc. in Philadelphia.
8   See *Moses and Monotheism* by Sigmund Freud and the *Book of Exodus*
9   See *Scota, Egyptian Queen of the Scots* by Ralph Ellis; and *Ireland: Land of the Pharaohs* by Andrew Power.

Preface

of the Eastern Star have very specific and undeniable reference to Ancient African civilizations. There is no lack of symbolic representation; our issue is a lack of symbolic interpretation.

Notice I say nothing of whether the use of the term African was a *consciously* placed cue for us to seek further into African symbolism as it relates to the Masonic craft. This I do not know and feel it is irrelevant (although it would be interesting if we could determine this). According to many African worldviews (and even Western adaptations of African worldviews such as those espoused by Freud, Jung, and others), symbolic truths may often arise from the unconscious minds and souls of their authors, without them ever being aware of its existence. This does not in any way weaken the credibility of the symbol's use and purpose for existence, it simply means the person responsible for its manifestation only served as a vehicle for its expression. For example, if you explore the lives of certain great inventors, they all similarly give credit to some "higher force" working *through* them; stating how they would enter a state of receptivity, and allow for the symbolic images of what they were to do, to come into their sphere of awareness. After recording these symbols, time is spent in contemplation and reflection on the symbols, from which meaning and instructions were derived[10].

It is my firm belief that the founders of African Lodge #1 were divinely inspired by higher forces (be they Ancestors, God, or their own subconscious minds), to reclaim their ancestral teachings which are now cloaked in the symbolism of the European and Hebrew cultures. The renaming of African Lodge to honor one of its founders, Prince Hall, served as a conscious or unconscious lowering of the veil; concealing the direction from which our truest and purest form of Light is to come. If we weren't taught to fear our ancestral culture and symbolism, we'd have a better chance of realizing how much we actually resonate with it and we'd be more apt to acknowledge the strange sense of familiarity we get, when in the presence of our own...hopefully we will all have this opportunity in the near future.

This book is my contribution to the work of our Ances-

---

10   George Washington Carver, President George Washington and Nikola Tesla are remarkable examples of this process.

tors, who during the time of war and enslavement, prioritized the institution of the African Lodge. They were not deterred by the racism and ignorance of those who opposed their birthright to be acknowledged as Master Masons. Our Ancestors toiled for centuries in the Americas, as entered apprentices, fellow crafts, and even master masons, but THEY WERE NEVER GIVEN THE NECESSARY INFORMATION TO TRAVEL AND EARN THEIR WAGES. Instead, the benefits were received and enjoyed by others.

Our nation's capital, Washington, District of Columbia, is affectionately referred to as "Banneker City" in honor of the highly esteemed Ancestor, Benjamin Banneker. To date, no definitive record of his being an Initiated, Passed, and Raised Freemason exists, however, his skill as a surveyor, architect, and multi-genius are signs of him having the "Mark" of a Mason and definitely being of the Craft, both speculatively and operatively. His ability to pick up the work of Pierre Charles L'Enfant and design the capital city of Washington, DC, in all of its Masonic glory, is evidence enough. As the story goes, Banneker was originally hired by George Washington to survey the boundaries of the city alongside Andrew Ellicott, however, once L' Enfant was no longer on the job, the story claims that Banneker recreated the plans from memory (because he [Benjamin Banneker] was supposedly untrained).

As another example of things being hidden in plain sight, and argued against, by pure intellectualism and rationalization, I present the asinine notion that Mr. Banneker was untrained and laid out the design of Washington, DC strictly from memory. This statement, which is so widely accepted by people of all races and walks of life, flies in the face of all the other accomplishments that Benjamin Banneker achieved in his lifetime. To attribute his architectural genius to a photographic memory[11], denies the possibility that he actually understood how to design and layout a city, according to precise measurements, and directional orientation. We must remember that Benjamin Banneker was a mathematician and an astronomer. He studied the movements and cycles of the heavens, mastering it enough to publish a series of almanacs, successfully predicting weather patterns, solar and lunar cycles, planetary influences, as well as medically-based experiences for people born under

---

11 A photographic memory is in itself a wonderful skill and tool to have.

Preface

certain signs. I'd be willing to bet he had more than just a good memory, which is probably the reason why President George Washington (a Freemason) hired him in the first place. Again, hidden in plain sight, only requiring a bit of thinking and accepting of what is right in our faces.

I can clearly remember the day that the Masonic Compass and Square were first pointed out to me on the back of a car. I must have been exposed to thousands of them by that point in my life, yet I could not recall having ever consciously seen one. I similarly recall someone pointing out a Masonic Lodge to me in Cincinnati. I had driven this route hundreds of times yet I had never consciously recognized that the building on the corner had any Masonic affiliation (even though the Square and Compass are clearly displayed). Symbols have a funny way of being concealed and revealed. The beauty is that once it's revealed, it is no longer concealed. I will never not see the symbols on the backs of cars; I will never not see the lodge sitting so beautifully on the corner in Cincinnati; I will no longer miss the quick and subtle gestures given as a sign of a fellow Traveler in passing. And perhaps most importantly, I will no longer be confused about the symbolism embedded by our Ancestors in the name African Lodge.

For this reason, I have intentionally focused on African Lodge #1, as opposed to the chartered African Lodge #459. It is the former Lodge that initially fought for the rights of African descendants to be Freemasons. It is the former Lodge that was birthed by the fifteen Brothers initiated in Lodge #441, as a result of their steadfastness and devotion to the ideal that we are Masonic by right of birth. It was, in fact, African Lodge #1 that petitioned the Grand Lodge of England for a charter, and thus, it was African Lodge #1 that was recognized by the Grand Lodge of England and that was "renamed" African Lodge #459. And thus, African Lodge #1 represents the true African spirit which birthed African Lodge #459. It is a supreme example of how our Ancestors functioned regardless of European recognition, although it was overtly limited by the lack of a charter. It is here that I draw my inspiration to continue forward on this journey towards embracing and unveiling more Light, especially as it concerns our ancient Ancestral legacy and its modern manifestations. By gaining more Light by way of our Ancestors, we will continue to improve our place in this world and in our own lives.

We will infinitely raise our legacy and our labor in the Craft, by continuing to unearth documentation such as the oration posted in an online Masonic group by Bro. Durrell Hodge[12], which some have stated is one of the most important finds in Prince Hall Masonic History, and which Brother L. Ken Upchurch Collins interprets to reveal the following points:

1. Although African Lodge was not a Grand Lodge, she acted as one, mimicking Lodge St. Andrews who birthed other Lodges.
2. African Lodge used the term Grand Master as a title for Prince Hall, although African Lodge was not a Grand Lodge.
3. African Lodge members had a lecture of the membership using an African language [Mandinka] as their native tongue, meaning they were at least bilingual.
4. African Lodge actually had a table Lodge with the proper accoutrements to support its meeting.
5. African Lodge clearly stated in 1788 that they were not acknowledged by their White Brethren.
6. African Lodge members utilized the proper understanding of Biblical knowledge relating to White (European) descriptions of Blacks as the Sons of Ham and internalized it as something good.
7. African Lodge had a firm grasp of esoteric and exoteric Freemasonry and expounded on it beautifully.
8. African Lodge was clear in breaking down Masonic Jurisprudence in 1788 to justify the validity of slave holder and slave being both speculative and operative with a prime example of Egypt as the backdrop.

I submit to you Symbolically Speaking, African Lodge #1, in service to our Brothers, past, present, and future, praying that we ALL meet on the Level, bearing gifts of Truth and Light.

Jeff Menzise, Ph.D.
St. Kitts, West Indies
October, 2014
(With Recent Edits Made in August, 2015)

---

[12]   See Appendix F *"The African Lodge, an Oration: Delivered Before the Grand Master, Wardens, and Brethren of the Most Ancient and Venerable Lodge of African Masons."* This jewel is neatly tucked away in the Columbian Magazine, August 1788 issue, under the "Columbian Parnassiad" section, which is usually reserved for poetry and other creative works. This oration is also classified as "Humor" when searched within certain scholastic and academic databases...this may be an attempt to discredit the profound implications of such a documented speech.

Chapter 1
Introduction
African Lodge #1

Freemasonry is a "peculiar system of morality veiled in allegory and illustrated by symbols."[13] This dense and perhaps vague definition is best understood by deciphering each of the main words found therein, and then regrouping the definitions. Let's begin with the word "peculiar." This term, in its more common use, means "strange," "odd," or "unusual." Equally common is its referral to some level of exclusivity or being distinct in character. Both of these references are applicable as we shall soon see, however, it is the third definition that brings the most interesting Light to the subject. Not as popular as the two previous definitions, the word "peculiar" is also used to identify a parish or church that is not subjected to the jurisdiction of the diocese where it is located, because it is subject to the jurisdiction of a monarch or an archbishop; an authority that supersedes that of the diocese.

This last definition, on the surface seems to not fit (based on its obvious religious reference), however, if one could glean the underlying meaning, the relationship becomes clear. The idea of not belonging to the "natural" order of authority, based on one's relationship to a higher authority, is the basic underlying principle of the Masonic craft, specifically for Free-Masons. In other words, Freemasonry is about developing yourself to become consciously aware of your inherent autonomy and sovereignty. This is done by aligning your purpose with the Supreme Being (i.e., God), and thus, you relieve yourself of the burden of being a slave to others.[14] This is perhaps why no slave can become a Freemason.

---

13   This is the "ritual" definition associated with the EA initiation.
14   This perfectly aligns with the Ancient Egyptian correlation of Heru with the "will." We will explore this further later.

Symbolically Speaking: African Lodge #1

Anyone who has been "initiated" knows, that by being divested of your "valuables," we were paying but a small price for the abundance of wisdom that was later presented to us. In other words, we detached ourselves from the arbitrary value assigned to material possessions, and thus freed from their influence and control, in order that we may be granted access to the invaluable and liberating wisdom maintained by our Craft.

    Going back to an earlier definition of "peculiar," we find what would typically be labeled as negative characteristics (i.e., strange, odd, unusual), however, the enlightened individual will see these as indications of the road less traveled. In today's world, populated by herds of sheeple (sheep-people, those that blindly/unconsciously follow subtle manipulation and coercion), it is with GREAT pride that one boasts of being un-usual, or odd, and even strange (unfamiliar). These attributes, especially when associated with the Masonic mission to go from being good to being better, are the very same attributes that have made all great women and men in history known and revered by us all. In the stories of Jesus' life, it was the strange and unusual events, his "odd" nature that made him stand out amongst the masses. The reason why we know who George Washington Carver is today is because of his strange and unusual way of conceptualizing agriculture and his ability to communicate with plants. The reason why our MWGM Prince Hall is held in such high esteem is because he too thought differently, and understood that peculiarity, in all sense of the word, was his purpose and birthright. So yes, the system of Freemasonry is odd, it is unusual, and it is strange to those who are accustomed to simply dealing with the surface, oft-times spoon-fed aspects of life. It's as strange and unfamiliar as the depths of the ocean are to an individual who has spent their time tanning on the beach.

    As pointed out above, the word "peculiar" can also be used in reference to a certain level of exclusivity, and/or characteristics pertaining specifically to an individual, group, place, thing, etc. This definition is equally applicable to the Craft of Freemasonry, but not for the reasons many of us may have previously entertained. It is believed amongst many Masons and non-Masons alike, that the symbols, processes, allegories, and reasonings found within

Introduction: African Lodge #1

Freemasonry are specific ONLY to Freemasonry (this includes its many auxiliary organizations, orders and groups). The reality is, the exclusivity and peculiar nature of Freemasonry is shared by ALL organizations that have sought to obtain and preserve the ancient wisdom traditions found amongst our earliest civilizations; specifically, those Universal Truths found amongst the ancient traditions on the African continent. This is the very reason why in EVERY regular lodge, there must be a V of SL[15] (be it the Quran, Torah, Holy Bible, Pert Em Heru, Odu Ifa, Bhagavad Gita, etc.). This represents the universal nature of Divine Truth. And thus, those that bicker about whose religion is the one and only True way to God are looked upon with great pity by those who know better.

It is a well known and undisputed fact that Freemasonry and its ancestral predecessors are all designed to be hubs, a sort of living container, designed to preserve, comprehend, and actualize the now obscure teachings found amongst ancient cultures around the world. Each of these groups naturally utilize their own cultural, racial, historical, and political references to clothe the wisdom, however, the wisdom being clothed is EXACTLY THE SAME. This equally applies to our various world religions, at least to those that are based on Truth and universal principles. This is the reason why there is such a direct and seamless interplay between the Saints of Catholicism and the Lwa of Vodoun, the NTR of Kemet, the Orisha of Ifa, etc.

This is what Carl G. Jung hinted at when he elaborated on the notion of the "collective unconscious" and his notion of "archetypes." A large minority realize that the present day "occult" and "esoteric" groups all have some relationship to the ancient "Mystery Schools" and secret societies of Africa. This was symbolically "brought out of Egypt" by the Biblical Moses as the Puat Neteru, then formed into the Hebrew Kabbalah, and subsequently further disseminated[16]. We will revisit this notion later. Suffice it to say that the goals of Freemasonry are peculiar to ALL groups that desire to actualize the higher powers latent in the modern human being

---

15   Volume of Sacred Law (i.e., Holy Book)

16   See *Moses and Monotheism* by Sigmund Freud; *The Moses Mystery: The Egyptian Origins of the Jewish People* by Gary Greenburg; *The Ancient Mysteries and Modern Masonry* by Charles Vail; and *The Initiatic Experience: Ancient Pathways that Led to Your Initiation into Freemasonry* by Robert Herd.

through spiritual, mental and physical cultivation.

The peculiarity of Freemasonry is:

> *unusual and specific, based on its adherence to a Wisdom designed to align the aspirant with the Will and Power of the Supreme Being, thereby freeing them from the bondage experienced by the uninitiated.*

The next term for our examination is "system." While not as complex as "peculiar," the word "system" is equally important to our understanding of Freemasonry. The notion of a "system" brings to mind an organized process, a structure containing various individual components working together for the integrity of the whole. The overall health of a "system" is predicated upon every aspect of that system functioning according to its purpose and design. This demonstrates the interdependent nature of the individual parts, meaning what goes on in one aspect of the system, impacts what goes on in all other aspects of the same system.

The human body is an excellent example. We are quite familiar with the various organ systems (circulatory system, digestive system, reproductive system, nervous system, skeletal system, etc.), and how each system is made up of various parts. Each of these individual parts serves a particular purpose and carries out a very specific and often highly specialized function. We all know how the oxygen breathed into the mouth and nose enters the lungs (respiratory system), and from here, is transferred into the blood in exchange for carbon dioxide. The heart then pumps the enriched blood throughout every part of the body (circulatory system), providing nourishment to, as well as removing wastes from, every individual cell.

On a smaller yet equally complex scale, the human eyeball is also a system, which is part of a larger system that actually connects to, and is dependent upon, an even larger system. The system of the human eye is made up of highly specialized cells and structures including the sclera, lens, iris, cornea, and retina (with its rods and cones). This system connects via the rods and cones, to the optic nerve which itself is part of the peripheral nervous system, connecting directly to the central nervous system. These systems combine to give us the sense we call sight. We could delve deeply into the make up of any one of these systems to further illustrate the point, however, that is well beyond the scope of the current volume,[17] and should be clear to the reader at this point. Let us be satisfied by acknowledging the human body as a prime example of systematic functioning and the microcosmic example of what takes place in the larger universe, and simultaneously a macrocosmic example of what takes place on a cellular and microscopic level.

In regards to Freemasonry, the systemic nature of the Craft is found in the organized and steady progression from one degree to the next, and in the methods by which the symbolism, allegories, lectures, and oaths are designed to work together towards the construction of a new Temple. Each "house" and degree serves a specific purpose to the whole organization, although not many actually function in this manner. The system of Freemasonry also exists across time, tying together wisdom that originated in the most ancient traditions known to mankind into a modern organization. This network of initiation holds true to the concept of a system as detailed above. It perfectly illustrates a principle of Maat, which states "all things are interdependent and interrelated." So it is the wise person that asks not "*are* these things related?", but, instead asks, "*how* do they relate?"

In a statement, the systematic nature of Freemasonry is:

> *identifiable by its ordered progression from one degree to the next, and is supremely exemplified in its interdependent structure of officers (with their respective stations), lectures, signs, passwords, and lodge structure. And especially by it's network of wisdom spanning both time and across cultures.*

We shall now deal with what is perhaps the most obscure term in the ritual-based definition of Freemasonry, "morality." Almost immediately upon hearing or reading the word "morality," the mind tends to drift towards religion, codes of ethics, and other "rules" to be imposed upon the masses by a tangible and/or intangible authority. These rules are often used to define what is right and wrong, while simultaneously defining a particular code of conduct and presenting the values held by a particular group or person. These codes are based on various aspects of the human experience

---

17   The five physical senses will be detailed as Masonic symbols in volume 2.

and are greatly determined by one's culture-driven worldview, one's upbringing from childhood, one's religious orientation, and perhaps most saliently, it is determined by how one *chooses* to live their life.

Morality can also be goal-oriented, meaning it can be defined and judged based on current needs and situations. For example, a person whose chosen system of morality places high value in "not stealing," may indeed find themselves in a situation where the only way they can feed themselves and/or their family is to take that which they have not paid for. This happens in crisis situations like the aftermath of Hurricane Katrina. In such a situation, the value of "survival" may trump the value of "not stealing," and thus temporarily overwrites that particular aspect of the moral code. In the system of Freemasonry, the moral code is one that is not flexible nor is it situation specific. The morality of the Freemason is based on the common goal of making *good men better.* Now, this is, in itself, a very small but dense statement. This notion of making good men better, is one that is supported by the millennia of Ancient wisdom traditions designed to awaken the latent divinity found in all humans. Going from good to better is literally the taking of someone, who has demonstrated themselves worthy of further instruction and training (good), and revealing to them the scientific practices necessary for becoming an individual that regularly and consistently demonstrates, through their thoughts, speech, and actions, the awakened nature of their innate divinity (better).

And thus, the Masonic notion of morality is:

> **based upon the science of awakening and developing the innate divinity found within each human. The code of conduct, values, and practices related to this system of morality are directly linked with the time proven processes maintained by the initiates of the highest orders in ancient times.**

The next word to be explored, "veiled," is perhaps the single-most concept that grants Freemasonry its highest glory as well as its lowest levels of disdain when it comes to public opinion. The term "veiled" provides this society of secrets with the label of being a secret society (along with all of the negativity that the uninitiated or soured initiates have ascribed to the Craft). It is the veiling of "se-

Introduction: African Lodge #1

crets" that gives the air of mystery to the modern Craft. Based on its common definition and understanding, the word "veiled" literally means to "cover," "conceal," "hide," or otherwise obstruct from view. An interesting point about veils is the fact that they are usually created using a very light, sometimes sheer, translucent material. The nature of such material is designed to allow some passage of Light, without needing to remove or lift the veil; while simultaneously obscuring the view enough to prevent one from gaining a complete and even comprehensible glimpse of the whole.

As an example, an elder initiate once taught me that literacy and comprehension, in any language, is the first veil shrouding the information contained within the written medium (assuming that the person has sight). He showed me how a person incapable of reading words could see them on the page (the passage of Light without removing the veil), yet they were unable to gain any benefit from that Light unless they did what was necessary to remove the veil, i.e., learn to read. The purpose of allowing a glimpse of the Light (even if incomprehensible), is to hopefully inspire the individual enough to motivate their quest towards "more Light." Think about the millions of Africans enslaved by European nations and held captive here in the Americas. Many were forbidden to read and write in the language of their captors. This veil was intentionally maintained and even thickened by the trauma endured. In many cases, the small exposures to Light were significant enough to motivate the enslaved nobility to seek and acquire "more Light." Incidentally, Prince Hall was one that advocated strongly for the education of Africans and their formal training for the purpose of removing these veils.

In some cases, the veil is a tool for protecting both the Light bearer and the Seeker. The veiling of one's Light is sometimes necessary in order to avoid persecution and unwanted recognition. This is thought by many to be the reason behind the so-called secret societies going "underground." In ancient civilizations, the initiated class of Light bearers typically had no need to hide from the rulers because in many instances, they were the rulers. In fact, a part of obtaining their positions of authority was to successfully pass your initiation trials, and to demonstrate worthiness of such a position—nowadays, we base the acquisition of leadership on the votes of the uninitiated masses, many of which are not thoroughly awakened enough to see beyond the surface of what they are looking at, and thus, incapable of making the best decision.

The veiling of Light in Freemasonry:

> *is not to conceal it from the non-initiated, but to protect both the Light bearer and the profane onlooker from being harmed; the former by ignorant zealots fearful of what they do not understand and the latter by looking too deeply too soon at the tremendous nature of Light. The veil is usually translucent, allowing just enough Light to pass through to peak and motivate the interest of those Seekers who have yet to intentionally embark upon their path towards enlightenment.*

In regards to the term "allegory," Freemasonry, like many other wisdom traditions, employs parables, stories, images, songs and tales in order to communicate its deepest and most profound insights. The use of allegory is a technique that forces students to think and process information with both hemispheres of their brain[18]. The allegory is a way of making the teachings come alive; it provides the movement of life that is most often missing from strictly literal, logical, left-brained, non-illustrative methods. The method of ancient societies, specifically those in various regions of Africa, was to begin teaching via allegory at a very young age, using what we now call fairy tales and nursery rhymes, to impress upon the memory of children the inner workings of their cultural worldview. As the child grows older and begins to develop in their cognitive abilities, more and more of the insight imbedded in the juvenile stories is revealed; this is very similar to how our degrees are designed.

For example, the stories of *Anansi the Spider*, originating in West Africa, are fun and often comical ways of transmitting lessons in morality, the stories of how natural things came to be, and even lessons on how to think and conduct one's self responsibly. Another set of moral stories originating in Africa are the Odu Ifa'. This collection of stories used alongside the divination tools found among the Yoruba in Nigeria are complete with prescribed rituals, offer-

---

18 Neuro-anatomy and it's relationship to symbolism and initiation will be explored further in volume 2.

ings, and specific actions necessary to successfully resolve and or prevent potential problems. A modern version of African wisdom, being transmitted via allegory, is found in the *Tinga Tinga* cartoon series. Here again we find very important life lessons being presented, except this time it is animated and packaged to reach very young children. Some would argue that the only reason why stories exist is to allegorically impart wisdom of some sort. Regardless of the message behind the allegory, it remains one of the most powerful means of subtly transmitting important information.

In the King James Version of the Christian Bible we find in Matthew 13:10 - 23 where Jesus' disciples ask why he speaks in parables (allegory) when addressing the multitude. In essence, he responded that he was intentionally veiling the wisdom in order that he and they may be protected, and that those who are earnest seekers after the Light, will devote themselves to the path of obtaining it. He identifies his disciples as being amongst those who have been trained to comprehend the allegories and likens their minds to good and fertile soil:

> **10 And the disciples came, and said unto him, Why speakest thou unto them in parables? 11 He answered and said unto them,** Because it is given unto you to know the mysteries of the kingdom of heaven, but to them it is not given. 12 For whosoever hath, to him shall be given, and he shall have more abundance: but whosoever hath not, from him shall be taken away even that he hath. 13 Therefore speak I to them in parables: because they seeing see not; and hearing they hear not, neither do they understand. 14 And in them is fulfilled the prophecy of Esaias, which saith, By hearing ye shall hear, and shall not understand; and seeing ye shall see, and shall not perceive: 15 For this people's heart is waxed gross, and their ears are dull of hearing, and their eyes they have closed; lest at any time they should see with their eyes, and hear with their ears, and should understand with their heart, and should be converted, and I should heal them. 16 But blessed are your eyes, for they see: and your ears, for they hear. 17 For verily I say unto you, That many prophets and righteous men have desired to see those things which ye see, and have not seen them; and to hear those things which ye hear, and have not heard them. 18 Hear ye therefore the parable of the sower. 19 When any one heareth the word of the kingdom, and understandeth it not, then cometh the wicked one, and catcheth away that which was sown in his heart. This is he which received seed by the way side. 20 But he that received the seed into stony places, the same is he that heareth

the word, and anon with joy receiveth it; **21** Yet hath he not root in himself, but dureth for a while: for when tribulation or persecution ariseth because of the word, by and by he is offended. **22** He also that received seed among the thorns is he that heareth the word; and the care of this world, and the deceitfulness of riches, choke the word, and he becometh unfruitful. **23** But he that received seed into the good ground is he that heareth the word, and understandeth it; which also beareth fruit, and bringeth forth, some a hundredfold, some sixty, some thirty.

Allegories are known as "extended metaphors," using the comparison of seemingly unrelated things to demonstrate a point or to convey a message. Ancient Egyptians knew this as one of the core principles of Maat, namely the principle of interrelatedness (all things are related); and is commonly exalted by the "Hermetic" axiom "As Above, So Below," or by the Law of Analogy[19]. The wisdom afforded to the person who learns to see how all things are related is invaluable and taps directly into that Triune aspect of God which we call Omniscience (omni – all, science – knowing). Cultivating the ability to decipher analogies is one of the early aspects of Freemasonic initiation, although many may never truly benefit from a rigorous training along these lines. As students, we require teachers that have devoted themselves to these levels of training in order that they too may be guided along these lines. Unfortunately, many of our Lodges today have somehow slipped into the habit of valuing "memory work" above cultivating various other cognitive skills and processes (as mentioned in the Preface). Nonetheless, our current memory work has a fascinating history rooted in the "method of loci[20]" currently attributed to the Greeks and Romans but whose roots are in African traditions.

Kabbalistically speaking, the use of Memory, Logic, Information and Linguistic prowess is relegated to the lower levels of human capabilities. The higher reflections of these same qualities are found in the ability to Know, to be Wise in action, to have access to all necessary information, at any time, based on analogy, and having a deep Understanding of the core and basic principles behind all things.

To further utilize the "parable of the sower" presented by

---

19 See *Ancient Future* by Wayne B. Chandler
20 See *The Art of Memory* by Frances Yates

Introduction: African Lodge #1

Jesus, let us see how knowledge of seeds and their growth capabilities relate to human cognition. Notice how in each example, the seeds are the same and always represent the hidden wisdom found in the lessons being taught. The seeds themselves are examples of a concealed power, a mystery, a natural principle that remains hidden from the profane eyes of the uninitiated. In true allegorical fashion, let us return to the living example of George Washington Carver. His historical significance to the advancing of the agricultural sciences and the survival of the United States is based on his uncanny ability to unlock the mysteries contained within the seed. He is literally responsible for revolutionizing agriculture in the United States by sharing and demonstrating the power inherent in crop rotation (a science that had been utilized for millennia by African and other ancient societies). He was able to produce many products from plants including dyes, fabrics, foods, and fuels. He claimed to have been taught these processes by the plants and seeds themselves[21].

The occult (hidden) nature of seeds is also exemplified in the teachings of Rudolf Steiner. In the Waldorf system of education, one widely utilized meditation is on the seed. The pupil is directed to visualize a seed in its various stages of the growth-decay cycle, extending from the initial sprouting to its eventual replication in the fruits of its own progeny. An even deeper level to understanding the seed is knowing that before it can grow into "new" life, it must first decay and die. The seed, once planted, literally decomposes and rots, making the necessary chemical changes to bring forth the organism it is destined to become. This is the same whether we are speaking of an apple seed planted in the Earth or a sperm cell planted in the ovum; in each case the original seed is "destroyed" and converted into something entirely "new."

On the surface, the seed of a sunflower in no way resembles the beauty from which it spawned nor the beauty it is to become. Thus is the case for the allegory. On the surface, it appears to be only a story, a painting, a song; while aesthetically pleasing (hopefully), at first glance, it seems to be devoid of any further depth and value to the uninitiated. Proverbs 26 : 7, 9 informs us that:

---
21   See *The Secret Life of Plants*, documentary and book by Peter Thompkins and Richard Bird

> 7 The legs of the lame are not equal: so is a parable in the mouth of fools. 9 As a thorn goeth up into the hand of a drunkard, so is a parable in the mouth of fools.

The concept here is that the allegory, by design, is quickened or brought to life by the substantive nature of the medium in which it is received. Thus, the individual who casually stumbles upon the wisdom of an allegory (by the wayside) has no understanding of its value nor of its meaning, and thus, is not likely to keep it as such. Those that receive the wisdom and feel the need to keep it totally concealed (as in a concrete place) will preserve it for a while, yet have cut off the life qualities of the seed, and treat it simply as hoarded information with little practical use, however, it's use is time-sensitive based on its shelf life, and will eventually rot with the hoarder's mind. The mind that is like the thorny place is a mind that is replete with conflict. A mind that is scattered and unrested, a busy mind that flutters from one thought to another as a butterfly from one flower to the next, an undisciplined mind filled with concern, worry, and preoccupation with yesterday and tomorrow while totally ignoring today (the here and now), while fertile with potential has no clear place to allow wisdom the necessary room (solace) to take root, grow and produce its fruits[22]. This is the person who is thinking of a response while listening to another person speak, as opposed to actually seeking understanding of what is being said. They tend to be quick to respond by diverting to a different point as opposed to dealing with the original point. The good soil is a mind that has been thoroughly trained and disciplined to be "silent" and still; a mind that is capable of deep, protracted thinking, and is capable of focusing upon a singular thought or no thought at all. A mind thus prepared is a vacuum that, by the Laws of Compensation and Magnetism, is designed to be filled with Knowledge, Wisdom, and Understanding, after its own quality, which is hidden deep within the seed being planted.

---

22   And thus, the reason for silence in the early stages of initiation. This represents the meditative and contemplative state of mind necessary to endure the processes to acquiring wisdom.

Introduction: African Lodge #1

Hence, the "allegory" in Freemasonry is:

> the rendering of Wisdom into palatable chunks concealed from the profane by its apparently unrelated nature to the lessons it thus imparts. The key to unlocking this hidden Wisdom is found by the earnest efforts of the initiate towards the cultivation of the necessary condition of their own vehicles (body, mind, and soul).

The next term is "illustrated." This word is the complement to "veiled." Based on the Law of Complements, something that is veiled must have a means of being revealed. To illustrate is to illuminate, to illuminate is to shine Light, to shine Light is to increase perceptibility, consciousness and to bring about an awareness and understanding of that which is being illumined. To point out, to demonstrate, or to place upon a path is the only purpose of a teacher, guide, or initiator. To forewarn of the dangers along the way and to expand the realm of known possibilities in a manner that not only informs the student, but also improves their ability to know for themselves, are characteristics of the evolved and skilled Master. Simply stated, to illustrate is to provide a means for making an obscure notion easier to comprehend.

When thinking of illustrations, visual cues usually come to mind. For example, an illustrated book is a book that contains pictures. An illustrated passage is a passage that evokes mental images of what is being written. The proficiency of words to illustrate a point is directly related to the skillful use of descriptive language (adjectives) to "paint a picture." Good writers, orators and marketers can make you "see what they are saying." The notion that a picture is worth a thousand words nicely illustrates my point (pun intended). To properly illustrate a concept is to efficiently and effectively present knowledge in a simplified form, that is widely accessible to those who are duly prepared to receive it.

From the earliest days of life, we are taught by way of illustration. During our birthing process, we are literally brought out of the darkness of the womb into the world of external Light. Our eyes are thus opened for the first time to the external world in which all other Light is to be illustrated. During the "awakening" and "birthing" process of Neo in the movie *The Matrix*, he states that his "eyes" are hurting. His initiator, Morpheus, tells him that the reason behind his discomfort is that he has never used his eyes before. All the while, in his "pre-awakened" life, Neo believed that his eyes were open and fully functioning; that he was actually seeing reality in its truest form. It wasn't until he was brought into a new understanding, and once Light was shed upon the old, through illustration, that he was able to better comprehend reality as being real, and thus able to more efficiently and effectively manipulate it.

According to Isha Schwaller de Lubicz in volume 2 of *Her Bak*:

> We enter an inner world…where all mysteries of the Word are at work, the Word whose face, hr, is a mirror. Your own face, Her Bak, opens to the outer world by seven doors: three are double, opening eastward and westward; the seventh is one and central, yet it has a double interior canal with double function. The air of Shu bathes them all equally; but each takes from this same air, by adaptation, a different quality. The eyes, ar-ti, receive Shu's light. The nostrils, sher-ti, breathe his air. The central door, the mouth, ra, has a dual function, to admit offerings of food and to let the Master of the House, the active Word, emerge and show himself. Each door is specialized as to name and function; but the central door is known by the generic name of ra, opening, entry. Note that the eye, ar-t, the nostril, sher-t, and the ear mesdjer, have the same letter, r. You must learn the meaning of each door and, if you want to know where it leads you, study its form, name, place, and symbolism and it will tell you its function…you can speak of Shu's air, his light, his shadow, his dryness, because Shu is a primordial, elemental Neter. That is to say, with his twin Tefnut, without whom he couldn't have existed, he contains the four constitutive qualities of the world; but he causes the manifestation of the Word which becomes word, voice, kherw, all the voices of nature. That is why the ears are said to be living, for they are the doors that receive him. (pp. 28-29)

The above illustration of the various ways by which one may become illumined or enlightened is directly in line with our earlier discussion regarding the various ways we can illustrate (audio, visual, tactile, olfactory, gustatory), and how the effectiveness of such illustrations are directly related to the condition of the vehicle (body, mind, and spirit) of the receiver. Schwaller de Lubicz's illustration derives directly from the Ancient Egyptian worldview which, in superior fashion, recognized the human being as the true living symbol (allegory) for EVERY known and unknown divine

Introduction: African Lodge #1

principle (Neter), and through the decipherment of this allegory, one can become Master of both his personal and the Universal Lodge.

Based on the above discourse, we find that "illustrated," in true Masonic understanding is:

> to shine Light onto seemingly obscure and abstract representations in order to render them visible, comprehensible and practical to the aspirant. The true and living Word is the highest example and manifestation of Universal Truths, and thus shining Light on the same, constitutes the method used by Initiates of the highest Order.

We now come to the final term in our ritual-based definition of Freemasonry, "symbol." Symbol is the main tool of an allegory and represents a substitute for the reality underlying its message. The widespread use of symbol to represent reality has reached every culture and every creature on the planet. From the dance of the honey bee, to the utterances of the new born baby, and yes each and every letter of each and every word that you have read in this book thus far, are all symbols. By definition, a symbol is ANYTHING that represents something else. All symbols communicate messages, regardless of an individual's ability to decipher and/or recognize the symbol or the message. A symbol can be an object that represents a concept, such as a ring worn on a particular finger representing the union of two people in matrimony (marriage). A symbol can be a collection of symbols, joined together to represent a larger symbol that then represents a concept: the letters of various written languages, join together to form words, which themselves represent a concept (the letters "p," "e," "a," "c," and "e," come together to form the word "peace" which is also represented by the hand gesture "✌" or by the "☮" symbol itself, which is a representation of an abstract concept, specifically, the absence of war).

Movements can represent concepts, and thus are symbolic as well. For example, the dance of the honey bee tells other bees precisely where nectar has been found; there is also a dance amongst the Dogon in Mali, West Africa, that represents the orbit of the stars in the Sirius star system. Sign language is another symbolic movement that utilizes hand gestures and positions to represent letters, words and phrases. Patterns of light, hues, and shades are other forms of symbolism used to communicate and represent concepts. These include naturally occurring colors and patterns in wildlife, the complicated processes governing bioluminescence as found in fireflies and deep ocean fish, as well as the light emanating from celestial orbs (constellations and planets).

Perhaps the most beautiful aspect of symbols is their high degree of flexibility and utility. This allows for one symbol to have an infinite number of meanings and interpretations, which furthers their use by various cultures, organizations and even levels within the same organization or culture—in exclusivity and under veiled conditions. These properties are what allow symbols to both conceal and reveal (the Law of Complements). Every symbol is teachable and through the Law of Analogy, is capable of invoking higher order thinking and thus awakens cognitive abilities otherwise dormant (this idea will be explored in more detail in the second volume). The most powerful aspect is in their ability to subconsciously deliver encyclopedic amounts of information, in both simple and complex ways. In a word, symbols are the epitome of communication efficiency.

Thus, we find that the Masonic use of symbol is designed:

> *to train the mind of the initiate to develop the higher order thinking, discernment, and insight necessary to actualize the potentials purported by our Craft and the processes thereof. The use of symbol both conceals and reveals the Light to Seekers, according to their degree of devotion to the process.*

Based on our above treatment of the ritual-based definition of Freemasonry, I now provide the following translation of the original:

Freemasonry is a distinguished adherence to Wisdom designed to align the aspirant with the Will and Power of the Supreme Being, thereby freeing them from the fetters of enslavement. It is identifiable by its ordered progression from one degree to the next, and is supremely exemplified in its interdependent structure of officers (with their respective stations), lectures, signs, passwords, and obligations. It is based upon the science of awakening and developing

Introduction: African Lodge #1

the innate divinity found within each human. The code of conduct, values, and practices are directly linked with the time proven processes maintained by the initiates of the highest orders of ancient times and is exemplified by the various V o SL. The "secrecy" or slight obstruction of Light is not to conceal it from the non-initiated, but to protect both the Light bearer and the profane onlooker from being harmed; the former by ignorant zealots fearful of what they do not understand, and the latter by looking too deeply too soon at the tremendous nature of Light. The obstruction is usually translucent, allowing just enough Light to pass through, to peak and motivate the interest of those Seekers who have yet to intentionally embark upon their path towards enlightenment. The Light is regularly disseminated via palatable story chunks and ritual dramas, concealed from the profane by its apparently unrelated nature to the lessons it thus imparts. The key to unlocking this hidden Wisdom is found by the earnest efforts of the initiate towards the cultivation of the necessary condition of their own vehicles (body, mind, and soul). In true complementary fashion, Freemasonry shines Light onto seemingly obscure and abstract representations, in order to render them visible, comprehensible and practical to the aspirant. The true and living Word is the highest example and manifestation of Universal Truth, and thus shining Light on the same, constitutes the methods used by Initiates of the highest Order. Symbols are used, in any initiation system, to train the mind of the initiate to develop the higher order thinking, discernment, and insight necessary to actualize the potentials purported by our Craft and the processes thereof. The use of symbol both conceals and reveals the Light to Seekers, according to their degree of devotion to the process.

    The above working definition provides us the understanding necessary to push forward through the rest of this work. To see Freemasonry as a process for cultivating divinity within the individual, using the practical application of very specific techniques, including both allegory and symbol, we are more capable of using the Craft as it was intended to be used.

Symbolically Speaking: African Lodge #1

Let us now revisit the main thesis of this volume:

> *Prince Hall and his co-founders of the African Lodge of Freemasonry left instructions for their African descendants to seek Light by way of African spirituality, culture, and science. This directive is symbolically embedded in the name "chosen" for the embryonic or should I say resurrected Order of Masonry and was subsequently changed to further conceal this message.*

It should become more clear that Brother Prince Hall and his fourteen Brothers recognized certain powers within the Masonic Order and sought against all odds to (re)establish the Masonic bloodline and lineage for those whose ancestors hailed from the great civilizations found on the African continent. During the late 1700s, when American Africans were still locked away on plantations and the system of racism/White supremacy was deeply embedded within the fabric of society, the "Founding Fifteen" pressed White Masons to adhere to their own Masonic doctrine, and not reject an applicant based on race. They were initiated as Masons but were limited in their abilities to function beyond that of marching and burying their dead. When their attempts at equality failed in the racist womb of an embryonic United States, they continued in defiance of the existing social structure, and sought the authority of the "Mother Lodge", the Grand Lodge of England, the same authority to which the local White Lodges had at one time submitted.

It is from here that they were finally "accepted" to be Freemasons, entitled to all rights and privileges of every other regular Masonic Lodge. As stated by Past Master Alton Roundtree in the Foreword, up until this point, the "Founding Fifteen" were members of African Lodge #1. Once they received their charter from England, they became (were renumbered) African Lodge #459. I have intentionally honored African Lodge #1 in the title of this series because it was the ORIGINAL formation of our "Founding Fifteen" and it is the structure that was recognized by England, found worthy of a charter, and who received the necessary validation to receive and perform the duties of any regular Lodge. Perhaps most importantly, I am acknowledging African Lodge #1 because it is what we named ourselves. Even after the various number changes,

Introduction: African Lodge #1

we maintained our heritage as African descendants, by proudly waiving the banner of the African Lodge. I personally feel that by changing the name to honor PM Prince Hall, we have risked losing sight of what the "Founding Fifteen" left us: a clear sign identifying from where our spiritual and Masonic legacy extends.

This is significant because it is the very place that many Africans living in the "New World" can trace their genetic and spiritual legacies. The importance of this fact will be better understood once the reader explores the chapter on the psychology behind symbolism[23], for now, let me simply say that the affinity of a symbol makes it more likely to have a deep and lasting impact on those being trained by their use. It is part of the reason why it took so long for Greek aspirants to finally be admitted into the "mysteries" of ancient African societies; they had to become better acclimated to the culture and its symbolic sciences, which meant they had to first loosen their own culturally-implanted biases before being able to learn the ways of their African teachers.

For those of African genetic descent[24], specifically those of more recent African ancestry who continue to carry the phenotypes of their African ancestors, the Hebrew-based symbolism of the Masonic allegories of today serves the purpose of transmitting certain messages and enlightening those initiated through their use. This symbolism is effective, however, I maintain that there is a more powerful and spiritually relevant set of allegories and symbols that will better serve Seekers who are descendants of the African Lodge (keeping in mind that the process is intended to be transformative[25]).

For the purpose of this volume, I have decided to highlight various aspects of worldview (ontology, epistemology, and axiology) in narrative form, in order to set the context for a more in-depth and technical discussion of worldview in volume two. The depth found in our use of symbolism is either strengthened or weakened in direct relationship to the worldview by which we engage them, and thus, it is important for us to seek an understanding

---

23 See *Symbolically Speaking: African Lodge #1, Volume 2.*
24 Some will argue that this includes everyone based on the archaeological findings of the "oldest" human remains in Ethiopia
25 Transformation has three dimensions: psychological (changes in understanding of the self), convictional (revision of belief systems), and behavioral (changes in lifestyle).

of the general ontology[26] found on the African continent. Yes, there are many, many cultures found on the African continent, however, it has been well demonstrated that at the core of each, their worldviews are basically the same. Keep this in mind as you read the next chapters, which explore African-centered ritual, spirituality, and initiation.

    Much of what we consider to be Freemasonry today, is but a mere shadow of the power enjoyed by the ancients. Many of our Brothers and Sisters approach the Craft as if it is simply an extension of some of the more popular "Greek letter organizations" enjoyed during their college days[27]. There couldn't be a grosser mistake made. To relegate our Craft to the role and identity of a mere "social" and "charitable" order is to totally betray the sacrifices made by our modern "founders" who risked life and limb to bring forth our birthright as descendants of great ones, at a time when racists were promoting the idea that we weren't even human! It makes no sense that our more recent and modern ancestors would invest the amount of time and resources to the founding of the African Lodge for mere political, fraternal and social privileges. But instead, it makes perfect sense that the statements made within our ritual, lectures, and lessons (i.e., that human beings are capable of divine awakening by a prescribed process of initiation) are real, and that many have demonstrated this via their own application of the tools therein presented, and that THIS is what PM Prince Hall and his Bredren were seeking to reclaim for the fallen Hiram Abiff, whose story is interestingly similar to that of our African ancestors.

    The modern history of Freemasonry is replete with evidence of our craft being a true system of spiritual cultivation, culminating with the awakening of "God-men" and "God-women," by preserving and implementing the wisdom teachings of ancient cultures and civilizations (i.e., African, Indian, Chinese, Native American, Sumerian, etc.). The core philosophy of each of these civilizations

---

26   Ontology is the study of reality, the nature of being, and how things come to be. A more thorough explanation and exploration will occur in *Symbolically Speaking: African Lodge #1, Volume 2*.

27   This is not a slight to the "Divine Nine", all of which have done excellent work, and were founded by Masonic Brothers and Sisters. In a later chapter, we will look at them as Rites of Passage processes that assist with refinement and certain aspects of character development.

Introduction: African Lodge #1

is that humans are in fact divine beings that have, via creation and birth, descended down the proverbial "tree of life" and thus, have become ignorant of their divine capabilities while becoming concretized in their physical being. Additionally, the process of "awakening" is fully possible and has been methodically preserved by the various initiation traditions including that of Freemasonry.

In the next chapter we will look briefly into the science of ritual, and in the following chapters look into the core concepts of African spiritual traditions and hopefully shed more Light on what the founders of the African Lodge were possibly and symbolically leading us to. This journey requires a sort of flexibility of mind, as we attempt to expand our current conceptual paradigms and understanding of reality, because the information and concepts are based on an entirely different worldview (ontology, epistemology, and axiology).

Symbolically Speaking: African Lodge #1

Chapter 2
Ritual

What if Prince Hall and the other founding fourteen Brothers fully intended for us to recognize and utilize an African understanding of Freemasonry while practicing our Craft? What if we left everything the *way* it is, and simply shifted our perspective and understanding of *what* it is? What if we viewed our various Rituals, from an African worldview and perspective? What if we collectively understood ritual to be a tool for bringing together the various aspects of reality (social, personal, divine), melding them into one total experience? This perspective of ritual ultimately serves to expand one's understanding of the sacred, in order to encompass ALL aspects of experience, making everything in everyday life, a symbolic expression of limitless truth and an opportunity to commune with the divine. And thus, we'd return power to our practice.

Instead, many adopt the Western view of ritual, which isolates it within proscribed boundaries, limiting it to certain times, days, and settings...and thus the "holy" and so-called secular are made separate and are given room to exist as individual realities. This segregative notion of ritual and reality is what allows for the removal of sacredness from various aspects of life, leaving institutions and individuals vulnerable to the infectious agents of baseness and banality. It's the very thinking that rationalizes and formulates excuses for the "pedophile man of the cloth" who attempts to fulfill his sick cravings on his unsuspecting congregation.

According to Evan Zuesse[28], and what he calls the "ritual vision of life":

> Ritual itself is concerned first of all with ordering bodily movements in space, and clearly the body is the foundation for all awareness. But ritual not only provides for classifications of

---
28 See *Ritual Cosmos: The Sanctification of Life in African Religions*, p. 9.

Symbolically Speaking: African Lodge #1

bodily, social and especially cosmic space, it also seeks to interrelate these spheres in a harmonious and fruitful manner, so as to transform and renew the universe.

This understanding identifies another very important purpose for ritual, the lofty goal of transforming and renewing the universe. For the initiate, the constant participation in ritual helps to strengthen their understanding of the universe while simultaneously equipping them with the necessary knowledge and practical skills to produce harmony within their respective worlds (internal and external).

We are currently functioning under a very limited understanding of science and knowledge. The current paradigm is highly externalized and very much dependent on materialism for both evidence of Truth and comforts. If only we understood that our ability to "know," and knowledge itself, exists well beyond what is currently referred to as *the* scientific method[29], and that our Light can shine exponentially brighter simply by shifting perspective. But what are the methods used to make this shift? What are these ritual practices? And how does one cultivate and develop them? I'm glad you asked. These questions and many more will be explored throughout this chapter and in volume 2.

The internal and external tools available to an African initiate are many. Their accessibility depends upon the degree of initiation, and they manifest uniquely in each individual. Amongst the repertoire of tools are intuition, direct knowing, mind over matter, telepathy, telekinesis, prophecy/foresight/foreknowledge, etc. These tools are commonly lumped into the somewhat "conspiratorial" category of extra-sensory perception, or ESP. The thing about ESP is many people misunderstand what it is, and thus believe it to be some sort of spooky pseudo-science. This couldn't be farther from the truth. ESP by definition is the ability to perceive without the use of the known physical senses.

Making it more plain, ESP is when you had a "hunch" to do <u>something and</u> it proved to be beneficial. It's when "something" told

---

29 I emphasize "the" because many erroneously believe it to be the one and only way to know and utilize science. It is, in fact, only "a" scientific method, one of many that are equally valid. Evidence of a scientific method beyond the one currently used by modern science is found in Western science's inability to understand how the many ancient pyramids were built, and their inability to duplicate it. Much in the same way that modern science cannot "create" life.

Ritual

you to call someone, go somewhere or stay at home, and as a result, proved beneficial. The converse is also true: the thought "crosses" your mind to do something or be somewhere but you *don't* follow through, learning later that if you had, it would have benefitted you. Have you ever been thinking of someone or something and it shows up either in a commercial, conversation, or the person calls, texts, or otherwise makes contact with you? That too, is ESP[30].

Now of course there are times when one has actually "sensed" something and was not aware of having seen, heard, smelled, tasted, or touched it; this is separate from ESP. This is simply unconscious sensing, or sensing beneath the threshold of conscious awareness. The way to hone, develop and cultivate these talents is similar to how one would develop themselves physically, via exercise and practice. There are two main vehicles for exercising these mental and spiritual "muscles": ritual and symbolism.

By Western definition, a ritual is: 1) an established or prescribed procedure for a religious or other rite; 2) a system or collection of religious or other rites; 3) observance of set forms in public worship; 4) a book of rites or ceremonies; 5) a book containing the offices to be used by priests in administering the sacraments and for visitation of the sick, burial of the dead, etc.; 6) a prescribed or established rite, ceremony, proceeding, or service; and, 7) prescribed, established, or ceremonial acts or features collectively, as in religious service. These definitions pale in comparison to the one offered at the opening of this chapter; it seems to lack the depth of the African perspective.

On the surface, they describe ritual as a standard and regular way of doing things. We also see that the term can refer to a written description of the various stations within a group, including their roles and responsibilities. Additionally, many of these definitions refer to some sort of religious organization or ceremonial rites, or the book containing a description of these ceremonial rites. So from the Western perspective, ritual is a step-by-step process; a way of ensuring uniformity, consistency, and establishes familiarity; in other words, it is formulaic. From an African perspective, the

---

[30] There is a well-established body of academic research into the mechanisms of ESP and its various manifestations. See *New Frontiers of the Mind - The Story of the Duke [University] Experiments* and *The Reach of the Mind* by J. B. Rhine.

consistency, and prescribed methodology is there, however, there simultaneously exists the understanding that the ritual goes beyond the formula; in fact, it exists *for the purpose of* going beyond the formula (i.e., the physical boundaries of reality). The processes, scripts, songs/sounds, required movements, scents, colors, etc., *all* serve as ritualistic tools; they are the forms through which the actual work is being done. It's similar to how the amount of water in a crystal wine glass, coupled with the shape and density of the glass, produces the range of sounds one gets by plucking it or running their finger around the rim. In other words, its movement (vibration) is manipulated by its physical make-up. The sound is the true work, while the glass and water represent the form(ula) through which the work takes place. Try hard to visualize and understand this concept, because it is key to looking deeper into, and broadening our understanding of, how powerful Masonic ritual could actually be, when approached from the African worldview.

    It is true that the work gets done with or without our knowing what is being done. And thus, a person can listen to a symphony and be emotionally moved by the harmonics, and may even develop lucidity of thought, all the while not understanding a thing about the relationship between music, cognition, and emotions. On the other hand, the person who is consciously aware of this relationship is capable of employing this knowledge to their own benefit. They can consciously establish intention and come prepared to take full advantage of the situation by coming with a particular problem in mind, about which they wish to gain clarity and insight through the course of the performance.

    This is intuitively, and perhaps instinctively, done by people everyday. For example, people choose a certain music for the sole purpose of altering their own mood and/or that of another. People have certain music they use to exercise, to relax, to become aroused or otherwise set the mood, increase mental focus and clarity, etc. These are all examples of how music is used in an everyday manner, for ritualistic purposes. Now, imagine this mental and emotionally manipulative tool being intentionally employed for the purpose of spiritual self-development. In essence, that is the function of religious hymns and chants. They are tools for manipulating thoughts

Ritual

and emotions, and thus behaviors. It's the reason why in movies, the music often shifts to some sort of "hip hop-ish" beat when the scene switches to a "dangerous" or otherwise "urban" environment. It sets the tone for how you will feel watching that scene, and in similar environments in real life.

This same level of subtle influence is found throughout society and especially in our religious institutions. The masses fail to realize that everything from the songs they sing to the construction of the house of worship (church, temple, lodge, synagogue, etc.), create the experiences they have while in attendance. Without knowledge of this fact, the participant may still receive some benefit, yet based on their lack of intentionality, when it comes to using the tools present during the ritual, they are unlikely to take full advantage.

It's similar to the ever-growing features found on smart phones. Between the "apps" and the hardware, these pocket computers can impact almost every thinkable thing that people do on a day-to-day basis. Let's say a person has 5,000 features on their phone but they are only aware of and only use the call feature. Sure they are able to accomplish a lot with this single tool, however, they have come no where near maximizing the potential of the device. Compare this to the possibilities once they learn to text, browse the internet, take pictures, record videos, produce music and movies, play any number of games, shine a flashlight, pay bills, invest money, learn a language, etc.. etc., etc., all from the same device. Their world and life experiences will become totally different, perhaps expanded, or maybe even contracted. This phenomenal and life altering difference is exactly what we find between the person who intentionally recognizes and uses ritual, beyond the surface motions and outward expressions, and those who maintain only a limited, concrete and superficial understanding.

In exploring the concept of ritual further, we will go both deeper and more superficially in order to cover its mundane and spiritual aspects. It is important for us to discuss both extremes in order to develop a well-rounded understanding of ritual, its power, as well as its familiarity and accessibility. By the time we finish with this chapter, our comprehension of ritual should be expanded and we should understand that everything we do can be ritualized, and thus, can possess the power to transform.

On the mundane or surface level, we participate in rituals without needing to think about it. From the way we wake up, to how we go to bed, we are constantly performing some task in a set, consistent and prescribed way. Think about what you do when you first wake up. Do you typically pray upon rising? Do you drink a glass of lemon water? Brush teeth? Shower? Exercise? Meditate? Whatever your morning routine, it is a ritual. In some schools of thought, the morning ritual is what sets the tone for the remainder of the day, hence the saying "woke up on the wrong side of the bed." This conveys that something was off in the morning ritual and thus has negatively affected the rest of the day.

Once awake, people tend to continue in ritualistic fashion. We typically eat breakfast in a consistent manner; some have a cup of coffee and read the paper, others make smoothies. Children may have a bowl of cereal while watching cartoons and/or reading the cereal box. Our morning commute is really no different. We typically travel the same way, be it on public transportation (bus, train, taxi) or personal vehicle, this routine also comes with it's ritual and consists of various elements like road rage, crowds, smells, traffic, radio programs, and sometimes the stress of being early, on time, or late.

Once we arrive at our destination, we continue to ritualize. Do you open the office? Do you have to change into uniform? Do you open and read email? Check phone messages? Have a morning staff meeting? Again, this is all ritual. It is a set routine or mode of operating. It contributes to how you function and how you experience your workplace and job. Your co-workers and clients are co-players in your ritual and they contribute whatever they bring from their wake up and early morning rituals too. In these public spaces, ritual can easily become a tricky pot of gumbo with a little bit of everything thrown into it. This can be distracting, confusing, or fantastically beneficial, all depending on what the people are bringing, and perhaps more importantly, how you view what is taking place around you.

Once our workplace rituals have concluded, we typically

Ritual

return to the commuter phase, sometimes it is simply the reverse of our morning travels, other times it may come with it's own special nuances. Some people habitually go to happy hour after work, some times everyday, sometimes on a specific day of the week (when their favorite restaurant or bar offers drink specials). Some will stop by the grocery store or market in order to pick up food to prepare for dinner once they get home. You may have to pick up kids from a day care center or school; there may be evening meetings or conferences you have to attend. One main difference between the morning and evening commute (or vice versa depending on if you work in the mornings or nights), is you typically are more energetic going in than you are coming back, having expended your mental and physical energies at work.

Finally, we have our night time ritual. We typically use this time to wind-down, prepare for bed, cook dinner, watch television, and spend time with our families. Just like the previous steps, this phase is also full of specific experiences and procedures. Take a moment and think about what you did last night before going to bed. Did you brush your teeth? Did you iron your clothes for the next day? Did you prep dinner? Eat in the same seat you always sit in? Watch your favorite TV shows? Help a child with their homework? Browse social media? Was this consistent with the night before? I'm betting it was consistent in more ways than not. Humans tend to be creatures of habit and thus, we readily lend ourselves to participating in and benefitting from ritual.

We can take this same concept and apply it to our exercise routines. Do you wear specific clothes to workout? Do you go to a specific gym? Start with a particular machine or muscle group? Carry a special water bottle? I'm betting you do. The same goes for our sexual and intimate lives, where we also typically have rituals that we perform. Folks may take a shower, drink some wine, put on some sensual music, dress a certain way, use a particular oil or perfume, prepare special dishes, take sexual enhancement supplements, etc. The actual sex act tends to also be routine for many. You start with the same act, move to a particular position, and if you are lucky, you get a few more positions in, then climax. After which, is the "clean up" where folks use the bathroom, take showers, put on clothes, and if you're at home, go to sleep, if not, you go home. Whatever your routine, if it is routine, it is ritual.

The main thing that takes our ritual participation from being superficial to a more in-depth process, is our intention behind the routine. What do we intend to accomplish? What is our understanding of how our mind, body, and spirit all participate in each of these activities? How are we benefitted, mind, body, and spirit by participating in these daily routines? If for any of these tasks we say there is no benefit to mind, body, and spirit, then we are only dealing superficially.

I tend to place some of our more intentional rituals like funerals, births, and weddings, at the mid-point between the superficial and the deepest of ritual practices. These events naturally carry a more obvious sense of sacredness because they serve as clear points of transition in our lives. When a person is expecting a child, we intuitively know that this is a powerful and divine process. Of course we don't always consciously and overtly acknowledge this fact, nonetheless, we feel it. From the non-ritualistic standpoint, the process of birth, for many, entails an unplanned conception, a medically-based pregnancy, and a hospitalized birth. In modern times, this is the norm. Technology has "advanced" to such a point that we are now capable of selecting our child's birthdate (within a certain range) and scheduling the delivery of your child with as much confidence as you would place an order with your local pizzeria.

Remember, anything that is routine is also ritual. In the case of the hospitalized birth, the medical staff also functions based on a ritual. They will even call it a "routine procedure." Their process is complete with consistent visits and checkups, each of which carries its own specific protocol. Expecting mothers are advised to carry on in a certain way, following certain protocols including prenatal vitamins, birthing classes, and the development of a birthing plan.

When labor occurs (either naturally or medically induced) the mother will either experience a natural vaginal birth or cesarean section (C-section). In the former, the attending medical staff will constantly check the cervix to measure how far it has dilated. They will also determine the position of the baby to see if it is

Ritual

in proper form (head down, facing backwards), or in one of the breach positions (sitting up facing forward with legs crossed or loose). Each of these variations determines what protocol to follow.

Regardless of the method, most women that give birth, and their families that witness it, see it as a miracle. Women have described it as being indescribable. The process of pregnancy, where a woman actually grows another person inside of her own body, gives women a direct experience of God. The moment that the developing fetus awakens in her womb and moves for the first time solidifies the miracle in her heart and mind. The flashes of communication, understanding and knowing that a mother shares with the child in her womb, is how God must feel with each of us. That moment when the baby is born, and the mother meets and touches him or her for the first time, is like a reunion of long lost relatives who play catch-up for the remainder of their lives. In some African cultures, this relationship is exactly that; the child is a returning Ancestor, while the parent is also a relative from times long ago. When one makes their transition (dies), they continue in the cycle of familial relationships, and thus, the circle remains unbroken.

This relatively new process of "medicalized" birth can easily take away from the deeper ritualistic aspects previously associated with birth. In ancient times, and still amongst those who carry on tradition, this process was governed by a midwife who is likely to have learned her craft from an elder, more experienced midwife, who has likely been initiated into the mystical sciences. Birth, as a ritual, begins with conception where two people have undergone training and preparation to become the healthiest and most capable woman and man they can be. Having gone through their respective rites of passage/initiations, the man and woman thus joined in matrimony, would ritualize sex, ritualize conception, ritualize pregnancy, ritualize birth, and ritualize the raising of that child.

According to Simon Ottenberg in ***Boyhood Rituals in an African Society, An Interpretation***:

> The baby is born onto the ground. It should cry; this is taken as a sign of health and vitality...When the placenta appears the umbilical cord is cut by the midwife or another female. The child is then rubbed with sand to wash it, or often nowadays with soap and water. The skin is smoothed with palm oil and

white chalk is put on it. The chalk cools the skin and it is also employed at Afikpo as a multivocal symbol of good health, fertility, good life, and happiness. The placenta and cord are buried in the courtyard—a practical procedure which also connects the child with the spirits of the ground, *ale*, associated with human welfare and fertility. The mother bathes in a special solution of water in which certain leaves have been soaked. A secret ritual is performed over the child by the women present. I could find no male who knew it, nor did any female inform me of what it was about. Men are forbidden to view it. The rite differs according to the infant's sex; and so begins the lifelong recognition of the importance of gender and of secrecy at Afikpo.

As revealed by the author, the ritual aspects of birth are secret and are entrusted only to those who have been initiated into these rites. This is how serious we once took ourselves. Fortunately, there still exist those who acknowledge the sanctity of conception, gestation and birth. Many still use midwives and have "home-births," "water-births," and otherwise ritualized births. People continue in the traditions of their Ancestors as much as practically possible. There are even those who go the medicalized route and still maintain their awareness of the sacredness of the ritual taking place.

Both of my children were born to ritual. In one case we were with an African-centered organization with initiated priestesses present along with a midwife. In the other case, we also ritualized, but this time my wife and I were the priest and priestess and the midwife was one of European descent, who had been initiated (formally or not) into her Craft, specializing in the natural delivery of babies that are in breach position. During this particular pregnancy, we consulted several Oracle systems[31] and were able to identify that there would be an unexpected occurrence with this delivery. We checked the Oracle to see the most beneficial place and method for us to have our child. We had our preferences, but the Oracle advised against each and every one of them. It told us to visit *The Farm* in Summertown, TN. At the time, this was about a 2 hour drive from our house.

---

31 In the speech by John T. Hilton quoted in the Foreword, he endorses, in true African fashion, the use of Oracles, "Let us be directed to that sure and invariable guide, the divine Oracles of God..."

Ritual

The midwives at this farm are the authors and contributors of the popular book *Spiritual Midwifery*, and are among the few who would dare to deliver a "breach" baby, naturally (meaning vaginally, without drugs or C-section). At the time of our consultations with the Oracles, we did not know that our baby would come breach. We did know that we were being guided to this particular group for the safe and healthy delivery of our child. During labor, as things began to intensify, my wife and I went into a mutual ritual space, within our conjoined souls, and began to call on all of the female deities of our Ancestors, and we called on all of the women who have successfully walked this path before us, in order that we may draw on their strength and support during this difficult and potentially dangerous process. When it came time for the midwife to bring our baby's head out from the womb (in a breach birth, the head is the last part to come out aside from the placenta...so imagine a full body up to the neck extending from the womb), the room was absolutely silent. You could feel the energies being drawn into the midwife as she took on a sort of blank and entranced gaze. She was calling on her source of wisdom for this most important part of the birth. She suddenly, and with one swift movement, reached in with her fingers in a scooping motion and brought our child completely into this world. We finalized this part of the ritual with the cleansing waters from our tears of joy. We continued to ritualize for our children by divining their purpose for being born, and subsequently naming them based on this purpose[32].

Marriage is another ritualized process that many still hold with some level of sanctity. Most perform the ceremony in the presence of family members and other important individuals. There is hardly a wedding ceremony that does not include someone who is considered to be a "holy" woman or man officiating. These ceremonies often occur in a place of worship or some natural setting, both of which are designed to inspire a feeling of God's presence as witness to this "holy matrimony."

The importance of this union is understood and is conveyed by the vows claiming to stay together until "death do you part." The

---

32   According to many African traditions, the naming is what reminds the child and community of the person's life purpose. See *African Names* by Hehi Metu Ra Enkhamit.

marriage of man and woman serves as the foundation of the new family-to-be. It is from this union that new life is generated, families formed, and the human race continued.

In relatively modern times, people have begun to spend enormous amounts of money for elaborate and beautiful marriage rituals. For example, the typical wedding in the United States costs between $19,833 and $33,055 not including the honeymoon. The average American marriage lasts about 8 years before divorce, with divorce rates improving slightly and marriage rates decreasing. Statistically speaking, women file for the majority of divorces, albeit for various reasons ranging from sexual dissatisfaction to abuse. Some contribute the preponderance of failed marriages, high cost of weddings, and declining instances of matrimony to the increased exposure to fantasy romance found in children's cartoons and movies. These media often provide an unrealistic expectation of romance and imagery of what "good" relationships are, to the point that folks either mistake courting, and all the bliss associated with it to mean "real love" OR they mistake the lack of "fairy tale" experiences to mean that love does not exist.

The African-centered perspective of marriage is one that goes beyond the sometimes superficially based notions found in Western societies. Instead of the romantic notions of "love," people who share the African-centered worldview often see matrimony as a means for cultivating and experiencing unconditional love. The African-centered perspective sees marriage as the uniting of two families, as opposed to two individuals coming together. To go a step further, beyond uniting two families, they are also uniting two bloodlines, two lineages, both of which trace all the way back to the most ancient of Ancestors, God. In essence, the marriage of man and woman reconciles the separation we experienced, from God, during our creation process, as outlined in the majority of the world's great religions.

The reunification of these complimentary aspects of God via the marriage, in an African-centered community, begins with the conception and birthing rituals outlined above. It continues with the rites of passage initiations experienced by children as they approach adolescence, and then from adolescence to adulthood.

Ritual

Another amazing observation of non-Western perspectives on marriage is that many cultures actually see the current union as a continuation of previous relationships, which have existed from the beginning of time, amongst the various generations of Ancestors.

Perhaps one of the most profound aspects of marriage from an African-centered perspective is the notion that it has a divine purpose for the individuals involved. This purpose being to once again realize and actualize their divine nature. This is done through the work that will inevitably arise as two people become intertwined in holy matrimony, especially in ritual, in front of God, the Ancestors, and their families. I have often jokingly stated that it is a cruel joke for us to have to work out ALL of our "baggage" with the same person we are supposed to unconditionally love and grow with. It also makes the absolute most sense! Think for a moment all of the time we spend with our spouses and those we are in relationships with. This person sees you beyond the dressed up, smelling good, looking good, sounding good, feeling good public person you appear to be to the less intimate people in your life. They know what your morning breath and "number 2" smell like. They know you when you are sick and when you have a bad attitude. They see you without the latest fashions and know your hygiene styles and habits.

This is enough for anyone to break up with another person with whom they have not made a deep, marriage commitment. This is the person whom you vent to, the person who must experience your work-based stress along with you. This person is also the one with which you may generate your own feelings of stress, burden, disagreement and frustrations, in addition to all the other things that have already been spelled out. This is separate from the other energies that come with having children, and growing older. As you can probably see, marriage from a Western perspective does not equip individuals to undertake such a task with any measure of success and happiness. From the African-centered perspective, we gain a measure of hope.

According to Ra Un Nefer Amen in his book *An Afrocentric Guide To A Spiritual Union*:

Symbolically Speaking: African Lodge #1

The consummation of the wedding takes place at a ceremony which may take place anywhere from several weeks to over a year after the consent has been given. An important part in preparing for the marriage is the families getting to know each other, the education of the couples, improvement of the girl's health through enhanced nutrition as she is prepared for pregnancy, and the groom's efforts to raise the dowry. It is important to realize that the difference between the African dowry versus the European resides in the fact that in the latter the woman brings it to the man, while in the former man brings it, not to the woman, but to her father and family. While in the European version, it can be construed as a token that one may give to another for showing favor towards one, the African dowry is more like a bond...To raise the dowry, they have to be in good social standing—an important quality that the dowry system was invented to test. A boy of good social standing would have no problem getting help from his uncles... father, married sisters, cousins, grand parents, and the boys of his age set (this is the group of boys with whom he underwent his Rites of Passage, and share other social responsibilities)... This dowry will thus act as a potent force to pressure the married couple to do right in the marriage, for the faulted party in the event of divorce would forfeit the dowry.

    Once married, the husband is expected to spend more of his time with his uncles, father, and older men, than with his wife, and the wife is expected to spend more time with her mother, aunts, and older women than with her husband. In fact, it is customary for them to keep separate households. This expectation, which carries the force of law, which is to say that they cannot circumvent it, accomplishes several things. For one, it physically cuts back on the possibility of sexual overindulgence, and for another, it forces the young married couple into a situation which will guarantee their education into manhood and womanhood. You just can't give information on the subject, however scholarly, and expect it to take root in the behavior of the majority of people. You have to have [a] means of inculcating it. Since a man cannot learn how to be a husband and father from his wife, he has to be made to spend the appropriate time with the only ones who can teach him that—successful husbands and fathers. The same is true of women. Their husbands cannot teach them how to become wives and mothers. They must be made to spend the required time with their mothers, and aunts. Unlike western wives and husbands who expected each other to share and solve the emotional heavies that can come along in life, in spite of their

Ritual

lack of preparation and experience, the African couple knew to place such burdens on their more experienced relatives.

In line with the above, I experienced an aspect of the African perspective and practice of wedding two people. Back in 1999, while in Gambia, West Africa, I was blessed and fortunate to participate in a wedding ceremony of two good friends who also traveled from the U.S. The ceremony was held in an African compound in full tradition. As we sat observing the ceremony we all received a shock when the officiating elder suddenly stopped the ceremony and proclaimed that the couple could not be married because the groom had not produced the required dowry. The audience went into a fuss. The American Africans present were distraught because apparently no one was told of this custom beforehand. Instinct kicked in for me and one other friend as we began to go around and collect money from everyone our friend had invited. Putting my own money into the pot, I walked over to the officiating elder and asked if this was satisfactory and if they could now continue with their ceremony. Without counting the money, the elder accepted the offer and continued the service. In hindsight, I realize, as outlined above, the dowry was not to pay for any specific thing, nor was it necessary to have any specific amount, but only to show that he was, in fact, in good standing and that his community of friends and family had his back. Two babies and fifteen years later, they remain happily married.

The third level of ritual I'd like to acknowledge are those that are fully intentional ceremonies, designed to, and fully expected to, have an impact on the mind, body, and spirit of the participants. These are our religious services including weekly church meetings, Catholic Mass, Islamic Jumu'ah, the Bah'ai services, Egbe of the Ifa groups, Akom of the Akan, monthly full moon rituals of the Ausar Auset Society, etc. In our mainstream experience, we have various levels of intensity and intentionality that these rituals bring to the practitioner, and thus we have differing outcomes. For example, we have witnessed scenes from a Pentecostal ritual where the participants are deep into trance, handling snakes, and perhaps speaking in tongue. We have witnessed the solemn Catholic rituals where the priests are swinging the thurible[33], singing in low tones, deep in prayer. Some of us have felt the chills associated with the Islamic call to prayer, beautifully sang over the loud speaker for all the town to hear. Many of us have even experienced first hand, in a Baptist church, where the organ accompanying the preachers voice is capable of bringing certain members of the congregation to such a frenzy that "Church Mothers" dance and whirl about, totally possessed with the Holy Spirit.

I recall a story once shared with me about a particular church experience. There was a congregant that was known to be susceptible to being "possessed" by the Holy Spirit. This particular elder would get possessed, slide down from her pew onto the floor, and slide all the way down to the front of the church, going under each pew in front of her. The congregants came to expect this occurrence and prepared themselves accordingly by picking up their bags and whatever else may be in her path in order to keep them from being dragged down to the altar with the possessed Elder.

Many who participate in this level of ritual do so with intention but without a sense of personal power. We often go to church, the mosque, the temple, with a sense of deference and passively appeal to a higher power that may or may not answer our calls, cries, and prayers. This process is how many of us have been taught to use these intentional rituals. We are guided to give all of our personal power over to the Minister, Preacher, or Imam. We are taught that they are the intercessor on our behalf, based on either education and/or a divine calling they have received. We place our faith, trust, and power in their hands, and follow with full confidence. The dangers in this are self-evident and go beyond the scope of this book; suffice it to say, it is the very reason why potentially brilliant and thoughtful people are easily converted into submissive and subservient "sheeple."

In this version of ritual (where we passively participate), we have periodic and perhaps sporadic glimpses of spirit. We have "miracles" that occur when our prayers are answered. We acknowledge the "miracles" when someone is saved from harm and death in ways that our rational minds cannot comprehend or explain. We <u>faithfully give </u>tribute money to our houses of worship, in order to

---

33   An incense holder (censer) suspended on a chain.

Ritual

secure our favor in the afterlife. We trust our religious leaders to be worthy of our unquestioning obedience to their selective preaching, partial teaching, and even community leeching; accepting their flaws to be normal and within the circumference of human frailty. I like to look at this form of ritual as being more artistic than scientific. It has the forms, sounds, smells, gestures, and feeling of a deeply spiritual process, but is by any measure, almost completely devoid of intentionally and scientifically directed spiritual power, on the part of the participants. This is what separates even our most powerful forms of ritual in the mainstream West, from the African-centered perspective and practices.

Before we explore the African-centered forms of ritual, let us place our Lodge practices into the three aforementioned levels of ritual. With all do respect, our Lodge ritual has been relegated mostly to the first two forms of ritual. Like the first level, we get "dressed" in regular fashion, we show up to our regularly scheduled meetings, we play our role depending on what station we are currently occupying. We go through the physical motions, verbalize a consistent script, deliver and receive memorized lectures and degree work, and have our annual functions, conferences, and special forums like clockwork. Many times we do all of these things, and many of us have been doing these things for decades, to the point to where it becomes automatic, with very little conscious thought required on our part. It's very similar to how we brush our teeth without thinking about it, or how we drive to and from work without thinking about the route.

Then there are those of us who experience our Lodge work as described in the second level of ritual described above. We automatically give a degree of sanctity to being present in the Lodge. We have an innate respect for the presence of the GAOTU[34] as evidenced by the V of SL that MUST be present for us to perform our works. We open and close with prayer; we see and recognize the beauty in our form and the eloquence of our Grand Lecturers as they deliver the allegories and historical citations for our Craft. We see the Light awakened in our EA at their I, we witness the strengthening of that same Light as they are P on to the degree of a FC, and finally, we see the divinely inspired joy as the Light is "ful-

---

34   GAOTU = Grand Architect of the Universe = God

ly" revealed to our Brothers as they are R as MM. The sanctity of our Craft permeates everything that we do within our Lodges. It is deeply embedded, although codified, in our allegories and symbolic expressions. From the rituals experienced by our new candidates all the way to our Funerary works, we recognize there is something deep about our practices.

    Our Craft, just like all ancient institutions, is a hub designed to keep, protect, and conceal immense spiritual power. Those of us who know this, utilize our time in the Lodge with the intentions of utilizing this power. We find ourselves, to whatever degree we are capable, intending to gain "more Light" by participating in the various ceremonies and rituals. Just as I described above in the third level of ritual, we tend to be more passive than active in this pursuit. We relinquish our personal power to a higher being, separate and distant from ourselves. The difference between the Lodge expression of this level of ritual and that of our religious institutions is the fact that we in the Lodge, do not ascribe to a "middle-man" that intervenes on our behalf for the sake of communicating with God (i.e., preacher, etc.). Everyone in the Lodge is on equal footing, as men, regardless of the individual socio-political stations they hold both in and outside the Lodge. While the WM conducts and leads us in instruction and business, and the Chaplain leads us in prayer, it is the duty of every man there present to work on their own behalf, and simultaneously for the benefit of their Brother, the Lodge, and the Craft as a whole. This is regardless of our individual religious affiliations.

    We too, have the sporadic experience of "miracle" and have our "unexplained" occurrences that we ascribe to divine intervention. We have there, hidden in our allegories, many examples of miraculous feats, especially the story of the resurrection of H.A., by the King of Israel. The building of a particular temple without the sound of tools and without any discarded materials is another miracle highlighted in our Craft. And even the notion that it only rained at night and when the Craftsmen were taking a break, but never when they were working on the Temple[35]. While we have certain advantages over many of our religious institutions, in regards to accessing our spiritual powers, we still fall short of becoming

---

35   The significance of these symbols will be explored in great detail in volume 2.

Ritual

the spiritual scientists that our more ancient Ancestors of the Craft were. They functioned as spiritual chemists in the laboratory of Nature, learning and utilizing the spiritual anatomy of Man as their chemical tool, and creation itself provided the ingredients for working the formulas outlined in our legends, allegories, and V of SL. This my friends, is what separates these three levels of ritual from the African-centered understanding of the same.

Relatively few of us here in North America have been exposed to the moving energies of an African-based ritual, wherein we find people performing physical feats seemingly impossible under ordinary conditions. For example, while in Africa, I participated in a ritual with the Jolla. During this performance, the Jolla men blew on whistles and danced their signature dance while the women followed behind in procession, clapping pieces of metal together creating a powerful rhythmic melody. Individual Jolla men, women, and children would dance around demonstrating the power of their "juju[36]" by taking swords and cutting across their arms with no injury, or by taking a razor blade, shaving the bark of a tree to demonstrate its sharpness and then running the same blade across their tongues, eyelids, or other body parts without penetrating the skin. I was later told that this same spiritual science is what Toussaint L'Ouverture, Dutty Boukman, and others used to successfully liberate Haiti from the French military. It was a spiritual protection that prevented metal from piercing the body,[37] allowing the Haitians to fight fearlessly against the firepower of the French.

Once, while attending an African ritual here in the United States, I observed one of the High Priests going into trance. The energy of this ritual was intentionally martial, and thus there were swords, fire, and a "fiery" drum cadence being played. This High Priest danced around an iron pot[38] for a few minutes before inverting his body into a "handstand," then slowly lowering his head into the pot, which was burning incense and herbs. As he lowered himself, his legs arched over the rest of his body in such a way that he was seemingly off balance, yet was totally stable. He remained absolutely still in this position for a few minutes before raising him-

---

36   Spiritual magic sometimes in the form of a talisman, etc.
37   I personally tested each of these tools...they are real.
38   Called a "Ting" in the 50th Hexagram of the I Ching

self back up and continuing to dance. In association with this same group, an elder once boasted to me about having undergone lung surgery, without anesthesia, by going into trance, and using only a machete in the hands of a powerful African healer/priest.

Masonically speaking, everything we do in the Lodge is a ritual. The way we open and close, the way we go form l to r, the way we perform our funeral rites, and most definitely the way we do our degree work. Each and every degree has a ritual very specific to the work and goals to be accomplished. In each of these degrees we have very specific symbols, colors, scripts, movements, and characters being portrayed. Every cap, every jewel, every geometric shape, every sign, password, grip, penalty and due-guard, are all symbolic representations of some underlying philosophy, truth, belief and/or purpose.

Our ritual is so dense and varied, even volumes such as *The Scottish Rite Ritual Monitor and Guide* by Brother Arturo de Hoyos, fail to scratch the surface of their inherent power. As stated in the opening pages as a quote from Albert Pike's *Morals and Dogma*:

> We teach the truth of none of the legends we recite. They are to us but parables and allegories, involving and enveloping Masonic instruction; and vehicles of useful and interesting information. They represent the different phases of the human mind, its efforts and struggles to comprehend nature, God, the government of the Universe, the permitted existence of sorrow and evil. To teach us wisdom, and the folly of endeavoring to explain to ourselves that which we are not capable of understanding, we reproduce the speculations of the Philosophers, the Kabalists, the Mystagogues and the Gnostics. Every one being at liberty to apply our symbols and emblems as he thinks most consistent with truth and reason and with his own faith, we give them such an interpretation only as may be accepted by all…To honor the Deity, to regard all men as our Brethren, as children, equally dear to Him, of the Supreme Creator of the Universe, and to make himself useful to society and himself by his labor, are its teachings to its Initiates in all the Degrees.

Nothing of the mystical aspects of our Masonic ritual is touched upon in any plain or direct fashion. The intellectual and historical significance of the ritual is detailed and repeated across

Ritual

various sources, yet our modern literature seems to shy away from even the possibility of our ritual practices having any spiritual significance. The African-centered scholar in me has an issue accepting the notion that ritual, of any kind, is completely devoid of spiritual significance. Pike, in the above quote taken from de Hoyos' wonderful book, clearly eludes to several spiritual traditions from which Freemasonry has developed it's lore, symbolism, and even certain practices, but it is left up to each individual Mason to delve as deeply or as superficially as they so desire.

Imagine if the rituals on the Scottish Rite "branch," as well as those on the York Rite "branch" of the "Masonic tree" were all conducted in such a way that the rituals intentionally had a spiritual and psychically transforming impact on the candidate going through them. What if at the conferring of the highest degree in Masonry, the newly Raised Master Mason actually resurrected to a new state of mind and purpose? To our credit, many do actually report such a transformation, similar to what is experienced when a Muslim makes his Hajj, or when a Christian is baptized in the Jordan River, however, this is not the norm, nor is it the real expectation of many Brothers that go through the process.

Before, during, and after taking my Masonic degrees, I was familiar with and actively participating in several ancient African spiritual sciences. These initiations allowed me to experience, first-hand, the power of ritual when done according to the wisdom traditions of our ancient Ancestors. Prior to becoming a member of the Blue Lodge, I was initiated as a Kemetic Priest and had participated in a host of traditional African rituals and ceremonies. I had also been initiated by the Jolla in Gambia and the Ewe in Ghana, both of which contained their own spiritual sciences and ritual ceremonies. The African-centered initiation that followed my becoming a member of a Masonic Lodge was with the Ifa spiritual tradition as a priest of Olokun. The culmination of these various African initiatic experiences, and their proximity to my Masonic journey, afforded me the unique opportunity of understanding and experiencing the similarities between the two, as well as a comparing and contrasting of what some believe to be a missing key to our Masonic journey as descendants of the African Lodge, currently called Prince Hall Freemasonry.

According to the African Shaman Malidoma Some', in his book **Ritual**:

> The abandonment of ritual can be devastating. From the spiritual viewpoint, ritual is inevitable and necessary if one is to live...The young ones are the future of the old ones. To allow this future to happen, the old ones must work with the Otherworld. When an elder fails to perform his work with respect to the spiritual, the future of this elder is threatened, not the present. Where ritual is absent, the young ones are restless or violent, there are no real elders, and the grown-ups are bewildered. The future is dim.

It is obvious that the consequences forewarned in the above quote are already upon us. As American Africans, our intentional and consistent use of African-based rituals has been systematically diminished. All manner of mechanisms have been deployed in order to get us to abandon our innate desire and need to perform rituals from the perspective of our Ancestry. For a while, and it still remains in certain pockets, regardless of who's religion and/or culture was being forced upon us, we found a way to link our ritual ways to the forms and processes of the alien culture. When forced into Catholicism, our Brothers and Sisters in Haiti, Dominican Republic and Puerto Rico linked the Orisha of Nigeria to the Saints of the Catholics creating Santeria. When the Protestant and Baptist forms of Christianity were infused into our worldview during the seasoning phase[39] of European enslavement, our Ancestors figured out how to continue to use the natural elements, divination practices, herbal remedies, and the art and science of "juju," to maintain a level of sanity in the insane conditions of the plantation. Now that we are "free," it seems that we are further away from implementing these traditions than ever before.

The fraternity of Freemasonry is one of the oldest and largest in the world, with diasporic Africans making up a significant number (be they Prince Hall Affiliates or members of other Grand Lodges). I recall being in a remote village in The Gambia, sitting in

---

39   The portion of enslavement where Africans were broken down and literally trained (in the behavioral psychology sense of the word) to become slaves in their thinking and behavior.

Ritual

a Brother by the name of Lamen's compound. Lamen did not speak English but he spoke four African languages and French. He was translating through a small child as he spoke to us about his experiences in life. The one word I was able to comprehend coming from his mouth was "mason." He told of his initiation and gestured as he described that he was the builder of the house that we currently sat in. His story helped me to understand that the way we, in the West, have separated the Operative from the Speculative, in more recent times, has actually diminished our ability to function in a truly free fashion.

This dichotomous, either/or way of thinking and reasoning is a deficiency acquired by our assimilation of the Western mentality and worldview. It forces us to draw separations where, in reality, there are none. Instead of asking "does" something relate, we would ask "how" does it relate. Instead of ascribing to one way of "knowing" we'd understand that there are several. This is the stuff that "worldview" is made of, and what we will cover in greater detail in volume two of this work. For now we will spend the rest of this volume detailing the general concepts of African spiritual science and initiation, in order to build the context for the symbol interpretation, psychological implications, and other high sciences found in volume two.

I leave you with this quote from an address delivered by Brother J. Harvey MacPherson, Lodge Spey, No. 527, entitled: *Antient Landmarks and Daily Advance* as found in the *Year Book of 1967*, Grand Lodge of Scotland:

> ...My personal belief is that the Craft, as we know it, goes far beyond the bounds of Freemasonry in its understood form... in the course of a somewhat chequered career in many parts of the world, I have encountered extraordinary instances of Craft S____ns being used over and beyond the bounds of Masonry.
>
> In action, in Palestine, a wounded Syrian member of a Dervish sect[40] gave me the sign of G. and D., unmistakably and obviously, dropping his h____s in t. d. m____ts. I took him aside and, later, questioned him. He informed me that the S____n was one which belonged to his own particular Moslem sect. He

---

40   For more information on this Dervish sect, see *Secret Practices of the Sufi Freemasons: The Islamic teachings at the heart of Alchemy* by Baron Rudolf von Sebottendorff.

was certainly not a Mason—but he had the S___n, and it had exactly the same meaning for him as it has for us.

Amongst the Pare Mountains, in East Africa[41], I watched two tribal elders greeting each other with a handshake. When one had moved on, I spoke to the other and gripped him in the same way as his companion had done. I have never seen a man more astonished. "When" he asked, "when were you accepted into our fetish?" He had never heard of a European being initiated into his order of things, and I told him that I had not heard of any of his tribe being initiated into my own order. His final question was staggering. He asked, "Bwana[42], where did you learn mshiko wa simba?[43]" Which means, quite literally, the g. of the l. This G. is the recognition sign amongst members of a tribal society who have adopted the l. as their emblem; and it is significant that the tribe concerned is not of Bantu origin but is Nilotic.

Again in East Africa, on a height overlooking Lake Nyasa[44], I was given the privilege of initiation into a tribal society of the Wanyakyusa[45]. The Signs which were imparted were given under a similar Obligation to our own, with similar, though not identical penalties attached. I feel, though, that the nature of the preparation of candidates lies outwith the obligatory secrets and it merits consideration. I myself was allowed to continue to wear a pair of light pants. The tribesmen who were initiated with me, however, were stripped of clothing. I was instructed to remove a signet ring from my finger so that I should carry nothing metallic. Together we stood on a sand 'pavement' which had been marked out in squares. We stood upright, our feet were squared, our arms were squared at shoulder and elbow, our thumbs were squared—and our right hands rested on the most sacred object of the tribe—the skull of a former chief.

---

41   In the Kilimanjaro region of North East Tanzania.
42   Ki-Swahili word for "master."
43   This phrase is spoken in Ki-Swahili.
44   Also known as Lake Malawi and Lago Niassa in Mozambique, is the southernmost African Great Lake in the East African Rift system, located between Malawi, Mozambique and Tanzania.
45   Also called Ngonde or Nkonde, this group of East Africans trace their Ancestry to a Nubian princess named Nyanseba.

Chapter 3
African Spiritual Systems

Although there are hundreds of cultural and ethnic groups throughout the continent of Africa, there seems to be one underlying premise to all indigenous African philosophy: the element of spirituality. This underlying premise is the focal point from which all other cultural manifestations radiate. This unifying theme of spirituality is defined as the belief in the direct and empowering relationship between God (Creator and Sustainer) and Its creations/manifestations. This relationship is both active and passive, meaning its influence is present regardless of consciousness and awareness of the fact (passive), and it is also something that can be consciously manipulated towards specific goals and purposes (active).

The ancient and indigenous African belief is that God IS all that has been created because all that has been created is taken from the initially unformed aspect of God (called Amen/Amun in Kemet, Ain/Ain Soph/Ain Soph Aur in Hebrew Kabalistic terms) and manifested to infinitude by Its Will. Simply stated, all of creation contains the essence of its creator, God (by whatever name people use to refer to the Supreme Being). To the uninitiated and thus unaware, this is simply a philosophical notion to be stated, inspired or confused by, and perhaps, used to articulate their belief. For the initiated, however, this is a scientific formula.

In popular terms, this knowledge is summed up by the idea that God is Omnipresent; meaning God is in all things and in all places, at all times; hence nothing is beyond God. Plants, animals, minerals, microorganisms, stars, planets, and humans alike are all composed of the essence of God—that unseen force and consciousness that generates life and life force. An analogy using present day scientific terms follows: all known creations are made of elements, which in turn are made of atoms, which are made of protons, neutrons and electrons, each of which is made of smaller, more subtle "things." The only difference between and within atoms and elements is the configuration of the aforementioned atoms and subatomic particles. Furthermore, there are distinct and purposeful relationships between the subatomic particles, readily understood in the language of polarity and charges, both of which determine the possibility of the particles bonding and forming the variety of universal substances, both known and unknown.

Think for a moment about the implications of this fact. If the above is true, and I am suggesting it is, then the only difference between gold and silver, platinum and helium, carbon and radium, is the configuration and quantities of the subatomic particles. Similarly, what makes the difference between a cat and a dog, as far as physical expression is concerned, is a slight variation in its DNA; the same holds true for the difference between a sperm whale and a housefly. Just as with the atom, a slight modification in DNA produces a drastically different manifestation of the infinite realm of creation; the source too, must be infinite[46].

African sages and master teachers of high culture and scientific treatise were well aware of the facts of modern day science (including: chemistry, physics, geometry, calculus, biology, botany, psychology, anatomy and physiology). They were the original chemists (Khemet) who practiced the science of matter and its changes; the pioneers who would perform surgeries and highly sophisticated medical procedures centuries before they would be attempted by Western civilizations (even prior to the advent of Western civilization). The many scholars who have given thought to the early practices of indigenous cultures of continental Africa have agreed that the seeds of civilization and high culture were first germinated and developed to its fruit bearing stages amongst the highly spiritual and especially practical Africans of the Nile Valley, from Uganda to Kemet (modern day Egypt), and spread in all directions.

These Africans are acknowledged as the first "modern" humans to formally identify, develop, and live according to the principles of cosmogony and cosmology; eventually spreading the knowledge and wisdom to other parts of Africa and the broader

---

[46] For an excellent commentary about DNA, knowledge, and ancient initiates, read *The Cosmic Serpent: DNA and the origins of Knowledge* by Jeremy Narby.

world.

Ra Un Nefer Amen describes cosmogony as a blueprint that provides a unified and holistically ordered view of God, Man, and the Forces that administer and sustain the world[47]. He suggests that one can utilize this blueprint to identify the interrelatedness of all things, as well as all experiences of life, and to guide one's thoughts, beliefs and actions in such a manner that it yields the maximum life benefit for all involved. The understanding of this blueprint comes from the study of cosmogony, or the science of cosmology (the study of order). This high science is what leads to understanding the many creation myths, and stories of the ancients; it is also a major part of the multitude of initiations and so-called "Mystery Schools" found throughout the African continent and ancient world.

The cosmology of indigenous African cultures has developed and manifested in a variety of ways. If one studies the cosmology of different cultures, much of which is recorded in the form of myths and various codifications (i.e., allegories), it becomes easy to see that they are identical in function, varying only in form (i.e., language, culturally specific customs and references, method of transmission and verification, and application of the knowledge). Cheikh Ante Diop, Oba T'Shaka, Ivan Van Sertima, Fergus Sharman and Laird Scranton have thoroughly investigated the direct relationship between the languages of many African ethnic groups and have determined that in spite of the observable differences in the many languages, they are directly related and maintain a high level of functional correspondence; a fact that further demonstrates the cultural connections between the various and varying groups. This direct correlation is perhaps most identifiable via their symbolic expressions, which also have direct correspondences with our Masonic symbolism[48].

The cosmological systems found amongst the ancient Nile Valley civilizations, as well as other ancient and indigenous Africans, is based on the belief in two basic realms of existence, the formed and unformed. Amen uses the term "Objective" to identify the realm in which all things have form, and "Subjective" to

---
47   See Metu Neter Vol. 1 by Ra Un Nefer Amen
48   See Symbolically Speaking: African Lodge #1, Vol. 2

denote the realm that contains only unformed energy/matter and consciousness/will (which the ancient and indigenous Africans described as being "under, unseen, or hidden"). This was later adopted by the Hebrew cultures and is evidenced by the relationship between Ain, Ain Soph, Ain Soph Aur[49] and Kether. The two realms are viewed as two sides of the same coin, with the Objective realm coming from the Subjective realm. A concrete example of this idea is found in the potter's clay[50]. Prior to the potter extracting a certain amount of clay from the bulk, there is an "unformed," "undefined," and "undifferentiated" mass of substance (energy/matter). The potter (conscious/will) determines what will be created and how much clay (energy/matter) is needed to accomplish the task.

The removal of the clay to be utilized in the project is the beginning of the transition from the "Subjective" to the "Objective" realm; the first Manifestation is personified as the NTR Ausar (Osiris), Obatala in Yoruba (Ifa) and called Kether in Hebrew Kabalistic terms. The formation of the clay into a specified object is the completion of the process (Geb - Kemet, Malkuth – Kabbalah). The process of going from the undifferentiated clump all the way to the clay bowl used to hold food is identified by the various spheres (Sephiroth) and paths along the "tree of life" extending from the top to the bottom; mastery of the manifested object is done from the bottom to the top.

In the Bantu cultures of southern Africa, the word for the "Subjective" realm is Ntu. In the Kemetic cultures it is known as Amen/Amun and in certain cases, Nu (Nu-t). Many cultures acknowledge that humans are a direct extraction and formation of a portion of God. These cultures also maintain that during the shaping process, humans have "forgotten" their true nature as unconditioned aspects of God, and have ignorantly began to take on the characteristics of their "Objective" manifestation and conditionings (i.e., body, personality, etc.). It is through the process of initiation, and the use of cosmology that humans are able to remember their

---

49   A reference to eternal Light as internally experienced.
50   This is not a truly perfect example because it is virtually impossible to express what exists in the Subjective Realm because it is indeed no-thing. Thus the clay is more of an example of the first manifestation from the Subjective realm into the Objective realm called Ausar or Kether, however, we will use it as an example of the Subjective realm for this discussion.

African Spiritual Systems

true nature and live up to their full potential[51].

But what is the full potential of humans? According to the indigenous and ancient people of Kemet and various other cultures around the world, humans, in their spiritually and mentally unconditioned state, share in the three main qualities ascribed to God; that is, humans have the potential to function in an Omniscient, Omnipresent, and Omnipotent manner. This knowledge is what sheds light on the detriment of using statements such as, "we are only human," to excuse limitations and mistakes.

African spiritual systems, and those of other cultural and racial groups, tend to differentiate humans based on their level of awareness and the culmination of their experiences with Nature, outward forms of creation, as well as their internal environment (mind, emotions, thoughts). These distinguishing factors are usually divided along the lines of the initiated vs. the non-initiated. While there are many different labels and levels used to identify various levels and degrees of "awakening" (initiation) found throughout the vast amount of African literature, we will use Ra Un Nefer Amen's categories (Sahu, Ab, and Ba) as found in the Metu Neter Vol. 1.

It seems that the masses of people always make up the lower tier of human consciousness, called the Sahu or "animal spirit." This level consists of people who, for the most part, are not initiated into a higher awareness of reality, making many of their life decisions based on emotions, beliefs (true or false), attraction to superficial pleasures (i.e., taste, touch, sight, smell, sounds), the avoidance of pain, loss, and the gain of material things. Humans functioning at this level are usually unaware of their greater potential and will often resist influences towards the unveiling of their current state of functioning. This level of existence exemplifies the phrase "ignorance is bliss," regardless of the fact that ignorance rarely produces true bliss. Don't misunderstand and believe that the ignorance being referred to here is purely of an intellectual nature, and thus can be corrected by mere intellectual workings. On the contrary, many intellectually astute people will be totally ignorant in regards to reality and how we can function in it, in a superior fashion. A shin-

---

[51] This is what was meant in my earlier statement of working the tree from the bottom to the top in order to master the creations.

ing example is the medical doctor that smokes cigarettes or does anything else to bring harm to their own physical health or that of their patients. Or how about the learned preacher, the good reverend doctor who has finished Divinity School but has not emerged Divine, and actually knows nothing of it.

The second tier, called Ab[52] or "human spirit", is the level at which humans who have made a conscious choice to pursue their higher nature, begin to get in touch with the moral, noble, and just aspects of their existence. The key to benefitting from the abilities found at this level of existence is to consciously choose to overcome the urges set forth by the Sahu nature (i.e., emotions, false beliefs, superficial pleasures), by being devoted to self-refinement and the exploration of your belief systems, for the sole purpose of realigning what we find with what is morally correct AND true, while simultaneously cultivating the ability to resist being blindly led by the emotions and lower nature.

The next and highest category of spiritual development for humans is called the Ba[53] or "Divine spirit." This is the level at which humans align themselves with the three attributes of God (omniscience, omnipresence, and omnipotence) and begin to reflect this experience in their daily lives. It is at this level that sages and spiritual masters are fully awakened. Those who have reached this level of spiritual development are able to intuit (know directly), manifest (power), and exist (be) in the world as if they are one with the whole, meeting no enemies or strangers along the road. The manifestation of this level of spiritual development is readily identifiable by simple observation of the billions of cells found within the human body. Although each cell is an individual, and some varying tremendously in form and function (i.e., a neuron compared to skin cell), they all typically function in proper order, physiologically supporting and existing for the sake of the entire organism. It is only when this harmony is disrupted that disease (dis-ease) is capable of negatively impacting the body.

Arabs (both Christian and Muslims) identify this state of being as "din," or living and functioning according to divine law

---

52   "Ab" refers to the heart, the organ to which human morality was assigned, and was weighed during the judgement of the person's soul after death.
53   Loosely translated as the "soul"

African Spiritual Systems

and order. What many ancient and indigenous cultures have realized is that nature, when in its uncorrupted state, seems to always function according to its din; a notion symbolized by the mummified body of Ausar (Osiris). The trees never cease to produce breathable oxygen for humans and animals, just as the lungs of these same creatures never cease to produce the carbon dioxide necessary for the photosynthesis processes of the trees and other plants (an example of the interrelated aspects of Nature – Maat). The planets and sun are also following certain paths and are considered to be functioning according to their din. Of all of creation, it seems that humans are the only creatures possessing the ability to consciously make a decision to go against its nature (its true and highest potential), and manipulate other aspects of creation to do the same; a characteristic that represents the God-quality of human beings (i.e., Free Will).

The ancient and indigenous spiritual masters of African societies realized the importance of cultivating and maintaining a conscious awareness of the higher aspects of what it is to be human. In order to guarantee the proliferation of this knowledge throughout society, various systems of initiation (commonly referred to as rites of passage or secret societies) were constructed and implemented. The sole purpose of many initiation processes is and was to "awaken" the human being, to become consciously aware of their spiritual powers and to initiate a process of re-membering all that has been forgotten (fragmented) through the creation process (the concretizing of the spirit into the more dense physical form).

Many cultures in Africa, and throughout the Diaspora, have their own variation of the awakening process and ushers its citizens through their own unique rite of passage. Dr. Raymond A. Winbush, for example, speaks of how during the initiation rites of the Poro society of West Africa, the boys are/were removed from the village at a designated age by the elder initiates in order to formally undergo their "manhood training."[54] According to some sources, these boys are/were removed for approximately six months, during which they learned how to become responsible and able men to their society, this included lessons in hunting, cooking, husbandry, specific skills and trades. What is not discussed is the spiritual

---

54 See *The Warrior Method* by Raymond A. Winbush

and so-called magical training that also takes place during these mystical rites. This is for good reason. Like most true initiation processes, the details and specifics of their power-filled initiations is held secret and can only be known by those who have undergone the process.[55] Another reason is that much of the spiritual cultivation that occurred pre-European and Arab invasion and influence, has been "lost" to the more modern religious expressions found in Christianity and Islam (both of which also carry their own versions of mystical rites of passage and magical initiations which is unfortunately not typically shared with their conquered groups).

The female counterparts to the Poro are known as the Sande society. They too, serve to develop the female youth into responsible women in their society; coaching them at the development of skills and a trade, the meaning of being a wife, puberty rites and the rearing and raising of children—again, the true depths of their initiation processes are also hidden from the profane and uninitiated. In both societies, the training focuses on spiritual, as well as mental and physical development; the individuals are also taught to respect the complementary sex, and to see them as an intricate part of society as a whole. Both groups are taught the laws of their village and are groomed to become responsible adults in the community.

Jawanza Kunjufu cites an indigenous "African" society located in the highlands of New Guinea who carry the name Busama. This particular group is known for their use of fire during their initiation processes. The male initiates must pass a trial in which they are required to run along a path of hot coals in order to "prove" their readiness to become a man in their society. This trial is one amongst many that requires both mental and physical abilities, including courage, endurance, and perseverance. It is unfortunate that much of what we have available to us regarding the depth of indigenous African initiation is for all intents and purposes akin to blurbs in National Geographic magazine; the perspective of an outsider, a non-initiate. With the exception of European archaeologists like Simon Ottenberg[56], Placid Temples[57], Beryl Bellman[58], M.

---

55   Beryl Bellman does a study of the Poro and Sande societies published as *The Language of Secrecy: Symbols & Metaphors in Poro Ritual*.
56   *Boyhood Rituals in an African Secret Society: An Interpretation*
57   *Bantu Philosophy*
58   *The Language of Secrecy: Symbols and Metaphors in Poro Ritual*

African Spiritual Systems

Griaule & M. Dieterlen[59], and others, many modern researchers do not submerge themselves into the cultures and thus do not obtain the necessary initiations to receive direct knowledge of what actually takes place. Even for those that do, oft times their worldview and role as a researcher limits their ability to gain a true understanding of what they have experienced.

Fortunately, Malidoma Some' gives a brief overview, as an indigenous African, of his direct cultural experiences with initiation. According to Some', the Dagbara of Burkino Faso, West Africa, utilize five elements (Water, Earth, Mineral, Fire, and Nature) to teach and test their initiates' worthiness of becoming a responsible and respected adult in their community. Each element represents a stage and a quality of initiation, each involving its respective element and their respective energies. The rituals performed are discussed to the extent that he is allowed to reveal them, based on an obligation of secrecy that every initiate must take. The lessons that each initiate masters throughout the process are phenomenal and serve as a staunch reminder of what is missing throughout the Diaspora.

In his book, "***Of Water and the Spirit***," Some' gives a detailed story of his own experience during his initiation process, which he received after he was thoroughly indoctrinated by a French Jesuit school, to which he was stolen away (literally kidnapped). He explains how much of the hardship and turmoil experienced in his pre-initiation life, specifically while being instructed under the culture of the colonizers, was directly related to him being forced to live "off-purpose." His life took a complete turn toward a divine and healthy improvement once he was reconnected with his indigenous culture and allowed to initiate. The stories told by Some', to the untrained and uninitiated, seem to be incredulous and totally fictitious. However, as one who has experienced initiation both on the African continent (in Ghana amongst the Ewe, and in Gambia amongst the Jolla) as well as here in the United States (initiated into a Kemetic priesthood and Ifa as a priest of Olokun) I have witnessed and experienced things that totally blow back the walls of what many believe to be reality[60].

---

59 *The Pale Fox*
60 Some of these experiences are discussed in a future chapter.

Symbolically Speaking: African Lodge #1

One of the oldest records of rites of passage/initiation processes is found in the Nile Valley in the land formerly called Kemet (Egypt). The people of these great and ancient civilizations are known to have descended from the more ancient African cultures found along the Nile, headed to the south (including Sudan, Uganda, Kenya, and Ethiopia), and have surely inherited the seeds for their science and spiritual knowledge from these more ancient groups. The social fabric of these societies was constructed around the process of spiritual development to the extent that even their buildings and temples were designed to facilitate their growth[61].

The initiation process was on-going, with its marked beginning existing prior to conception and the forming of the physical part of life. Indeed, their process was understood to have began with the spiritual journey of the soul towards the gathering flesh, and continued with the soul's journey back to its source (God) after the flesh was no longer animate (death). The understanding of this ancient and powerful process is vital to our comprehension of modern day rites of passage programs and systems of initiation, including Freemasonry, and thus we will briefly outline it.

The Kemetic initiation philosophy, like many other ancient cultures, was ingeniously recorded as a myth (allegory); theirs is specifically contained within the ancient story of Ausar and Auset (called Osiris and Isis, respectively, in Latin), as well as the various Pyramid Texts and Pert em Heru[62] (Book of Coming Into the Light). Auset, representing the personality (individualized soul) is married to Ausar who represents the true and Divine Self of humans, that is, the God within. In most versions of the story, Ausar was tricked by his evil brother Set (the separating and destructive aspect of creation). The goal of the deception was to get Ausar to lay down in a coffin in order to kill him and take over his kingdom. Set and his confederacy were successful and later chopped Ausar into fourteen pieces, scattering his parts around the world. Auset, through her love and devotion for Ausar, traveled the world in order to re-member the dis-membered body of her husband Ausar. Upon re-membering the body of Ausar (minus his reproductive

---

61   See R. A. Schwaller de Lubicz' *The Temple In Man*, as well as Volume 2 of *Symbolically Speaking: African Lodge #1*.
62   Often mislabeled *The Book of the Dead*.

organs which were swallowed by a fish), Auset magically conceived a child, Heru, whose task it was to reestablish Justice and Order to his father's now chaotic world.

This story is the blueprint of the initiation process. Auset, who symbolizes the masses of people, was once wedded to her true Divine Self, Ausar. This is symbolic of the African belief that all of creation is of the Divine. Through the experiences of life, she eventually became weakened and was overthrown by the base and carnal desires of the lower, "animal spirit" (personified by Set in the story). This represents the creation process and the unguided soul's battle with the experiences of their physical nature. The lower nature caused Auset's connection to, and memory of, her divine nature to become severed and scattered amongst the chaotic movements of the lower self. This part of the story is used to symbolize the pain, trials and tribulations of the uninitiated human experience, which is transient and dependant upon certain physical criteria before "peace" is experienced. Some have also equated the scattering of Ausar's body with the scattering of the truth throughout the world as presented in the following statement:

> "All Faith is False, All Faith is True. Truth is a Mirror broken into Many Pieces, Everyone Claiming their Bit, to be the Whole."

She eventually, through devotion and sorrow from the experience of hardships, began to remember the Divine aspects of life and renewed her experience with those parts of her true nature. This is representative of the rites of passage process, during which initiated elders guide the neophytes through a process of trials and tribulations akin to those projected throughout life, in order that they may, once again, gain an understanding of their divine nature.

In traditional African societies, the external process of initiation begins at the onset of puberty, around 12 years of age. During the first seven years of life, the human is primarily developing the anatomical and physiological structures necessary for future survival, which is heavily based on physical coordination, communication skills and adaptability. The next seven years is usually when the socialization process becomes the focus. Typically, in the previous stages, the developing human has learned to talk, develop motor skills enough to ambulate, and has began to become familiar with their surroundings and primary caregivers and perhaps family members. Amen labels the human trait responsible for this development as "indiscriminate imitation." It is theorized that humans in this stage of development, utilize models in their environment in order to emulate and imitate. This is consistent with various theories of developmental and cognitive psychology.

Initiation, in the form of rites of passage, is the key to unlocking the developing human's mind from this mode of operating. Up until the time of initiation, it is believed that humans function at a level that lacks the consciousness and the spiritual sophistication needed to successfully and consistently overcome many of the forthcoming situations in life. The vast majority of people living in indigenous societies are formally initiated; beginning the process with an awakening ceremony that was well documented by the ancient book entitled Pert Em Heru (Becoming Awake), and continued amongst many cultures throughout the continent and the world. This book is mistakenly referred to by many as the **Egyptian Book of the Dead** because of its use to guide the souls of the deceased through their next rite of passage. The Kemetic people believed rites of passage occurred at many stages of life (including death), and that the instructions for the living were the same as those for the deceased (As Above, So Below).

The awakening ceremony is utilized to bring the individual out of the perpetual state of trance that has engulfed them since physical conception. This stage is often related to water, dreams, nighttime, moonlight, and the womb. It is believed by some cultures that if this state of trance is not overcome and henceforth controlled, the individual remains in a childlike state for the rest of their existence[63]. It is similar to the phenomenon of sleepwalking, or hypnosis, a state in which an individual is highly susceptible to suggestions and is likely to blindly follow the trends, movements and influences of others. The dominant cognitive function of this stage of initiation is memory and altering states of consciousness at will.

After the initial awakening process, the main focus of the

---

63 Alfred "Coach" Powell calls this Prolonged Adolescence Syndrome. See *Hip Hop Hypocrisy: When Lies Sound Like the Truth*.

African Spiritual Systems

initiation is to challenge the false beliefs and limitations that have been adopted over the uninitiated lifetime, and to replace these beliefs with information and knowledge of the true and divine self through mental exercises and the learning of a trade. These false beliefs and limitations are self-imposed roadblocks to the actualization of the true potential of humankind. These roadblocks can manifest from early life trauma, from adverse stimuli, the learning of false information, and/or the indiscriminate imitation of uninitiated people.

The information and knowledge acquired during this stage of initiation is based on the cosmogony of the culture and is often only transmitted via the spoken word or highly codified writings. The trade the person is initiated into, is directly related to the life purpose of the individual, which was identified prior to their birth, and was sometimes determined by the family in which they were born, and their role in the overall community[64]. Verbal communication skills are further developed at this stage with the intention of equipping the initiate with a vocabulary and knowledge of language that will allow them to negotiate their condition in an "adult" world. Amongst the Dogon, various stages of their initiation process are defined based on how the individual engages the word.[65]

The third stage of initiation is the last of the stages utilized to raise an individual from the depths of Sahu existence to the noble and upright position of an individual living at the Ab level of existence[66]. This stage focuses on the visual images entertained by the initiate, their utilization of creative expression, as well as their ideas pertaining to the experience of pleasure and joy. People tend to utilize their visualization time imagining joyful and pleasurable situations, however, many who are exposed to negative imagery and experiences are easily inundated with dangerous and even scary imaginings. For the neophyte and uninitiated, a major goal is to

---

[64] This concept of learning a trade as part of initiation is beautifully illustrated by Isha Schwaller de Lubicz in Her Bak volumes 1 and 2. It is a peculiar coincidence that Freemasonry is based on stonemasonry as a trade, and how much of our rites are based on speculatively learning this trade.

[65] The giri so (word at face value), the benne so (word on the side), the bolo so (word from behind), and the so dayi (clear word).

[66] Similar to the EA degree in Freemasonry, the Sahu level is designed as a preparatory phase, and as a primer for what is to come.

assist them in recognizing and controlling their visualizations, in order to utilize this tool for the manipulation of their situations and behaviors, ultimately to improve the overall quality and experience of life.

In regards to the pleasure aspect of this level of initiation, the goal is to teach the initiate to utilize temperance in order to control their desires and pleasure seeking behaviors. This is important because it reduces the likelihood that children will participate in high-risk activities, which can compromise the physical health and well being of the individual and the community as a whole. The initiate is taught how to utilize their imaginative faculty during meditation and trance work in order to manipulate the life force and manifest, through spiritual cultivation, desired outcomes. This ability becomes instrumental in the later stages of initiation[67].

The fourth stage of initiation is the first stage where the formal awakening of the initiate takes place. Previously, the initiate was taught how to recognize altered states of consciousness (trance, meditation) to alter certain beliefs and behaviors. They were led in all of the tasks by the initiator. In this stage the initiator teaches the initiates to become self-determined; they engage in exercises geared towards increasing their life force to the degree where it is strong enough to "awaken" their previously dormant Will[68].

In order for the initiate to raise their life force to a level sufficient enough for awakening the Will, it is necessary to engage in certain breathing techniques (Dummo Breathing, Naddi Madi Shudi) and physical exercises (Qi Gong, Tantric Sex, Yoga). Over time, the initiate becomes more aware and sensitive to their environment, giving them a higher state of receptivity and a perspective that is more keen than the uninitiated. The animal totem of this stage of initiation is the hawk, which is known for its ability to fly at great altitudes and its superb eyesight. Its celestial correspondence is the sun, which is known as Ra, the heavenly version of the internal life force of all human beings.

The ability to make decisions free from emotional coercion

---

[67]   This is the underlying philosophy to sciences such as Qi Gong, Reiki, Tantric and Kundalini Yoga, etc.
[68]   The Will is a human attribute that allows a person to make choices, free from emotional influences and persuasion from personal desires.

is a major factor separating the initiate at this level of consciousness (Ab) from those of the former (Sahu). It is due to one's functioning at this level of consciousness, that we must accredit the moralistic and upright functioning associated with this stage of initiation. When an initiate can no longer be coerced by base desires, and solicitous temptations, they are able to freely act according to principles and codes taught to them in the second stage of initiation, which are then reinforced in the following. It is clear to see how this type of training could greatly benefit society, especially given the numbers of celebrities and "leaders" getting caught up in sex-based scandals and other situations that call their characters into question.

The fifth stage of initiation is simply a higher degree of the previous in that it further substantiates the idea that one is free from emotional coercion, and that their choices, throughout life, should be based on moralistic codes and principles. It enforces the idea that one must willingly function according to divine law and correct living in order to gain the maximum benefit and reap the finest of rewards in life. Africans who utilize this particular spiritual system believe that when someone lives according to the principles of this stage of initiation, they are endowed with spiritual protection and divine immunity. This same belief is cited in many religious systems in the form of divine protection[69].

Taken to a deeper level, this stage of initiation also correlates with the physical immune system of the human body. It too functions according to the properties of divine law, meaning if someone violates the "laws" of healthy human living (i.e., sleep deprivation, overeating, under eating, introduction of "poisonous" substances into the body) the body will become more susceptible to infection and the person becomes ill. Likewise, if a person follows the laws of healthy living, they will have a strengthened immunity and will not succumb so easily to illness. Following divine law yields physical and spiritual protection.

It is important for the initiate to realize that while some things may be harmful to their well being if it is handled incorrectly (i.e., ingested, carelessly, ignorantly), they all have their place, pur-

---

69   We see it spelled out in the Bible as "No weapon formed against thee shall prosper." (Isaiah 54:17)

pose and role in the scheme of creation. For example, the properties of bleach make it beneficial for use as a cleaner and harmful if it is ingested and/or inhaled into the human body. This chemical is not a bad chemical; it just has its specific function and use. All things can be explained in the same way according to this particular African spiritual science. All things have a purpose, and no thing has a property in and of itself; it is all relative to that which it is relating to. For example, hot water is only "hot" as it relates to waters found at lower temperatures, how it relates to human body temperature, or how it registers on a thermometer. Sit it next to lava, and all of a sudden it is quite cool.

Upon administration of the physical, mental and spiritual exercises of the fifth stage of initiation, the initiate should understand that there are certain consequences (equal and opposite reactions) for every choice and action that they make and take. In order to further enforce this principal, the initiate is graduated to the next stage of initiation, which elaborates on the interdependency, inter-relatedness and inter-connectivity of all things in creation.

The sixth stage of initiation is the final stage in the Ab level of consciousness. This is the stage where the initiate begins to thoroughly understand the underlying principles of creation. This is also the stage where the initiate begins to develop the cognitive skills that drive their ability to synthetically (synthesis) conceive and think of the world. Mastery of this stage is the truest form of holistic functioning because it allows one to categorize elements based on mutual relationships, characteristics, and the effects they may have on other things. For example, one who has mastered this stage will become proficient in their ability to identify and categorize all things that have similar qualities as fire, i.e., centrifugal activity, increase in temperature, increase in speed, rapidly and violently destructive situations, etc. They realize that fire corresponds with summer, fever, rage, cayenne pepper, horseradish, passion, skin eruptions (rashes), violent assaults, and high blood pressure amongst other things.

The importance of this ability lies in the fact that initiation is simply a means of introducing the initiates to the macrocosm (big picture) by isolating similar experiences into a microcosmic

African Spiritual Systems

experience (their individual life). In other words, initiation serves the purpose of exposing the young initiates to situations that they will inevitably face throughout their adult life, in order to give them experiences in which they have successfully and efficiently negotiated the matter, in a relatively safe environment. This stage of initiation is the key to success when it comes to understanding the macro-cosmic experience. Strength and mastery here, allows the initiate who mastered the "water" aspects of initiation by successfully swimming across the "Great River," to approach a seemingly dangerous situation involving a large body of volatile water with confidence and success (i.e., a mid-water rescue). It is this stage of initiation that really fortifies the initiate's deep understanding of the initiation process, demonstrating how their performance within this closed cycle of experiences, is applicable to the "random" experiences of life and the forthcoming responsibilities of adulthood. It gives them knowledge of the tools they have and practice using them.

The seventh stage of initiation is the first of the Ba or divine level of awareness. It is within the experiences of this stage that the initiate "dies" to the world. They must forsake all worldly things in order to gain spiritual power. This is perhaps the most difficult of all stages because the initiate begins to experience exercises that are designed to draw their consciousness away from the tangible things in life (i.e., material wealth, interpersonal relationships, and external conditions), towards the more unseen, spiritually-driven, and selfless aspects of the responsible initiate. The planetary correspondence of this stage is Saturn, which is a large and slow moving planet. This correspondence helps the initiate to understand that while life is moving at its respective pace, one's mind must always function in a relatively slow and calculated, cool and concise, focused and concentrated manner.

During this stage, the initiate's attachment to their physical body is severed by sometimes harsh and dangerous exercises. For example, some groups "bury" their initiates for a period of time in order to give them the experience of being dead. Other cultures utilize this stage to force their initiates to overcome certain self-imposed limitations by placing them in situations in which they have to overcome an obstacle or perish. This stage is implemented in an amazingly calculated manner. It comes only after the initiate has proven the ability to detach his or herself from certain qualities that will surely cause them failure at this level. The main objective of this stage of initiation is to awaken the spiritual power that lies dormant within the human individual. The initiate, once given the official title of being "dead," takes on a new name to signify their purpose and newly discovered spiritual powers. This is known as their initiate name, and its use is reserved only for those who have also been initiated. The initiates are also given access to the powers of mantra, or spiritual sounds that are uttered by the mind and/or mouth. These mantra, or hekau, are believed to be vehicles for spiritual powers, which manifest the qualities of certain divine intelligences when uttered by one who has "died" and become awakened through this stage of initiation.

The eighth stage of initiation focuses on the development of the intuitional talents of the initiate. During the previous stage, the overcoming of the distracting nature of worldly things and conditions was proven; this accomplishment allows for one to still the thinking process in order to receive the direct wisdom of what Amen calls the "indwelling intelligence," and what Isha Schwaller de Lubicz calls the "permanent witness." This intelligence is believed to be divine in nature, and to directly reflect the omniscience of God. It is this same divine faculty that Oracle systems (Ifa, Metu Neter, I Ching, Afa, Dilogun, etc.) are believed to harness and manipulate in order to reveal the underlying structure, implications and meaning of life events. The initiate is given tasks that require them to successfully utilize their intuition to solve problems, answer riddles, complete puzzles and exit labyrinths. Many of the tasks are presented in high risk and high pressure situations in order to limit the likelihood of the initiate utilizing their thinking and intellectual abilities instead of exercising their intuitive gifts.

The master of this stage is considered to be a sage, the personification of divine wisdom. The sage is one who gives guidance to the community and its leaders. The sage is thought to be the most noble of all positions in the community because they have intentionally opened a conscious and direct connection with God.

African Spiritual Systems

In these cultures, the kings would have obtained this degree of initiation and hence would be considered the representation of God on earth. This is very different from how "leaders" come to power here in Western Civilization and cultures[70].

The tenth stage of the initiation process is where the initiate, through their previous accomplishments and acquired skills, are able to realize that they are *one* with all of creation. They literally are able to engage in such a state of consciousness in which they experience the fact that there is only one being dwelling in all of reality, and that all of creation is merely an expression of the one being, God. This is considered to be the second highest development in the life of a human. It is at this stage that an initiate is perceived to be a true unifier of the upper and lower self, yielding the same power and abilities as the indwelling intelligence, which is responsible for the maintenance of the heart beat, the digestion of food, the division of cells, and all other miraculous and "automatic" functions of the universe, micro and macro.

The eleventh and final stage of initiation is where the initiate is able to, through the practice of meditation and trance work, experience what is called Amani (Peace) in Ki-Swahili or Amen in the Kemetic language. This stage is considered the highest of human spiritual achievement, which upon mastering, one enters the realm of the ancestors shortly thereafter, and become what is referred to as an "ascended Master." According to the authors of this particular spiritual system, the final stage takes years, perhaps several lifetimes, to achieve and is the underlying purpose and goal of all human existence. In the classic Kung Fu movie, *The 36 Chambers of Shaolin* (also known as *Shaolin Master Killer*), this high level of initiation is depicted as the final "chamber." The monks at this level were all sitting meditatively, while in many of the previous chambers, they were engaged in rigorous physical activities. When the initiate ambitiously attempted to by-pass all previous stages, in order to experience the highest and final level, he soon realized his error and was incapable of experiencing such power.

The initiation system detailed above, is an iteration of what

---

70 In the last chapter of *Her Bak*, Her Bak as an initiate is introduced to the Sage as the TRUE power behind the Kingdom as everybody, including the King, bowed in reverence to his presence.

is found in Metu Neter vols. 1 and 2, by Ra Un Nefer Amen. While not an exact replica of the Ancient systems, it provides the scientific framework upon which many past and present rites of passage and/or initiation programs are based. This framework has been adopted and modified by many cultures throughout Africa and the Diaspora, providing for the multitude of variations in rites of passage initiation processes. Many modern day rites of passage programs utilize portions of this framework, combining it with modern resources and themes, which are necessary for the programs to be effective in the present context. One very empowering aspect of many modern rites of passage programs is that they often combine lessons, proverbs, themes and procedures from a variety of African regions and cultures, providing for a well-rounded experience to those who participate. We will now take some time to briefly explore the rites of passage concept as it relates to Freemasonry.

Rites of passage processes are generally defined as transitions from one phase of life to another, marked by an identifiable experience or experiences, and a change in perspective and related outcomes. It is safe to say that everyone experiences several rites of passage all throughout their lifetimes. For example, a person as a developing fetus is experiencing the rite of conception and life as a fetus. The mother who is pregnant is undergoing the rite of pregnancy. The birthing process is another rite of passage. Puberty (nocturnal emissions/menarche), first sexual encounters, marriage, buying first home, high school graduations, prom, obtaining driver's licenses, first job, first smoke, first drink, reaching legal age to purchase and consume intoxicating substances, etc., are all examples of rites of passages, to which many are attentive and consciously manipulating.

In comparison to the original concept of the rites of passage process[71], our modern day focus is lacking in substance, meaning, and purpose. For many youth in African American communities, the rites of passage process is relegated to haphazard, media-driven, and violence-ridden experiences, through which one stumbles behind a guide who is also lost, and sometimes deliberately misdirecting the naive. Young ladies bear the scars of years of unad-

---

71 To awaken the consciousness of individuals to the level at which they obtain a greater awareness of God and Self.

dressed molestation and the subsequent promiscuity and failed relationships, while the young men continue in the example of the absentee father, replaced by a televised image of Black men that are criminal, oversexed, violent, and uncaring. Both are doomed. Many scholars and community workers have recognized this sobering fact, and have reacted by developing programs designed to restore a conscious awareness of other aspects of life, that are diametrically opposed to the identified problem behaviors.

According to Brookins' model, rites of passage programs "are designed to provide a structured and formalized process through which youth develop the basis for a strong self-concept that will prepare them for coping with the many challenges they will encounter as they enter adulthood." His model presents rites of passage as a means for developing skills for dealing with the everyday stressors of life. This method is a defensive approach, which benefits the participant by arming them with the awareness that: 1) there is an element that attempts to steer them wrong, and 2) there is a way of protecting yourself from this element. Brookins' model entitled the "Adolescent Developmental Pathways Paradigm" (ADPP), is a program that links ethnic identity with the self-concept and developmental processes of adolescence. This is achieved by providing an understanding of ethnic identity and through the intentional socialization of its participants towards an identity that is stable and healthy.

The ADPP provides a process through which its participants develop: a) knowledge of American African history and culture; b) positive perspectives towards American African history and culture; c) belief in the inherent ability and strength of American African people; d) adherence to an Africentric value system that emphasizes the positive principles of African philosophy, as reflected by the recognition of their spiritual connection with nature and other humans; e) demonstrable competencies and skills that are consistent with these principles and that provide the child with the ability to adequately function within the American system on a social and economic level; and f) a commitment to activities that promote the development of the American African community and its legitimate integration into the wider social system.

Symbolically Speaking: African Lodge #1

This model assumes that the degree to which an individual can counteract negative images, attitudes and behaviors perpetually projected upon their sense of identity, determines the degree to which a person is able to successfully perceive and negotiate the world. This powerful and detailed model provides the framework through which an individual may develop beneficial strategies for resisting the aforementioned detrimental factors, which, in turn allows the person to develop an awareness of racial and oppressive realities, the likelihood of experiencing such realities, ego defense techniques to defend themselves against these realities, an orientation that finds faults in the overall context and systems as opposed to within the individual, active participation in one's own community, as well as a spiritual orientation of life in order to recognize the non-material nature of creation and all events therein.

Brookins provides the following list of psychological objectives that modern day rites of passage programs should accomplish in order to be most effective:

1. An expansion of the identity and knowledge gained during earlier developmental periods.
2. The completion of and separation from childhood roles.
3. Coming to terms with the fears and anxiety produced by the anticipation of previously unexplored roles and responsibilities.
4. Learning to attach meaning to personal and group based knowledge and experiences.
5. Exploring and developing commitments in a variety of identity domains.
6. The re-emergence of a new outer identity.

In summary, the author states that "rites of passage initiates, structures, and formalizes the process of achieving an ethnically-conscious self-concept." In the world of Prince Hall Freemasonry, we have youth organizations, namely the Pythagoreans, that are typically sons or relatives of Prince Hall Freemasons. These young men are brought together under the tutelage of Freemasons that serve as their mentors and guides. While this process is greatly beneficial to both the Craft and the youth, it seems to be lacking in structure and form that would make it a genuine Rites of Passage process as outlined above. Part of the issue stems from the fact that many of the Brothers in the Prince Hall family, and men in general,

African Spiritual Systems

have never oriented their own experiences as being part of a rites of passage process, and thus fail to consciously acknowledge the benefits and power of such.

In order to structure a rites of passage program for our youth, we as adults must have experienced a conscious awakening to the fact that these are even necessary. Having been I, P, and R as MM, each of us has participated in rituals and a rites of passage process. Unfortunately, many of our initiators have failed to make it plain and clear to us, the potential powers latent in what we are doing. Much of our current practice as Freemasons, specifically those of us descending from the African Lodge, is devoid of spiritual science. It is full of religious art, but severely lacking in the step-by-step, scientific protocols that are designed to, in deed, make "good men better." Based on the brief outline of African spiritual science presented in the previous section, we can clearly see what we are missing as adults, and thus are incapable of giving to the youth: 1) a knowledge and practice of improving our physical vehicles (body); 2) intentional processes for improving our cognitive skills and utilization of our minds (including memory, analytical & synthetical thinking skills, creative visualization, etc.); 3) the strengthening of our ability to choose without emotional coercion, in a holistic manner, based on truth; 4) the ability to discern and subsequently live truth, and therefore consistently behave in a just and correct manner; 5) cultivate and embrace our true spiritual powers; 6) further develop our ability to "know" beyond available "facts," opinions, feelings, thoughts, and apparent contradictions; in other words, to be truly wise; 7) to be a unifying and strengthening force in our organizations and communities, beyond superficial differences; and lastly, 8) the ability to generate and maintain a true state of peace, regardless of circumstances.

Being truthful with ourselves, take a moment to review the above list. Be honest about your position in each of these categories. Be honest about when, if, and where you received training along any of these lines. Was it merely information or was it knowledge and understanding, accompanied by practical skills development through specific techniques? Are you able to teach young Brothers and Sisters in any of these categories? Can they look at you as a living example of any of this? At a glance, we seem to have all these bases covered; upon deeper exploration, we are found wanting.

When exploring the process of enslavement, many of our historians and political activists emphasize the political, economical, and even the physical aspects of the Maafa[72]. Rarely do we see a spiritual analysis designed to help us understand how deeply the experience has impacted us. This is not to be confused with the religious discussions where scholars will identify how missionaries came to Africa to spread their religious beliefs, and how they forced and coerced conversion, and weakened the social and organizational structures of Africa (which is also a valid and necessary discussion). We should ask: "What were our practical tools for applying our religious beliefs?" and, "How were these impacted by the traumatic and ongoing assaults related to enslavement and colonization?"

A shift in worldview seems to be at the core of this disruption. Our worldview is what determines and dictates how we view and understand reality (ontology), how we place value on things (axiology), and how we know what we know (epistemology). When changing just one of these, you can totally reorient an individual's or group's interaction with the world. This seemingly simple shift is at the root of all non-organic mental illness[73]. When, for example, you are able to convince a person, that they are being cursed by an unseen and unverifiable force, and that they will live their lives this way, and perhaps their "after-life" too, unless they believe a certain thing, you can then create an obsessive-compulsive personality that is stifled by the anxiety associated with doing that "certain thing."

As an example of shifting an individual's worldview, we will once again refer to the scene in the movie *The Matrix*. Neo, in the first part of the movie, is living his life under one set of assumptions about "reality." He has a job, political views, hobbies, and even a particular look about himself. When he begins to experience things that challenge his existing worldview, he starts to slip into mental instability. The more his present worldview is disrupted, the more

---

[72] Maafa is a Ki-Swahili word that means "the great destruction" and is often used to describe the enslavement and colonization of Africa and her peoples by Arabs and Europeans.

[73] Non-organic meaning not dealing specifically with brain structure issues, or neurochemically-based maladies.

unstable he becomes until eventually, he is left with a decision: totally shift his perspective of reality, or forever live in this uncertainty that has been created for him. He chooses to totally shift his paradigm and worldview which is the point where his conscious and intentional rites of passage begins.

When he is "raised" from the dead level to a living perpendicular, his hoodwink is removed and he is assisted to a standing position. He exclaims that his eyes hurt...this is due to the Light he is seeing for the first time. While he was unconscious, he was receiving the necessary physical and energetic treatments designed to strengthen and heal is atrophied physical body[74]. Once physically capable, he was then ushered along to the mental training exercises designed to improve his physical efficiency. Knowledge and information were directly downloaded into his brain, which gave him access to the actual skills related to this information and knowledge. To his own surprise, he now knew things beyond what he knew before.

At this point it was necessary for him to demonstrate that he actually knew what he claimed, and was capable of taking it further on his own. This is related to the later stages of initiation as outlined earlier, where the initiate is required to use their spiritual powers and apply their knowledge in various situations. As the movie progresses, it becomes apparent that Neo must identify with the deeper and more spiritual aspects of himself, in order to be successful. This is directly in line with the outline provided earlier in this text. It was necessary for him to detach from his personal identity and limitations, in favor of his divine self, in order to tap into the powers necessary to accomplish his goal. I strongly recommend reflecting on or re-viewing and perhaps studying ***The Matrix*** from the perspective outlined thus far in this book. One last point as it relates to our ability to "initiate" others, only after we ourselves have been initiated: Neo's initiator, Morpheus, himself had been initiated and awakened to the reality of the world. His paradigm had been shifted and his worldview brought closer in line to reality. Without this experience, he would not have been able to assist the others.

Goggins, in his work on rites of passage, defines it as a mul<u>tifaceted process</u> that preserves cultural self-consciousness along

---

74   This was done via acupuncture treatments.

with the collective cultural wisdom of a society, while marking the transition from one stage of life to another, inclusive of the change in expectation and responsibilities. He identifies a variety of rites (biological, philosophical and social passages) culminating in the formal celebration and acknowledgment of birth, puberty, death, marriage, adulthood, and self-consciousness. These rites may be applied to communities, families and individuals.

In his small but detailed book regarding rites of passage, Goggins conducted interviews with five people who have had personal experiences with rites of passage, either from Judaism or the African-centered perspective. He sought to gain an understanding of the purpose of the rites of passage processes, as well as to gain an understanding of how self-concept and education influence rites of passage. His results indicate that rites of passage processes promote continuity, trans-generational connections, a way for understanding life's circumstances, self-awareness, self-identity, and parental involvement.

One other major aspect of rites of passage as identified by Goggins is that of cultural awareness and identification. He notes that the essential function of culture is to: "1) provide a lens of perception or cognitive framework in which to view the world; 2) delineate standards of evaluation by which to measure worth or legitimacy, beauty and truth; 3) define the conditions and means that motivate or stimulate a member (institutional or individual) of society and prescribe sanctions for disruptive digression; 4) define collective and individual identity, roles, and responsibilities; 5) Provide a common language or means of communication; 6) provide the basis for social organization; 7) condition the mode of production; and, 8) delineate a process for perpetuation of the culture." Goggins maintains that through the development of culture, according to the aforementioned functions, a child, and their direct community will be capable of eradicating current problems and prevent future ones from developing.

Goggins later identifies the disruption of indigenous African societies, the dispersal of its people and the discontinuity of their culture as the sole factor leading to the current negative state of African descendants worldwide. He cites "public schools, debutante balls, beautilions, gang initiations, and incarcerations" as some of the detrimental non-African centered rites of passage processes that have been used to replace the missing culture of the American African community. He considers these forms of rites of passage to be detrimental due to their focus on material, as opposed to spiritual development.

What is perhaps most interesting and most relevant to our discussion of Freemasonry as a potential rites of passage program is found in the eight points listed by Goggins on the previous page. We can line up each point with an aspect of Freemasonry, which demonstrates that we are indeed engaged in a rites of passage process that potentially yields great benefit to its participants (See Table 1.). Goggins' study on rites of passage relates in another, less obvious way. In his interview, he questioned two basic groups of people: 1) American Africans, and 2) Jewish Americans. For anyone knowing our Masonic ritual, we are heavily inundated with Hebrew symbolism, allegories and culture. In fact, it is into the Jewish "way" that we are Raised, by the King of Israel himself. This represents a shifting in worldview from that of our own to that of another. It gets tricky because without this shift, we'd still be mentally dead, however, with this shift, we have overwritten our own worldview which sustained us up until the point where the deathblows were delivered.

As descendants of the African Lodge, it would benefit us tremendously, to seek out and fully embrace the worldview of our Ancestors, the ones we maintained before the traumatic experiences of the Maafa (allegorically, our meeting with the Ruffians). There are many interesting and applicable correlations between Africans and Hiram Abiff, many of which will be further explored in volume 2 of this series, which promises to bring a major Light and understanding to our Brothers in the Craft. From the fact that his people once migrated to Egypt, to the fact that he was the "keeper" of Ancient Wisdom, the hidden clues are amazing.

Symbolically Speaking: African Lodge #1

Goggins' Rites of Passage	Masonic Expression
1) provide a lens of perception or cognitive framework in which to view the world	1) Found in our allegories, history, current rituals and degree work.
2) delineate standards of evaluation by which to measure worth or legitimacy, beauty and truth	2) This is found in our various proficiency exams, our memory work, signs, tokens, obligations and Tyler's Oath.
3) define the conditions and means that motivate or stimulate a member (institutional or individual) of society and prescribe sanctions for disruptive digression	3) Brothers are motivated by their desire for more Light found in "higher" degrees and sanctions are illustrated by our "penalties" and implemented by internal judiciary processes.
4) define collective and individual identity, roles, and responsibilities	4) The various "stations" in the Lodge define the roles of the Brothers, as do the various degrees and "houses."
5) Provide a common language or means of communication	5) This is found in our symbolism, degrees, signs, and tokens.
6) provide the basis for social organization	6) The existing protocol, constitutions, and V of SL provide for this.
7) condition the mode of production	7) The various Masonic committees oversee productivity.
8) delineate a process for perpetuation of the culture	8) By continuing to Initiate, Pass, and Raise more Brothers, via prescribed rituals and degree work, the Masonic culture is perpetuated.

Table 1. Comparison of Goggins' Rites of Passage Model with Freemasonry

Drs. Nathan and Julia Hare posit that locus of control and personal mastery are two of the most beneficial skills developed by African-centered rites of passage programs. The authors contend, "how one behaves in the struggle to mobilize one's resources for

African Spiritual Systems

self-fulfillment is dictated by whether one sees the center of the control of one's destiny situated in oneself (internal) or amid the snares and snarls of fate and fortune (external)." This notion is akin to the fourth and fifth stages of the African initiation/rites of passage process outlined above. Based on their perspective, Drs. Hare advise those interested in raising healthy American African children to focus on striking a healthy balance between an internal and external locus of control. The internal is represented by an individual's ability to determine their own fate through decision-making and personal awareness; the external is represented by environmental agents that influence the individual in both positive and negative ways.

    In our Lodge system, we all enter into the Craft of our own free will and accord. We make it through our various trials and tribulations based on our own drive, dedication and devotion. Many decide to discontinue their initiation due to feelings of inadequacy and not believing they have what it takes to complete the process. These all represent aspects of an internal locus of control[75]. Part of the external locus of control demonstrated in our Craft initiations is literally found in our Lodge environments. I have visited several White Masonic Lodges and have found their Temples laced with cultural relics, art, artifacts, and symbols related to our Ancestral heritage, specifically that of Ancient Egypt[76]. As I walked through the *Egyptian Room* housed within the Grand Lodge of Pennsylvania, I simultaneously felt excited and disappointed as I imagined our Past Masters of St. John's #3 in Cincinnati being able to sit in such a marvel and conduct Masonic business and carry-on our degree work. This example of an external locus of control puts a bit of a spin on the concept because it refers to how the external environment can be purposely designed and "allowed" to shape, mold, and influence one's circumstances, performance, and state of mind.

    I could only imagine how my cousin, Past Master Jerome Sanders, or his good friend and Brother Past Master Rufus DuHart would feel if they sat in the East with the sun disk of Ra above their

---

75   In a later chapter, I share personal experiences that demonstrate my training in regards to internal vs. external locus of control.
76   See "Image Gallery" beginning on pg. 99

heads, and ancient Metu Neter inscribing the Temple walls around them. Given my African-centered worldview, I understand that the Ancestors, whose energy is neither created nor destroyed but continually surrounds us, would have been elated and directly benefitting our Lodge work carried out in such an environment.

According to the more conventional view of an external locus of control, I will cite the experiences of MWGM Prince Hall and his fourteen accomplices when founding African Lodge #1, and obtaining the charter for the same. The "Founding Fifteen" seemed to be up against the most rigid system of racism and oppression when they sought to become Masons. They met obstacle after obstacle, hostility, ridicule, rejection, and neglect at the hands of society. If their collective locus of control was externally oriented, we may not have ever had an African Lodge and the current PHA family. Had Brother Hall been deterred by the lack of response from the Grand Lodge of England, once he received the Charter and Constitutions, he may have given up instead of functioning as a Grand Master would, by granting Dispensations for other Lodges to be formed under the Charter of African Lodge #459, which eventually led to the founding of the African Grand Lodge. The "Founding Fifteen" exemplify the notion of self-determination. They forged a road where none had previously existed; and they did it with courage and confidence.

Drs. Julia and Nathan Hare used Eriksonian stages to determine the optimal time for beginning what they call "the year of the passage." They say the best time for initiating the rites of passage process is at 11 years old. This starting point is designed to intervene at the moment when many American African males traditionally begin to deal with and succumb to peer pressure, insecurity-based self-consciousness, ambivalence about matters of life, and the all important physical changes that usually begin between the ages of 11 and 13 with the onset of puberty. The overall goal of this experience is to instill within the youth, an understanding of their cultural selves, their cultural legacy, as well as to provide guidance for the coming experiences of life. This goal is inspired by their (the authors') observation that many American African male children are left to their own devices when it comes to negotiating their development and interactions with peers and the society at large. What if we could provide the same for our young boys and girls who have Masonic affiliation? What if our youth organizations were modeled after the African-centered rites of passage processes? What outcomes could we expect for our youth?

Dr. Cherry, in response to this question, developed and implemented an Africentric rites of passage program in order to reduce risk factors and increase protective factors for alcohol, tobacco and other drug (ATOD) use amongst American African 5th and 6th graders. Her research objectives were to: 1) improve knowledge of and increase intolerance of drugs; 2) improve values; 3) increase racial identity; 4) improve self-esteem; 5) increase knowledge of African culture; 6) improve family communications; 7) improve behaviors in school; and 8) improve problem solving skills. They utilized Africentric philosophy and worldview as the conceptual framework for the study in which they recruited 85 American African fifth graders and 84 American African sixth graders from public elementary schools on the east coast of the United States.

Data were collected at pre-test to set a baseline and to control for certain variables amongst the participants. Each group was administered certain questionnaires in order to assess their pre-test standings across the aforementioned constructs. At post-test, it was determined that the rites of passage program yielded significant results in regards to protective factors such as: racial identity, knowledge of African culture, self-esteem, and school-based behaviors; changes that the authors expect to be reflected in the reduced risk of ATOD (alcohol, tobacco, and other drugs) use in future years.

In a separate study, Dr. Belgrave administered an Africentric model of substance abuse prevention to fifth graders. Their main focus was the effects of Africentric values, self-esteem, and Black identity on drug attitudes. The authors recruited 54 fifth graders and their parents from an east coast public school system and administered a drug prevention program sponsored by the Center for Substance Abuse Prevention (CSAP). The authors collected their data prior to the administration of the program based on their interest in the attitudes of the children prior to being exposed to a drug prevention program.

Symbolically Speaking: African Lodge #1

The results of their investigation did not support the notion that Black identity and self-esteem contribute to explaining drug attitudes. However, their findings did reveal a significant relationship between Africentric values and drug attitudes, meaning the more Africentric values are adhered to by an individual, the less tolerance they will have towards the use of drugs, which in turn, decreases the likelihood of experiencing the risk factors associated with drug use. This finding is used to support the claim that African spiritual systems in the form of rites of passage programs may increase one's Africentric values, as well as decrease the likelihood of drug use amongst school-aged children.

Obtaining such a strong foundation as children, makes it likely that they will maintain some of these values as they become adults. This means that within a generation or two, of having children experience these processes, we will have adults who know and understand the value of such an education. We should understand that what we do today, is not for ourselves, but for our future generations. If we adopt this idea and attitude as we work our Craft, we will slowly but surely begin to see the effects in our children and grand children. We will once again be giant pillars in our communities, shining Light for all to see and emulate. It is within reach, and worth the effort it will take to close the gap.

This brief treatment of African spiritual systems, rites of passage, and other concepts is for the purpose of building a context within which we may further explore the implications of viewing Prince Hall Freemasonry as an African-centered process of refining the character of men and communities as a whole. Using the original title of African Lodge as a "sign" directing us to explore African principles, processes, and systems while completing the unfinished Temple, provides us with an entirely new paradigm within which to re-form our tools, revisit our Temple's blueprints as laid out on the Trestle-Board, and continue to build in the way that our Ancestors intended for us to build. Viewed as a rites of passage process, African Lodge Freemasonry (PHA) takes on a powerful dimension with great potential. It's up to us to reclaim it.

Image Gallery

Symbolically Speaking: African Lodge #1

Image 1. Two dollar bill - notice the man in the circle and how clearly his face has been darkened as compared to the others found in the image.

Image 2. The original portrait - notice the man in the circle (Robert Morris) in the same seat as the man with the "dark face" found on the two dollar bill.

Image Gallery

Image 3. The "Egyptian Room" located in the Grand Lodge of Pennsylvania. It was the first room completely finished, and was designed based on exact replication of images found in Egypt.

Image 4. The Heru Bedhet, or "winged sundisk" found on the floor at the foot of the Worshipful Master's platform as well as at the foot of the Senior Warden's platform. This ancient African symbol represents spiritual ascension.

Image 5. These pyramids, serpents and Heru Bedhet are found on the walls in both the East and the West. The serpents represent stimulated life force, vitality, mental awareness, etc.

Image 6. This is the Altar minus the Volume of Sacred Law. In this context, the Volume of Sacred Law would be the Pert Em Heru, the Pyramid Texts and any of the other divinely inspired, sacred texts found in the Nile Valley.

Image Gallery

Image 7. This representation of Ra, the so-called Sun God, is found in the East, directly above the Worshipful Master's station. The rays extend across the Lodge in all directions. Notice the Ankhs (☥).

Image 8. A view of the Lodge from the East facing West.

Image 9. Side view of a Her-Em-Akhet (Sphinx) found in front of the House of the Temple, Scottish Rites Headquarters in Washington, DC. Notice the Bird head-dress, similar to Auset's (Isis) crown.

Image 10. Side view of the other Her-Em-Akhet (Sphinx) found in front of the House of the Temple, Scottish Rites Headquarters in Washington, DC. This one has a serpent head-dress.

Image Gallery

Image 11. Front view of the Her-Em-Akhet. Notice the serpent around the neck, the Ankh between the paws, and the Metu Neter (hieroglyphic writings) on the platform beneath the statue.

Image 12. Front view of the 2nd Her-Em-Akhet. Notice the Kemetic (Egyptian) woman between the paws, and the Metu Neter (hieroglyphic writings) on the platform beneath the statue.

Symbolically Speaking: African Lodge #1

Image 13. One of two Kemetic Statues found in the main gallery of the House of the Temple. The black stone blocks were quarried in upstate New York, then transported by train to Union Station in Washington, DC. Additional tracks were laid to bring the marble to the Temple where the sculptures were carved on site.

Image 14. An outside view of the House of the Temple showing the step-pyramid at the top.

Image Gallery

Image 15. A Heru Bedhet "winged sundisk", found on the wall of the House of the Temple.

Image 16. A view of the main staircase with both Kemetic sculptures on either side, and a bust of Albert Pike in the center atop the second flight of stairs. Inconspicuously displayed are two "thrones of Auset" (𓊨). These are only visible as such from a certain viewpoint in the main gallery.

Symbolically Speaking: African Lodge #1

Image 17. Mud Masons of Mali exhibit at the Smithsonian Museum of Natural History. African "Traditional" Masons maintain a blend of both Operative and Speculative Craft.

Image 18. Various grains and other items used to "bless" the structures being built. This is very similar to the "cornerstone" ceremony practiced by the Western Craft.

Image Gallery

Image 19. Plumb line used by Mali Masons.

Image 20. Trowel used by Mali Masons

Symbolically Speaking: African Lodge #1

Image 21. This Heru Bedhet is found in the Washington Monument. Notice how it is positioned directly above this sculpture of George Washington as seen upon entering the Tekhen (Obelisk).

Chapter 4
Re-Claiming Our Stolen Legacy

*I*n his classic book *Stolen Legacy*, George G. M. James presents a vast amount of knowledge and information about ancient African history, its relationship to Greek philosophy, and the impact that it has on us today. Many who critique this powerful and enlightening work, have done so from an intellectual and historical perspective. Some have found issue with the accuracy of some of the information, while others have refuted the overall notion that Africans gave birth to Greek civilization. One analysis that seems to be missing is of the spiritual and initiation legacy that he also presents. Theoretically, this is the aspect of ancient African life that made the cultural, political, intellectual, and all other accomplishments possible. This chapter is devoted to such an exploration. The expansion of his points, found throughout this chapter, are based on my own experiences as an initiate into several African spiritual systems, as well as my expertise and research of the topic.

Professor James acknowledged three distinct levels of initiation within the Kemetic spiritual systems. He refers to the first degree of initiates as "The Mortals." These are individuals who are just beginning their instruction, gaining information about the deeper mysteries of creation. They are called "Mortals" because they have yet to realize, through conscious experience, the immortal aspects of their being, i.e., the spirit. At this level, the initiates were given tasks designed to heighten their understanding of their daily life experience. These tasks helped to distinguish the physical experience from the mental and spiritual. Control of the physical, specifically those "automatic" and reflexive functions, was the goal. "Conditionings," such as response to "hunger," lack of stillness (in regards to body movement), endurance under extreme temperatures and other forms of discomfort, control of breath and breathing, heart rate, and body temperature, as well as suppression of the "startle" response, were all key to growing beyond this level of initiation.

To get an idea of the kinds of trials experienced at this level of initiation, try eating but only once in a day and making that meal totally raw; try breathing at a slower rate taking only four breaths in one minute (inhale for a count of 5 seconds, hold for a count of 5 seconds, exhale for a count of 5 seconds…each complete breath takes a total of 15 seconds). For a more advanced practice, reduce the rate of breathing to 3 breaths per minute (inhale for a count of 5 seconds, hold the breath for a count of 5 seconds, exhale for a count of 5 seconds, then hold 5 seconds before inhaling again…each complete breath takes a total of 20 seconds). During this phase, male initiates learn to control their ejaculatory reflexes, meaning they are able to delay and/or altogether prevent ejaculation during sexual stimulation (this ability not only demonstrates mental control over the body, but also greatly benefits the overall health and well-being of the physical vehicle)[77].

Many systems of initiation also require the initiate to spend a certain amount of time isolated in darkness with restricted mobility. Some spend days in a coffin, others are buried up to their necks[78], some are kept in small closet type spaces where they remain quietly in deep trance, separating their physical sensations from their mental awareness. Some systems place the initiate into situations of extreme pain or physical discomfort (i.e., being bit by ants, enduring scarification, walking great distances, remaining awake for extended periods of time, various feats of endurance, stamina and strength, physical purging, etc.), as an opportunity for them to demonstrate and experience for themselves the abilities acquired throughout the earlier phases of this stage. Again, the main goal of this stage is to assist the initiate in realizing the difference between the physical (mortal) and mental aspects of their existence. Once this has been accomplished, the initiate moves on to further familiarizing themselves with the immortal parts of their being: the mind/soul and spirit.

---

77   The Taoist have done an excellent job of preserving this science.
78   Malidoma Some' details his experience of being buried in *Of Water and the Spirit*.

Reclaiming Our Stolen Legacy

Initiates at the next stage, according to George G. M. James, are called "The Intelligences." These initiates are in the process of developing their newly found tool, the mind, whereas in the first stage they were introduced to the mind by juxtaposing it to the experience of the physical body. The "Intelligences" work specifically to develop the ability to know beyond the physical senses through the development of what was called the "nous" by Greek philosophers. Nous is loosely described as an inner knowing and awareness; a sort of intuition based on discernment and an innate ability to determine reality from fantasy; a direct experiencing of Truth. With this talent, an initiate is capable of looking beyond the surface of a situation, and thus, recognizes the truth within. The level of insight gained, allows the initiate to base their decisions on truth, by-passing the useful but sometimes confusing indicators provided by the emotions and physical senses.

An "Intelligence" is an individual that is lucid in their thinking, and fully capable of maintaining their mental functions superior to their physical operations. An individual at this level is aware of an impending physical experience and through the use of the proper mental state, is capable of altering or avoiding it altogether. For example, an "Intelligence" is keenly aware that they have been exposed to a cold virus, they literally feel its introduction into the physical body. Through the proper "steadfastness of mind" they are able to keep their bodies from succumbing to the effects of the virus, thereby maintaining their physical health until the virus is naturally removed by the immune system.

In the early phases of this stage, the initiate may falter by keeping the illness at bay for a moment, then through the use of distraction and or a lack of trust in their new abilities, allow their physical vehicle to acquiesce to the "logical" procession a virus introduced to the body will follow; in other words, they become sick. The theme for initiates at this level is "mind over matter." In order for this to become a reality, they must further explore their mind and strengthen it to the point where it surpasses the primacy of the body and physical sensations. An "Intelligence" is also fully capable of manipulating physical situations outside of their physical bodies, this is done by the strict monitoring and regulation of

Symbolically Speaking: African Lodge #1

beliefs, emotions, and imagery entertained by the body and mind. For example, I was in a situation where I was surely going to miss a flight. I am literally driving back to the airport in a rental car with less than an hour before my flight is scheduled to depart. I have to refuel the vehicle but cannot find a gas station at the rental car exit. After driving around for about 10 minutes, I decided to roll the dice and return the car without refueling (this is a big deal because the rental car companies typically charge about $2.00/gallon more than the local gas stations).

For the sake of context, I must tell you, as I got into my original car (I reserved and prepaid for a midsize but was bumped up to a full size without request), I got a "feeling" that I needed to change to a small SUV. Following this flash of "nous," I left my luggage in the trunk, walked through the rain back to the rental car facility. I asked the young lady how much it would be to upgrade to a small SUV. She asked which one did I want...I looked out the window and pointed to a red vehicle parked in front of the building. She said, they were out of that vehicle but had several others... to which I responded, "Are you sure?" She surprisingly stated, "Oh, we have one left." She processed the upgrade and told me where to find the vehicle. I got my luggage out of the old car and made my way through the rain to the new car. It was nice, except for the chocolate chip cookie crumbs I found on the passenger seat. Later during my brief rental experience, I noticed an empty yogurt cup wedged between the armrest and the driver's seat as well as a banana peel and napkin between the passenger door and seat.

As I am pulling in to return the vehicle after leaving it on ¾ of a tank, I'm thinking "dang, they're gonna charge me about $40 to refill this tank..." Just then, I got back on my square and realized why the car had been left dirty, it was leverage to excuse my less than full gas tank. There was a young American African male there checking in the vehicles, a fact that made me feel better about my odds. Just then, an older White lady walks over and says "Hi, how was your rental?" I think to myself, "ok, this is interesting..." She jumps in, turns the key to check the gas levels, makes a notation, then gets out of the vehicle. I begin to tell her of the cookie crumbs, yogurt cup, and banana peel she will find on the passenger side. She smiles and tells me my total. She let me know that I would not be charged for the gas because they gave me a dirty vehicle. In addition to the flash of insight, this situation also demonstrates how our own biases as well as our expectations can potentially make or break our opportunities. But wait, the trip isn't over yet.

I am now more like 30 minutes away from departure and I am standing at the rental car facility awaiting the shuttle. The ride takes about 10 minutes and the trek through the airport is an easy 15 minutes, running. I arrived at the terminal and took off into a full sprint with a backpack and a roller bag. I get to security and am not selected for the pre-screen line which is a lot shorter and moves a lot faster…I maintain a level heart (stable emotions) and refuse to give into the panic of missing my flight and repeating what occurred on my last trip[79]. As I finally reach the x-ray belt and body scanner, I hear my name over the loud speaker as a final boarding call. I stand patiently in line visualizing myself seated on the plane headed home. Once cleared of security, I begin to run again with my suitcase on my head and backpack on my back. I bypassed the train to the B concourse and decided it was better to sprint. I'm winded by the time I get to the concourse and decided to ride the escalator up to the gates. My flight leaves from B3, oddly, the gates are beginning at 10 and going down to 1. I take a few deep, burning breaths and begin to sprint again. As I am approaching B3, I notice a door is still open so I run faster. I get to the counter and realize it was not B3 that was still open…it's the one that was just closed!!! The young lady smiles and says "Are you on this flight?" I managed to wheeze out "Yes…" she immediately calls on her walkie-talkie to hold the flight "I've got him…"

They NEVER open the doors after they have been closed,

---

[79] Earlier this same week I missed a flight due to traffic. That airline wanted to charge me over $600 to buy a first class ticket on the next flight or I could've stayed overnight and caught a flight the next day for only $250. Instead I bought a ticket on another airline that departed from an entirely different terminal requiring a shuttle ride. On my way through security, I realized I left my tablet under the driver's seat of the rental car I just returned, so I called the company and took the shuttle back to retrieve it. As I get back to clear security again, I see a familiar face in line, it's a professor from Howard University who sat on my dissertation committee as a last minute replacement for a member who decided to step down…he was present at my presentation at the conference we were both leaving. Long story short, the turn of events, and my level and steady clarity afforded me the opportunity to now work on a major project with this professor.

however, it occurred this time. I immediately went into one of my known breathing techniques to settle my physical body and proceeded down the ramp to board my flight. When I got to my seat, it appeared as if nothing happened. I sat down and relaxed, just as I saw in my visualization. I never doubted that I would make it, yet, I had to move as if I was going to make it.

I wholly attribute the success in the above situation, to my ability to hold the image in my mind that I would successfully board the flight, and also to my being aware of the insights provided to my emotionally-stilled mind. I never gave into the panic and I consistently appealed to a higher power than logic and physical "realities." I pushed my physical body beyond what were clear signs of fatigue and exhaustion, while simultaneously holding fast to the outcome I desired. Some may call it luck, and see it as a fortunate set of circumstances beyond my personal control. I, on the other hand, know better and am well aware of the role me being an initiate played in this scenario.

The talents awakened during the next and final stage of initiation, called "The Creators" or "The Sons of Light[80]" were demonstrated in the above example. It is the level at which the initiate becomes a conscious co-creator of their own experiences in life. They are fully capable of either actively manipulating their outcomes, or consciously recognizing the divine intervention taking place via the order of operations, and thus *allowing* it to play itself out, without regard to the personal desires and potential emotions that may arise when things seemingly are going wrong[81]. "Sons of Light" are those who seem to live a magical life; those for whom the Gods conspire; fortuna[82]. They are the ones who live their lives as exemplified by great sages, that is, the women and men of high wisdom.

As with each of the previous stages, initiates at this stage manifest their awareness and abilities in various degrees. Some are new to the gift and thus have yet to uncover how they may best use their talents via their own disposition, and the paths by which their talents are manifested; others are in full control of these abilities

---

80   Also a term used by early Jews to identify a class of priests.
81   This was more apparent in the scenario where I missed the flight and paid extra but ran into a colleague in line (see Footnote 76).
82   Fortuna is a Greek concept meaning God has conspired on your behalf.

and live as God-men and God-women amongst the "Mortals" and "Intelligences." The fully awakened "Son of Light," is capable of knowing how to make all things happen; at times they expose the illusion of time, space, and material existence by their accomplishments and feats. Outside observers may dismiss the experiences of a "Son of Light" as being "lucky" or attributable to happenstance (being in the "right place at the right time"); regardless of how others interpret the experiences, the "Creators" know, without a doubt, their role in the process.

In the earlier levels of this stage, balance must tilt in favor of the spirit in order for most initiates to eventually and totally take command of, and master, the mind and body. One very serious misunderstanding of the principle of balance is that something in balance is stagnant and stationary, not moving. Many wrongfully believe the best way to maintain balance is to keep still; in actuality, balance is a highly fluid and dynamic process, and is responsible for maintaining all things in the position in which they are. For example, a person standing on the toes of one foot, must find a balance in their posture much different from when they are seated on a couch. At times, the person on their toes may need to lean their body completely perpendicular to their leg in order to find balance; at other times, they may be found standing seemingly perfectly still except for the micro-movements of their foot, ankle, calf and other leg and core muscles.

Such is the same with balancing life. At times a person may have to go to an extreme in order to experience balance. Thus, an individual attempting to bring harmony to a tumultuous relationship may have to either become extremely passive or extremely assertive in order to find the balance; this adjustment may be temporary or necessary on a more permanent basis. The act of balancing, devoid of this fluidity of movement, is sure to end up in a broken state of permanent imbalance. This is similar to the hypothetical oak tree found growing on the beach of a tropical island. The tree, being fairly rigid, would surely break at the first sign of a hurricane; it is only the flexibility found in palm trees that will survive the storms and hurricanes of life. According to Lahleh Bakhtiar in volume one of her work on mystic Islam (***Spiritual Chivalry, God's***

Will Be Done), it is sometimes necessary to exhibit the extreme aspects of a particular energy in order to bring about its balanced state. For example, both courage and cowardice are manifestations of the fire element. In certain people, based on circumstance, training or natural disposition, fear may dominate their personality, making them timid, fickle and lacking in initiative. One prescription for correcting this imbalance involves the person entertaining and engaging in high risk, adrenaline-producing activities. The person should function as a sort of "daredevil" for a period of time, against their personal fears and contrary to their comfort zones, in order to expand the range of their expression of fire[83].

The same is true for any of the elemental states. A person with issues in the area of water, manifesting as a self-neglecting and depressed mood, may find themselves in situations where being outgoing and nurturing of self and others, is the path towards their balance and thus healing. The key is to monitor the extremes closely, to prevent the concretization of the opposite state or the other extreme (in the case of cowardice, a person may inadvertently become reckless, impulsive and dangerous).

The risk of dealing in extremes in order to bring balance is highlighted in the ancient Kemetic story of Sakhmet, the Lioness-headed Neter-t (goddess/natural energy). She was sent into the world, as a lioness, to combat the enemies of Ra (those things that disrupt and deplete the life force, bringing about chaos, disorder, disease, and death). While on her mission, Sakhmet began to enjoy her wrath and ability to destroy; she took delight and pleasure in the taste of her victim's blood and the smell of their fear. In order to bring her back into the balanced state, Tehuti, the Neter of Wisdom, transformed himself into a very small and meek animal and stood before the blood-lusting Sakhmet. In such a vulnerable state, Tehuti forced the compassion out from beneath the hardened shell Sakhmet had come to hide behind. Through their dialogue, Tehuti was able to remind Sakhmet of her original state and her original mission. And thus, her fires were cooled and restored to their balanced state.

When looking at a physical balance, such as the "Scales

---

[83] This is very similar to gradual desensitization and flooding techniques used to treat anxieties and phobias.

of Maat," the astute observer clearly sees the three aspects of the process: the active, the passive, and the neutral. Each scale oscillates between being active and being passive. This partially depends on which scale is receiving the weight for measurement and which one is serving as a counter-balance to that weight. The stand in the middle is the neutral component, and thus maintains its position regardless of the weights on either side of it. This image symbolically contains the previously discussed three stages of initiation encoded in its arrangement.

In addition to the three levels of the ancient Mysteries of Kemet, George G. M. James also points out the ten virtues that eventually become the four embraced in the Masonic Lodge[84]. Unlike many modern systems of spiritual cultivation and initiation, those of the ancients were more than intellectual talking points; they were actually states of being that must be demonstrated in the initiate's day-to-day life. These ten virtues are: 1) Control of Thoughts; 2) Control of Action; 3) Steadfastness of Purpose; 4) Identity with Spiritual Life or the Higher Ideals; 5) Evidence of Having a Mission in Life; 6) Evidence of a Call to Spiritual Orders or the Priesthood in the Mysteries; 7) Freedom from Resentment; 8) Confidence in the Power of the Master Teacher; 9) Confidence in One's own Ability to Learn; and 10) Readiness or Preparedness for Initiation.

The control of one's thoughts is of utmost importance, and thus, we will deal with it first. Thoughts are directors of energy. They are what guide and direct the powers of creation and manifestation. Similar to how a driver in a vehicle is the conscious entity directing the machinery, the mind/soul in humans is the "conscious-entity" of the body, directing its experiences via thought[85]. The degree of wisdom directly determines the type of thoughts that are entertained, as well as one's degree of thought control. In our everyday dialogue, we speak and hear of "focus" and its relationship to accomplishing tasks; now imagine what occurs when the level of thought is magnified and focused on accomplishing Godly goals?

What if instead of being motivated by, and focused upon,

---

84   Temperance, Fortitude, Prudence, and Justice.
85   There is an interesting correlation between the word "thought" and the Greek name for the Neter of Wisdom - Tehuti, "Thot".

political gains, intellectual prowess, and financial wealth, humans directed their mental energies and degrees of creativity towards the enhancement of themselves as human beings…having as a direct and tangible goal, the awakening of the divinity within? I am willing to bet it would be well worth the work. This shift from the "lower" to the "higher" aspects of being human, serves as the first obstacle for an initiate to experience, when it comes to initiating. Success at every encounter is dependent upon their level of focus, conscious awareness and mental stamina. To control one's thoughts is similar to controlling one's hands, eyes, or breathing, except it's totally internal and mental.

The power in spiritual cultivation is protected, or should I say the initiate is protected, by this first task, because it decreases the likelihood of the disciple having a fickle mind while handling powerful mental and spiritual tools that will be unlocked at later stages. There is no difference between this and requiring medical students to take various courses, develop certain skills, demonstrate those skills, and eventually master them, prior to being able to "practice" medicine. One main difference between the modern initiation/education process and those of the ancients is the latter required their aspiring physicians to also be initiates of the spirit, not simply academically and intellectually trained. A certain level of spiritual awareness and competence was required of all that were called to serve others. This helped to ensure that the mistakes commonly made by our modern professionals, were either totally eliminated or were few and far between. It would seem silly for a physician to claim to help others with devices and protocols that were harmful, if indeed, the profession were full of initiates; in fact, the Hippocratic Oath taken by modern physicians is derived from the "school" of Imhotep (Asclepius), and was used by the Ancient initiated class of healers, as a declaration of their reality and intentions:

> I swear by Apollo Physician and Asclepius and Hygieia and Panaceia and all the gods and goddesses, making them my witnesses, that I will fulfil according to my ability and judgment this oath and this covenant:
> To hold him who has taught me this art as equal to my parents and to live my life in partnership with him, and if he is

Reclaiming Our Stolen Legacy

in need of money to give him a share of mine, and to regard his offspring as equal to my brothers in male lineage and to teach them this art - if they desire to learn it - without fee and covenant; to give a share of precepts and oral instruction and all the other learning to my sons and to the sons of him who has instructed me and to pupils who have signed the covenant and have taken an oath according to the medical law, but no one else.

I will apply dietetic measures for the benefit of the sick according to my ability and judgment; I will keep them from harm and injustice.

I will neither give a deadly drug to anybody who asked for it, nor will I make a suggestion to this effect. Similarly I will not give to a woman an abortive remedy. In purity and holiness I will guard my life and my art.

I will not use the knife, not even on sufferers from stone, but will withdraw in favor of such men as are engaged in this work.

Whatever houses I may visit, I will come for the benefit of the sick, remaining free of all intentional injustice, of all mischief and in particular of sexual relations with both female and male persons, be they free or slaves.

What I may see or hear in the course of the treatment or even outside of the treatment in regard to the life of men, which on no account one must spread abroad, I will keep to myself, holding such things shameful to be spoken about.

If I fulfil this oath and do not violate it, may it be granted to me to enjoy life and art, being honored with fame among all men for all time to come; if I transgress it and swear falsely, may the opposite of all this be my lot.

Notice the difference between the above translation of the original version, and the following, modernized version of the oath written in 1964:

I swear to fulfill, to the best of my ability and judgment, this covenant:

I will respect the hard-won scientific gains of those physicians in whose steps I walk, and gladly share such knowledge as is mine with those who are to follow.

I will apply, for the benefit of the sick, all measures which are required, avoiding those twin traps of overtreatment and therapeutic nihilism.

I will remember that there is art to medicine as well as science, and that warmth, sympathy, and understanding may outweigh the surgeon's knife or the chemist's drug.

I will not be ashamed to say "I know not," nor will I fail to call in my colleagues when the skills of another are needed for a patient's recovery.

I will respect the privacy of my patients, for their problems are not disclosed to me that the world may know. Most especially must I tread with care in matters of life and death. If it is given me to save a life, all thanks. But it may also be within my power to take a life; this awesome responsibility must be faced with great humbleness and awareness of my own frailty. Above all, I must not play at God.

I will remember that I do not treat a fever chart, a cancerous growth, but a sick human being, whose illness may affect the person's family and economic stability. My responsibility includes these related problems, if I am to care adequately for the sick.

I will prevent disease whenever I can, for prevention is preferable to cure.

I will remember that I remain a member of society, with special obligations to all my fellow human beings, those sound of mind and body as well as the infirm.

If I do not violate this oath, may I enjoy life and art, respected while I live and remembered with affection thereafter. May I always act so as to preserve the finest traditions of my calling and may I long experience the joy of healing those who seek my help.

The classical version of the Hippocratic Oath is from the translation of the Greek by Ludwig Edelstein, "***The Hippocratic Oath: Text, Translation, and Interpretation.***" The modern version was written by Louis Lasagna, Dean of the School of Medicine at Tufts University. These two oaths seem to cover the same ground: do no harm, honor those that came before you and those that will come after, humility, confidentiality, etc. One major difference is that the Ancients, being an initiated class, in the truest sense of the word, appealed to the higher forces of nature for their strength, courage and wisdom. The moderns mention a higher being but only once. This is important because there seems to be no need for a warning against playing God in the earlier version, however, in the modern version, we see such a warning...many would argue that in these modern times, some physicians do just that.

For the sake of further clarity, allow me to provide another illustration of the very simple concept of controlling one's thoughts, using an everyday and common example. Look at the clothes that you are currently wearing. At some point they were a mere thought in your mind; an idea in response to a question of "what will I wear today?" This thought, in the form of a question, led you to imagine and/or physically look through your options, which eventually led to you putting the clothing on your body. This is a clear path from thought to action.

In the case of babies, it is my belief that they are fully capable of thought and fully capable of manipulating physical existence through the same. It is perhaps more difficult for us to recognize their manipulation because they are still working to master the physical world, and are incapable of having much of a direct physical impact (i.e., can't change their own diapers, can't open/close doors, etc.), until they reach certain milestones (this is heavily based on the growth and development of their nervous system). The evidence of this manipulation is verifiable by placing an infant in a room full of people. It is guaranteed that someone, if not several people, will come over to tend to the baby's needs within seconds of becoming aware that the baby is present.

The second task is to control one's actions and behaviors. In the world of cognitive psychology, one way to view the relationship between thoughts and actions is that the latter follows the former, that is, behaviors follow thoughts. This means that we act based on what we think, and perhaps how we think, regardless of whether or not we are consciously aware of these thoughts. This is the root of the sayings: "perception is everything" and "as a man thinketh." Behavior is what many psychologists use to infer what a person is thinking, feeling or intending. It is one of the few tangible cues of what occurs in the human psyche, and still much of it is speculation. For instance, a smile is usually interpreted to mean the person is feeling happy or amused by something; a frown typically means they are upset or saddened. A person in the throws of a fight is typically angry, afraid, and/or threatened and is usually defending themselves from some real or perceived threat. An individual experiencing sexual arousal is usually seen watching objects of their desire in a "lusting" manner, and doing things to eventually engage in sexual intercourse. Following these "cues" can be tricky because the source of the feelings and thoughts may or may not originate with the person experiencing and responding to them; in other words, they may have been conditioned to experience the thoughts/feelings and their subsequent behaviors by some external process or force.

Take the well known psychological experiment involving "baby Albert." Albert was a toddler exposed to a white bunny rabbit under normal conditions. In this situation, Albert naturally displayed interest in the animal and attempted to pet it and learn it through touch, taste and sight. In a later phase of the experiment, the rabbit was again brought out to Albert but this time it was associated with a loud noise that naturally startled and scared the baby. After repeated exposure to the loud noise, simultaneous to the release of the rabbit, Albert began to realize that there was a relationship between this rabbit, the loud noise, and his feelings of fear. In the final phase of the conditioning process, the rabbit was once again released without the loud noise. This time, Albert's natural curiosity was overridden by the fear response conditioned via the loud noise in the previous phase.

Not only was Albert now "afraid" of the rabbit, but anything furry and fluffy like a rabbit also generated fear. His thoughts and behaviors were no longer his own, but a product of the experimenters' desires and goals for their program. Had "baby Albert" been trained to control his thinking as well as his behaviors, he may have been able to resist their attempts to condition and control his cognitive and emotional responses to the experimental stimuli. As a toddler, he was far more susceptible to the ploys of the researchers simply based on his limited cognitive development at such a young age; hence the benefit of initiation as we grow older – it serves as a method for systematically "cleaning up" any adverse tendencies we have developed based on early life exposures.

Scientology has developed a process called "auditing" that is designed to address these early life traumas. In their lexicon, the conditioned behaviors are called "aberrations," and the traumatic experiences are said to create "engrams," or energy disruptions, which lead to aberrated behaviors. These behaviors are automated and usually unconsciously experienced and activated. During "auditing," the auditor assists the person to "re-live" the traumatic experiences by repeatedly recalling their earliest memories. There is no need to process the details of the experience, they are simply recalled and repeated. The trained auditor is skilled at identifying the signs that the "engram" has been released, and no longer has a negative effect on the person.

The goal is to find the earliest "engram" and release its energy; this theoretically frees up any and all engrams that came after it. It is further theorized that the earliest "engrams" came while in the womb – this is based on the Scientologist belief that the human begins to record events ("memories") soon after conception. Simple and often overlooked experiences such as parental arguments or a mother falling or becoming ill after eating something spoiled, can imprint the developing embryo or fetus with an "engram" and thus, create aberrated behaviors for the rest of their lives.

Similar to the ancient forms of initiation, the "auditing" process is thought to increase the human's functionality to its maximum potential. This is done by clearing the channels of perception, conserving energies otherwise wasted on erroneous response patterns, and refining an individual's thought patterns to the degree that they are capable of higher-order thinking, insight, and wisdom. These are similar to the goals stated by psychoanalysts, energy healers, and those who specialize in past-life regression interventions.

On a more common level, human behavior is the sum total of everything a person does (including: thinking, moving, eating, sleeping, fighting, laughing, loving, walking, talking, etc.), and perhaps more importantly, how they do what they are doing. The "how" of behavior also serves as an indicator of what a person believes. For example, the way a person prays, has sex, prepares their foods, choose their friends and recreation are all based on their beliefs. It may also indicate the source of their behavioral influence.

These are two very important concepts for the aspiring initiate to wrestle with. Both the source of influence, and the beliefs undergirding behaviors, are powerful indicators that help to identify the origins of problems and ailments in a person's life. This is the same philosophy shared by psychologists and medical doctors alike. In both professions, the etiology (source/origins) of the current condition is sought in order to better understand the condition and to hopefully restore balance to it. In the language of the Adinkra symbols found in Ghana, West Africa, this is called Sankofa – a symbol representing the power and benefits of looking to the past or origins in order to better understand the present, so that the future may be more actively and accurately determined and controlled.

Likewise, it is the function of marketing to influence, if not control, the behavior of the target audience. We are exposed to an inordinate amount of marketing ploys everyday of our lives. Prior to the advent of cell phones, 3 and 4G networks, the worldwide-web of the internet, commercial jets, and other technological advances, it was a lot less likely that many people in remote locations would be exposed to the tools of the trade. However, with this relatively new breakthrough, marketing firms enjoy an almost endless source of human capital, granting more opportunities for their subtle persuasion to impact more people. A theatrical example of this is found in the movie "*The Gods Must Be Crazy.*" This fictional account explored the impact an empty Coke bottle falling from the sky (from an airplane), had on a southern African village.

Once while riding down a rural road in Benin, West Africa, I noticed several billboards featuring the words beauty, lovely, and irresistible. The image on the billboard was of several African women, the one in the foreground was of a lighter complexion than the others in the background; those in the background were out of focus, drawing even more attention to the one in front. Of course I may have been reading too deeply into the add, except the product was a skin-lightening (bleaching) crème. On this same trip, I interacted with people who maintained their traditional ways of living (i.e., in a village without piped, running water, but plentiful with naturally, stream-sourced running water), that had cellular phones with data plans; granting full access to social media and "worldstar" fight videos. This exemplifies the far reach of marketing and how it can insidiously influence the behaviors of the unsuspecting masses.

One very common misunderstanding about marketing is that it is only used to market products for consumption or purchase, and that the methods used are ethical and not psychologically developed to maximize its effectiveness. On the contrary, marketing is also used to promote and model attitudes, beliefs, character traits, personality, standards (moral, sexual, intellectual, etc.), desires, tastes & preferences, prejudices, "norms," and expectations. This aspect of marketing is much less apparent because there is not a tangible product for sale. There aren't commercials explicitly telling you to think this way or another. The jingles and product placement are typically imperceptible to the viewer because they are otherwise distracted by the obviously placed cues. The all-pervasive nature of these subtle agents of influence (i.e., marketing), is the reason why initiators are required to demonstrate some form of self-control; otherwise, they will be as children playing with dangerous weapons or priceless jewels.

In many ancient civilizations, the people responsible for the health, safety, security, education, and overall livelihood of the masses were required to initiate for this very reason; it rendered them less likely to be manipulated into illegal and immoral behaviors, and ensured they would be at their peak performance regardless of the task and specific profession. We don't have to imagine because we have witnessed the medical doctor, working at a cancer center, who still takes "cigarette breaks." We have observed the mechanic who may fix one part of their customer's car and loosen up another in order to get more business. We have also, all to often, observed religious leaders who preach against "sin" while fully participating in the same, if not worse, abominations[86]. The uninitiated human tends to be more susceptible to subtle manipulations than initiates. This does not mean initiated people are beyond being influenced and always do good; the only thing I am pointing out is that we (initiates) at least "know" better (or should) and when we end up on the wrong side of the decision, it is likely that we have consciously chosen to be there, or were set up as such.

In the context of the initiation process, controlling one's behavior serves the purpose of further establishing control over the physical and mental parts of your being. The degree of control over the mind and body sought by initiates can seem extreme to the

---

[86] Sin is defined according to their own religious practice, and thus, is not the same for everyone.

everyday person – those who have given little to no thought to the concept of evolving as a human being – but for those on the path, it cannot be mastered enough. Imagine if instead of becoming fearful when faced with what appears to be an imminent car accident, you were able to stay focused, steady, calm, and under complete control of your mind and body. Imagine that instead of squeezing your eyes shut, clenching the steering wheel, and slamming the breaks in preparation for collision, you are able to recognize an opening in the lane next to you, accelerate slightly, and move over with only seconds and inches to spare?

Or how about the situation where an animal unexpectedly rushes you and your family while hiking in the woods. Instead of freezing with fear, you are capable of generating the necessary fire for evoking fear in the animal causing it to flee from the scene. As shown by these examples, control of one's behavior is not only about the preventing of behaviors but also about generating and eliciting the desired and sometimes necessary behaviors, on command. Unbeknownst to many, athletes, martial artists, and skilled professionals are inculcated with this process of behavior control via their repetitive training. Amongst athletes it's called "the zone," in the emergency room it's a "guided hand." This phenomenon is clearly demonstrated in the opening scene of Berry Gordy's classic movie, "*The Last Dragon.*" Bruce Leroy is training with his "master" and catches the appropriate arrow by "knowing without knowing."

For the beginner, it is impulse control, after a little mastery, it becomes the means for intentional movement. The skills and competencies developed during this phase of initiation are transferable to every aspect of life. A person that learns to control the so-called automatic responses of the body is now less likely to impulsively do things that they will later regret. The person battling addiction is less likely to revert back to the use and abuse of their substance of "choice." The number of "accidental" pregnancies will likely decrease because control over ejaculation and control over hormones that generate sexual desire, will assist in taming those aspects of the human animal, which is pre-programmed for reproduction.

Reclaiming Our Stolen Legacy

Anyone who has participated in the Armed Forces, police academy, or any other specialized organization has likely experienced trainings based on the notion of self-control of both mind and body, and are thus seen to be superior to those who have not. These are the women and men entrusted with high-stakes and high-priority activities that depend on their ability to maintain control and focus, under the most stressful of conditions. We thank you for your sacrifice, service, and dedication to training.

The third virtue is "steadfastness of purpose." The lack of purpose is perhaps one of the most important losses that we have suffered as a result of enslavement and colonization. To live without knowledge of your purpose, is to live a haphazard life. It's like driving to an unknown destination on an unknown route with little understanding of the vehicle used to transport you there. Riddled with confusion, this kind of living is usually very dangerous and filled with hardships, frustration, and a deep sense of detachment; a situation not easily corrected.

On the flip side, the person who is aware of their purpose has a standard against which they are able to measure opportunities and determine their activities. They are able to determine whether an option is in line with their reason for being born, and thus, if it is in their benefit to participate. This is different from having a desire to engage in a behavior or embark upon a journey. The sense of purpose supersedes desire; it also trumps comfort and popularity. A well-rooted sense of purpose brings to an individual the uncanny ability to persevere through the unattractive circumstances, while easily making what would otherwise be a tough decision. The sense of purpose serves as a road map for life planning and decision-making.

In ancient and indigenous cultures around the world, it is understood that an individual's life purpose is directly related to all other aspects surrounding birth including: physical disposition, place, day and time of birth, as well as the parents through which they are born. This is a powerful conceptualization of purpose and should not be underestimated. The value placed on this knowledge was worth more than all physical possessions a person can have, and maintains this level of appreciation even in modern times. It is the world of astrologers and diviners that now carry on this tradition. As the saying goes "Millionaires have Advisors, Billionaires have Astrologers." The entire science behind identifying a person's life purpose, via astrology and other tools, is based upon a person's spiritual disposition and life path as determined prior to birth (as mentioned in previous chapters). This determination is "sealed" by the date and time when the first breath is inhaled (inspiration). It is a way of more subtly and immediately understanding an individual's personality, their likely hardships and successes in life, as well as their overall temperament and personality disposition.

In traditional African societies, and various other indigenous cultures around the world, the high priests of the group would determine the newcomer's purpose and reason for incarnating. This was done by various means of divination, all of which are based on the high spiritual sciences of the respective group. It is a shared and common belief that we choose our destiny and parents based on life lessons that we intend to gain during our brief time as physical beings. This tradition is carried on today, throughout much of the world, albeit in a watered down, less spiritually-aware form.

For example, when a couple finds out they are pregnant, they often go to a doctor ("initiate" into the medical sciences) in order to determine the sex of the baby (receive divination regarding the forthcoming being). Instead of using cowrie shells, bones, coins, cards or other ancient tools for divination, the medical doctor uses the sonogram to answer the question. Instead of laying out the life path that will assist the parents in raising the child to his or her greatest and highest potential, the doctor tells the parents of the child's sex (male or female)[87]. Instead of selecting a name that will forever remind the child and community of their purpose and reason for being born, the family now buys either blue or pink clothing, welcoming the baby via stereotyped gender roles and naming them based on other reasons.

This represents a missed opportunity to know the most <u>important piece</u> of information a parent could ever share with their

---

[87] One of the earliest tools used to determine pregnancy status and the gender of the child, was found in Ancient Egypt. A woman would urinate on both wheat and barley seeds for a few days, if the wheat seeds grew, the woman was pregnant with a female child; if the barley grew, she was pregnant with a male child. If neither grew, she was not pregnant.

Reclaiming Our Stolen Legacy

child—knowledge of their life purpose. This void is soon filled with externally imposed guidance; a sort of blind leading the blind, or in some cases the ill-intentioned misleading the lost. We can all recall advice given to us by an elder, as we were growing up, that makes absolutely no sense now that we are adults. Tips like "never tell your mate everything," or "ride or die," or "all men are dogs," or "you can't trust women." The unsuspecting child may actually attempt to live based on this training, and end up no better for it. Parents that have reached an advanced level of awareness are at-least able to avoid giving this sort of guidance, and are likely to seek out and share the child's purpose with them; they are also likely to know and understand their own purpose, making them more stable and thoughtful in their own parenting styles, and less injurious due to ignorance and detrimental guidance.

  As with all things in creation, human beings can also be classified according to one of the Sephiroth or spheres on the "tree of life," each of which can also be categorized into one of the four elements: Fire, Earth, Air, and Water. For example, the child born with a "fiery" disposition, to parents who do not understand their purpose, may easily be labeled as aggressive, hard-headed, hyperactive and may be treated as if they have a psychological and/or social issue (ADHD, Oppositional Defiant Disorder). Depending on the gender, this presentation may be seen as stereotypically appropriate (for males) or stereotypically inappropriate (for females). The same child born to parents that understand and know their purpose will be given the proper training and guidance to accommodate and enhance the child's natural disposition. This sometimes happens in a haphazard way by noticing that this child is "athletic" and thus signing them up for sports; however, the haphazard method will almost surely be fragmented and leave the child void of other aspects of their training that are equally important (i.e., the development of the necessary mental aspects and spiritual discipline associated with their fiery disposition).

  A "fiery" child can manifest anywhere on the continuum of courage ranging from cowardice on one extreme to reckless on the other. The "fiery" disposition is one that can seem confrontational or always in some sort of drama. They may fight a lot, sustain a lot of injuries, flirt with danger, feel the need to protect and defend others, gravitate towards rough and tumble play, or avoid all of these things out of fear. The child that exhibits the "approach" aspect of fire, will likely be most suitable in situations where they have a respected "leader," whose directives they can follow (i.e., coach, ranked officer, supervisor, etc.). They will likely remain good soldiers, cops, athletes, and firefighters, never moving up the ranks to become the leaders themselves.

On the other hand, the "fiery" child with the avoidance approach tends to be a little more cautious and less likely to go as hard as their counterparts. They seem to have an element of insight that keeps them on the margins of danger without directly experiencing it as fully as those on the other extreme. This child is likely to have many "fiery" friends, who themselves exhibit the so-called "dangerous" behaviors, and who may see their cautious friend as the "weak one" in the crew. In time, the "weak one" may become the one the others take their directives from, having spent their childhood observing and subtly manipulating the group, they have learned them inside and out, and thus, know how to lead them.

The child born with a "watery" disposition may be sensitive and nurturing. Just like the "fiery" child, there are stereotyped expectations based on gender roles. The "watery" female child is typically more acceptable than the "watery" male child, and thus will be treated as such. In reality, the empathic and nurturing disposition of a water child is what healers are made of. These children are likely to have a destiny tied to the nurturing of other souls via education (teachers), medicine (healers), selfless sacrifice (religious and spiritual leaders), or via the process of birthing and caring for children (midwives, parents of many children). As seen via the natural expression of these elements, we recognize that neither is stronger nor more powerful than the other – water extinguishes fire and fire evaporates water; water carved the Grand Canyon, fire destroyed Rome.

Just as water absorbs and dissolves things into itself, so is the person with a "watery" disposition. They seem to have a deep concern for the well-being of others and often desire to lend a helping hand. As toddlers, they are the ones who attempt to soothe a crying baby. They may also be "foodies"—loving to eat as well as prepare food for themselves and others. They like to play doctor and want people to notice when they have hurt themselves, expecting the same level of concern *from* others as they have *for* others. For many years across various cultures, water has often been equated with emotions and how one feels.

Following this idea, we can recognize how stilling the emotions gives a clear view of a situation similar to how still waters give a better reflective image than the turbulent tides of the ocean. Hence the reason why still waters were gazed upon as a sort of oracle[88], and why ocean waves were used to send offerings and to cleanse (baptize) souls.

Opposite the extreme nurturing disposition (passively empathic) is the emotionally volatile (actively externalized). The word emotion consists of the prefix "e-" and the root word "motion."[89] The prefix "e-" carries the general meaning of something being externalized, in the case of emotion, it refers to the externalization of motion…literally something that moves. As we have seen, emotions are often associated with the observable behaviors (meaning they generate external movements) and sometimes can only be known concretely, based on these observable behaviors (unless articulated by the person experiencing them). The ancient and modern initiates recognized this with the saying:

> "Emotions make poor leaders but great servants."

Looking at the "e" in "emotion" as a symbolic representation of "energy" as physicists do[90], it becomes clear that we are talking about the same thing, the energy that drives movement. Freud called it libido when discussing his psycho-sexual stages of development, the Japanese call it Qi, the Chinese—Chi, East Indians—Prana, and the ancient Egyptians—Ra. Anything that carelessly spends and thus depletes this energy is classified as an "enemy." The emotionally-led person tends to expend their life-force by uninten-

---

88   Symbolized in Egypt by the Ibis bird standing on one leg staring down into the water. The science is sometimes called "water gazing."

89   We have already explored the importance of controlling one's emotional state as a prerequisite for further instruction on the path to initiation; nonetheless, we will briefly revisit the discussion for the sake of further exploring this very important topic.

90    $E = MC^2$

tionally vacillating between non-beneficial and typically non-productive emotional states, thus becoming their own greatest enemy.

The "watery" individual, of either extreme, runs the risk of being emotionally unstable, based either on their own internally generated emotions or from their sensitivity to the emotional states of others. One very profound and powerful gift of initiation is the ability to master emotions. The person who has reached this state is now capable of controlling emotions wherever they may manifest. This master of emotions is fully capable of eliciting or diminishing any emotional state, their own or that of another, at will…imagine the power.[91]

A child with an "airy" disposition may be talkative and have thoughts that seem to be "all over the place." Their curiosity may give the appearance of being "absent-minded" as they are capable of getting "lost in thought," sometimes making them oblivious to the cues, commands or directives of others. The "airy" child may be inquisitive and ask a lot of questions of the adults in their environment. If the child is born to parents of little patience or little confidence in their own intelligence, the child's questions may be met with harsh responses, designed to deter them from asking more questions. This scenario is sadly played out far too often.

With old school sayings like: "children are seen not heard," and "be quiet when grown folks are talking," children are often left to figure things out on their own, or with the insidious help of T.V., music, and other vehicles of popular culture. The "airy" child, thus treated, may have anxiety around expressing themselves and their innate desire to learn, and could subsequently develop a speech impediment (stuttering or stammering over words) or some form of social phobia.

On the other hand, the "airy" child whose gifts are recognized and nurtured has an easier road to travel as their questions are answered, either directly or indirectly, through guidance provided by people and the things in their environment. They are nurtured as they seek to satiate their insatiable curiosity. Their "gift to gab" is respected and hopefully guided, enhanced, and developed

---

91   Hence the reason why the Joker is the most powerful card in the deck; why the court Jester controls the audience; and why the ring master or clowns in the circus run the show—they control and manipulate the emotions in the room.

into an asset for the child. These children should have a library card and should have books of their own. They should be given support to write and read often. Language should be seen as valuable and interesting, and verbal and written communication their specialized tools. A child with this disposition may have an excellent memory and recall for what they have read or heard, and can be quite persuasive. Their command for language and factual information is exceptional, and they are sometimes labeled a "know it all." As with the other dispositions, this one carries its own set of unique strengths and weaknesses, and also benefits from evolved parents.

Finally, the child with an "earthy" disposition is one that is generally stable, yet oscillates through cycles similar to how the earth alternates seasons. The stability found in these cycles is as predictable as the winter cold, summer heat, spring blooms and the browning and falling of leaves in autumn. The "earthy" child is strong-minded which is sometimes confused with being stubborn. They are not easily moved and can be "set in their ways." Just like earth (solid matter), they are moldable and very practical. They have a propensity for being great nurturers, similar to the rich soil found in the organic farmer's fields. Unlike the nurturing of "watery" types, the "earthy" nurturer is more discerning and distinguishes what it gives to others. Just as the earth is full of a large variety of substances, the "earthy" individual has more than "emotional" support to give, and thus provides what is needed to who is in need.

This feature is further demonstrated by both the root system in plants, as well as the small & large intestines in humans. In plants, the roots are able to discern and discriminate what substances from the soil are required for the plant, and ingests only those things. Similarly, the intestines in humans have highly specialized cells, in various locations, that are designed to absorb and uptake very specific nutrients at specific points along the intestinal walls. These cells discern what is in the digesting foods as they pass by, absorbing only that which it is designed to uptake.

Resources tend to be plentiful for the "earthy" person, whether by hard work, saving, or inheritance. The physical world is either their playground or their prison; a veritable heaven or hell for them. Many of the "earthy" types tend to be either physically fit, or suffering from physical ailments. They can be centers of physical pleasure or have an aversion for physical contact. Loyalty is another of their known attributes along with steadfastness, stability, and a degree of deliberateness in thought, speech, and action.

People of this temperament often are aloof and can be natural loners. They tend to be reserved, private and conceal secrets (both their own and those of others). Just as the earth has many terrains, landscapes, textures, and degrees of solidity, the "earthy" type also has many moods, manifestations, movements, and modes of operating: some being stable, predictable, and allowing things to move around them, while others forge ahead like Juggernaut or a landslide, devouring anything in their path.

Parents of "earthy" children can best assist them by providing stability in their home environments; minimizing drastic changes, disruptions and all things unpredictable. "Earthy" children are great gardeners and caretakers of life. They should be allowed to nurture pets, grow plants, food, flowers, work in clay, and all sorts of arts and crafts, using their hands as the main tools for manipulation. They are deep feelers and are often empathic to a fault, directing their nurturing energies externally to others while neglecting their own needs. Like the other elements, "earthy" individuals are neither better nor worse off than the other types. They provide a specific and unique contribution to the whole, just as the others.

One of the main goals of initiation, as it relates to the various elements, is to get the initiate, with a specific disposition (earth, air, fire, or water) to a point where they are fully capable of manifesting any of the elements AT WILL, based on what a specific situation calls for[92]. So a naturally "watery" person, will be able to manifest "fiery" attributes in a situation where they are expected to perform with courage in a risky, and perhaps dangerous, scenario. A "watery" individual expected to work in a martial situation, may not have enough manifested "fire" to ensure their success. The initiate will have several tools (Qi Gong, Dummo Breathing, knowledge

---

92   This requires the ability to KNOW what energy a specific situation calls for. Early training requires the use of oracles or other systems of divining. Later, however, the initiate is able to directly recognize and interpret subtle signs and make a correct determination based on those.

of herbs, etc.) to assist in manifesting and utilizing the necessary fire.

The same goes for all dispositions and situations. In common everyday language, people tend to discuss these traits and dispositions based on zodiac signs and will excuse and expect certain behaviors based on this information[93]. As mentioned earlier, the zodiac signs are also categorized based on the four elements, and thus carry specific traits and dispositions related to the same. People believe that because they are Capricorns, they will always respond to situations as a Capricorn; or because their new love interest may be of a particular sign, they must manifest intimacy in a predetermined way. While this may be true for the masses of people, the initiated class is capable of flexing between them all, and thereby, are capable of manifesting whatever energy is necessary at any given time.

The fourth virtue or characteristic demonstrated by those that are ready for, or already in, the process of initiation is "identifying with spiritual life or higher ideals." This virtue is typically identified via the individual's perspective on things and their specific interests in life. People who demonstrate this trait tend to be more interested in the less tangible and unseen causes for events and experiences. They tend to think deeply about seemingly simple matters, and ask existential questions such as: "Why am I here?", "Where was I before I was born?", and, "What happens after I die?" People exhibiting this virtue, tend to be interested in fields that foster exploration, and provide understanding and deeper meaning to everyday matters.

You may realize and be thinking at this point that "almost everybody, at some time in their life, has asked these or similar questions." You are correct. The difference is found in the continuation along these lines. Many are deterred and discouraged from exploring these matters beyond a fleeting thought. Family, society, occupation, religion, and other things, can deter individuals from exploring these questions further. Thus discouraged, they may "abandon ship" and live their lives with a feeling of being

---

93   Many people are operating under false "signs," thinking they are one sign when they are in fact another. This is based on the difference between the Tropical Zodiac and the Vedic or Sidereal Zodiacs. This will be elaborated upon in volume 2.

unfulfilled, and a nagging that is barely perceptible but not easily ignored. On the other hand, some persist, no matter the cost and against all odds. They travel along the path seeking the answers to these questions, and find themselves willing to explore and seek out life experiences that lead to the answers. These people, once they consciously embark upon the journey, find that the "road map" and "street signs" become more clear and point them along certain causeways and avenues, which bring more enriching experiences to the Traveler; eventually leading them to knock at the door of initiation.

The fifth virtue is the "evidence of having a mission in life." This is readily identifiable by the person's focus and accumulated work and/or experiences in a particular field or discipline. They may not see it as being a mission, but once pointed out and examined more thoroughly, it is hard to deny. When you hear musicians in interviews answering the question "When did you first start singing?" They will often refer to a point in their early childhood and provide stories of how parents and other adults "always knew" they would be a performer.

The same goes for those that are excellent artists, builders, scientists, orators, etc. Parents tend to innately recognize an individual's mission in life and sometimes haphazardly, or unconsciously guide the child in the right direction for various reasons (helping their child to fulfill their dreams, monetary reward, social fame and acceptance, etc.). When these traits and qualities are observed and recognized by the initiating class, the potential initiate may be "encouraged" to consciously begin their journey. In some cases the unfortunate candidate, unaware of their gifts and talents as it relates to being an initiate, is taken advantage of by those who recognize their gifts and talents, and benefit from their ignorance.

I recall a story, shared by one of my Masonic elders, regarding his work as a chemist for a well-known paint manufacturing company. He was the ONLY person within the organization that could produce a particular color of paint. This was done by manipulating the chemical reactions used to produce the various colors.

The formulae they had available to them required the procedure to naturally run its course and thereby not producing the desired color. My elder intuitively knew to stop the chemical reaction at a very specific point in the process, and thus produce the desired color outcome. This, amongst other intuitively driven actions, made him a great asset to the company, although he was never openly made aware of his value. While conversing, I had a flash of insight. I was shown how the company used him, purposely stunted his level of awareness, and exploited his talents and ignorance.

During this period in his life, he was suffering from health issues directly related to his work in the laboratory, and the long-term exposure to chemicals. He was enraged by what his growing insight was showing him. He began to understand things about his professional life and how much more he could have done, if only he knew about *himself* what the company executives recognized in him. Fortunately for us, as long as there is consciousness and breath, there is still plenty of opportunity to evolve into our true destiny and glory. My elder and I both shed tears of sorrow, excitement, and a new sense of purpose and possibilities. We began working together to further understand his purpose and mission in life. In my eyes, he manifests the wisdom carried by George Washington Carver. His life took a drastic turn for the better. He began to seek out and apply natural remedies for his health concerns, all of which began to work and restore his body to strength and vitality. His mood improved and he began to be fulfilled by knowledge of his purpose and innate talents.

Sixth on our list is "the evidence of a call to Spiritual Orders or the Priesthood of the Mysteries." There have been at least two times where I have absolutely and without any doubt recognized this occurrence in my own life. One was the continued acknowledgement by Freemasons of my person as a Freemason PRIOR TO BECOMING INITIATED, PASSED, and RAISED as such. My elder cousin later told me that such individuals are considered "Marked" Master Masons (not to be confused with the Mark Master Mason degree). These individuals, by virtue of their "spirit," personality, and observable behaviors are often "mistaken" (or recognized) by others to be a part of their group, in this case a Freemason.

I can clearly recall several instances where I was asked certain questions, given specific handshakes, and afforded certain privileges based on this recognition, with no intent to deceive on my part. One such example occurred during my undergraduate studies at Fisk University in Nashville, TN. During that phase of my life, I was a deejay for many parties thrown by various organizations affiliated with the local universities. After one such party, hosted at Vanderbilt University, my "crew" and I went to a restaurant to get some food. While in line, a tall White man, wearing a "10-gallon" cowboy hat, a large chrome belt buckle and cowboy boots with spurs, got in line behind us. The man was standing right behind me because I was last in line behind my friends (I intended to pay for the food because they helped me with my deejaying equipment and records).

After a few moments of standing there, he got my attention. Among other things, he asked: "Are you a friend?" Confused by the question and its seeming randomness I stood quietly as he examined me with his crystal blue eyes. In my mind I heard a voice say, "well you are definitely not an enemy, so yeah," after which I verbally stated, "Yes, I am." He then made some statements and asked another question: "Are you a Traveler?" Again I stood perplexed by this question and wondered what that had to do with anything and why this dude was talking to, and taking such an interest in, me. Like before the voice in my mind provided guidance, "yeah, you love to drive to Atlanta." So I verbally responded: "Yes, I am a traveler." He then grabbed my hand, in what I now know to be a specific Masonic grip, and said: "Just remember along the way that anything worthwhile is not easy, but stick with it!" Now I was really confused, until he turned his hand and I saw his ring decorated with the Masonic Square and Compass. He furthered the gesture of Brotherhood by buying all of our food that night…I will never forget that experience, and now better understand it after being Raised almost 20 years later.

I now understand that this evidence of a calling is often first recognized by those that are already in the spiritual orders and priesthoods. They are taught within their orders what it means to be within. They are filled with the ideals of what they are striving for, whether or not they actually obtain the goal. By default, they are now capable of recognizing these very traits in others. The

Reclaiming Our Stolen Legacy

book *Her Bak: The Living Face of Ancient Egypt* by Isha Schwaller de Lubicz gives a wonderful example of how those from the inner temple recognize the gifts, talents and promise found in the "everyday" person, and subsequently lead them along the path towards initiation. Jesus the Christ is another shining example as found in the story where his parents "lose" him and find him again "teaching and learning in the Temple." His masters recognized his potential and invited him into the process[94].

Many of my initiation experiences have played out in similar ways: I get a flash of insight regarding my growth along a certain trajectory, and begin to act upon that flash. Sometimes I have encountered situations where the people responding to my knock are "hesitant" to answer because they are incapable of recognizing the one knocking; at other times, I am swept off my feet by those that recognize what I have yet to realize for myself. In both cases, the universe seems to conspire on my behalf, opening the way for my journey. Several times I have been granted fully paid opportunities to travel to some remote village deep within Africa, or somewhere else on the planet to be initiated. By understanding, for myself, that I have a higher calling to become a recipient of Light, I am strongly motivated to seek the same, and not easily deterred from my path.

Seventh is the "freedom from resentment, when under the experience of persecution and wrong." The opportunity to meet this particular test is common to anyone trying to live a more noble and evolved life. Oft times, those of us seeking to improve ourselves, are recipients of persecution from those that, for whatever reason, are not actively pursuing spiritual growth and development. For some, the persecution is a result of the persecutor feeling judged and negatively perceived by the one they persecute. In other words, because the initiate is beginning to do things differently (eating, thinking, socializing, dressing, etc.), and because the initiate believes these changes are beneficial and "better" than their former mode of operating, those that maintain the former ways, automatically assume they are somehow participating in lesser behaviors too, and that the persecuted feels the same way (that the persecutor is participating in lesser behaviors).

Sometimes this is real. There is often a point during the

---
94 Luke 2: 41-52

growth process where we can become super critical of all things that do not align with the new knowledge we are experiencing. As an example, people who decide to become vegetarian can sometimes shun and shame those that have decided otherwise. In the presence of vegetarians, or just a selective consumer/eater in general (no sugar, salt, dairy, hard liquor, tobacco), omnivores may feel as if the vegetarian is judging them, and thus they may begin to persecute the vegetarian with remarks like "I don't see how you survive eating that rabbit food." Or statements such as: "Why are you keeping your kids from eating candy…that's not right." Its very similar to hanging with people you use to drink with, after you become sober…they will "naturally" offer you a drink or even call you "square" because you don't. This is consistent with my personal experience, and for many who I have talked to about this very topic.

 When I first began to gather information regarding deeper aspects of creation, I then began to change my diet for what I perceived to be a better, and more healthy selection. This involved me eventually becoming a vegetarian, then a vegan. In addition to the dietary shift, I began to study and practice various forms of "energy" healing and exercises designed to cultivate, generate and direct the lifeforce (Qi Gong, Tai Chi, Pranic Healing, Tantric Practices, Yoga, Meditation, etc.). When certain people close to me saw my shift in diet, they began to challenge my decisions by sometimes verbally insulting my choice to eat "rabbit food," or by describing my food selection as "weird." In some cases, people who knew I no longer ate meat, would sincerely offer me a bite of their burger.

 Needless to say, the path got pretty lonely at times, and lent itself to feelings of being persecuted and wrongfully suffering from the ignorance of others. During my phase as a Rastafarian, I wore long locks and a long beard. My beard at one time contained 7 locks (dreadlocks) around which I would wear a ring made of hematite. I can recall with vivid memory a teacher (university professor) approaching me and stating: "Jeff, if you didn't open your mouth, I wouldn't know what to think about you." She meant that, based on my appearance, she would mistake me for someone that was crazy or ignorant, but my articulated intelligence allowed her to see otherwise.

Reclaiming Our Stolen Legacy

The "freedom from resentment" in the above illustrations is evidenced by me not feeling burdened due to the ignorance of others, when they decided to project and unload their ignorance onto me. Much of this unloading was in the form of insulting the decisions I made to consciously and intentionally improve my life: mind, body, and spirit. I could've easily, and sometimes did, feel shame. A few times, I sought to change or at least hide my decisions from others based on this persecution. It was not until I reached a certain level of confidence that I was fully capable of unapologetically being who I am. With this newly found stance came newly experienced and invaluable powers and abilities, which I wouldn't trade for the popularity that I once enjoyed.

Our children often have to endure a similar level of peer pressure and judgement from society. Nowadays, popular culture makes it "normal" for our children to present themselves in the image of hip hop artists. This image is not always a healthy and productive presentation. For the child that is not into the fashion trends, labels and brands promoted by this culture, they can be ostracized and made to feel shame about who they are. As initiates, they will be built up beyond the influence of pop culture and peer pressure, and thus will no longer be susceptible to the negative assaults subtly launched in their direction.

Our eighth virtue is having "confidence in the power of the Master (as Teacher)." This virtue is of importance because it allows a level of receptivity and faith in the sometimes difficult teachings received along the road of initiation. It is a prerequisite to, and sometimes the result of, the concept of trust and trustworthiness. Again, using my life as an example, I can recall many situations related to my various initiations when I was literally in a predicament where my trust and confidence in the process helped to alleviate and prevent what may otherwise have been overwhelming feelings of anxiety and fear. One such situation occurred as I was on my way to being initiated amongst the Ewe in Ghana, West Africa.

Prior to visiting Ghana, I was in Gambia, West Africa. I had connected with a Mandinkan brother I met during my previous visit to Gambia; he invited me to visit his village. I accepted and recruited six others to attend as well. On the morning of the journey,

Symbolically Speaking: African Lodge #1

all six people backed out and left me to go on my own. We were all going to contribute money to purchase gas for the boat we'd have to take up the Gambian River; needless to say, we were left with only my contribution. To make a long story short, there was a minor conflict regarding the amount of money I was able to contribute so we sat in front of the village chief (who happened to be the father of the brother I was traveling with). His father resolved the matter stating that I was correct in contributing the amount I had previously agreed on, and that it wasn't my responsibility that everyone else cancelled.

After leaving his father's compound, I was taken around the village by his older brother. We walked for a few hours visiting various people and seeing major landmarks of importance and spiritual significance. At one point we encountered a group of young children kicking a soccer ball around. One of the kids kicked it to me, and without thinking, I did a sliding kick that sent the ball hurling towards a tree, off of which it ricocheted into another tree, from there it bounced into a third, then right back to the kids…we were ALL amazed. At this point I noticed the overall energy beginning to change on the island. People began to arrive on boats carrying various pots, vessels, carvings and other undetermined goods. Men, women, and children along with goats, chickens and various other animals all began moving from their boats on the beach towards the center of the village.

At this point, I hadn't seen the brother I was travelling with since we left his father's compound. Before coming on the trip, I was very clear in telling them I must leave to be back in the town by a certain hour, he agreed. We were fast approaching this hour and I was beginning to feel uneasy. The intensity of the energy continued to grow as I was continually led around the village. I finally insisted that we find his brother and begin to head back towards the boat so I can get to town. His brother ignored me at first, to which I responded with a bit more fire. We eventually "found" his brother, to whom I reiterated my desire to leave. He stalled for a moment then we were headed back to the boat. Once on the boat, we began heading down the river. In my hand I had a box of matches that was given to me by the brother to burn some of the local herbs they were growing in the village. I had some of the herbs with me as well and was about to light some when a voice (similar to the voice when I was at the restaurant) clearly stated, "hold that match!"

    Surprised by the sudden command, I held the match and became super attentive to my environment. The voice then encouraged me to ask the following question of the two brothers navigating the boat: "If I had to walk down one of these roads to get back to the ferry, which side would it be?" To which the one in the rear of the boat responded: "The one over there," (pointing to the left bank). The voice immediately said: "just in case you end up on foot without them." Then another question came to me: "How long have you all been navigating this river?" To which the one in the front responded: "Since we were small boys." The voice responded: "So there should be no mistakes!" At this point I am confused and the intensity of the vibe was becoming unbearable. The best way I can describe this feeling is one of imminent danger. Within the next 5 minutes I was shown exactly why I was guided to ask those questions.

    The boat somehow ended up crashing into the bank of the river (the mistake that should not have happened). The brother, laying down in the front of the boat, jumped up as if surprised. He began to look at the brother in the back of the boat, where the motor was, as if they were beginning to execute a plan. Now I leave room for me to have been paranoid, overreacting to a situation, or just plain hallucinating, but what happened next leaves no doubt in my mind that I was reading the situation correctly. The brother in front finally spoke by asking: "What happened?" To which the one steering says: "We must've run out of gas." At this point I notice the two 5 gallon gas cans on this boat; one is between my feet and is full, the other is a couple of rows behind me and already a quarter empty.

    I have now turned sideways in my seat, in order to see both of them as the one from the front began to approach me. As he got closer, I instinctively placed my hand on top of the gas container at my feet as if to open it (remember I still have the box of matches and a match in my hand). When he finally got close to me I gestured as if I was going to open it. He looked at me and said: "I need

Symbolically Speaking: African Lodge #1

that gas can so we can refill the motor." To which I responded: "Use the one that has already been used." Again, they look at each other, then proceed to refill the motor with the can I suggested.

We are back to moving on the river for another five minutes or so when we crash into the other bank. This time, I realize that there is something really wrong with this situation, and that I need to treat this as if my life depended on it. As the one from the front approached this time, I literally took the top off the gas can, and held the match as if I was going to strike it. They looked at each other, pressed the primer on the motor and started it back up. We eventually got to the docking point, after which we had about a mile and a half walk through the bush to get back to the main road.

As we are walking, one of the brothers kept trying to lag behind me, at one time claiming he had to use the bathroom as he walked off the path into the bush. I said and did the same thing except on the opposite side. I waited for him to come out before I did, and fell in line behind him. We eventually reached the main road where I found some elders at a little shop brewing atiyah (green tea). I immediately walked over to them and yelled back to the brothers "I'm gonna take tea…let me know when you have a car for me." The elders chimed in by telling them to go and leave them with their new friend…I was in good hands.

I finally made it back to the ferry, got across the river and jumped on the back of a motorcycle and rode another hour to the town I was staying in. As I arrived back to town, several of the people that were supposed to accompany me seemed to be utterly surprised to see me. When I look back on this situation it reminds me of the Tupac interview in Vibe Magazine where he describes getting shot in the lobby of the NYC studio. He spoke of when he made it upstairs to where the others were, and how they all looked as if they saw a ghost; like they didn't expect to see him again. I was shook. I didn't know how to take what just occurred. Was I crazy? Was I delusional? Was I overreacting? One thing I was clear about is that I was alive and in good shape…feeling strong and secure, guided and protected. When I replay the boat ride, I feel confident in my interpretation, if for no other reason than the fact that the brothers never once asked me if I was okay. They never reacted to

Reclaiming Our Stolen Legacy

the fact that I was CLEARLY going to ignite a five-gallon container of gasoline on their boat; if I was tripping, they would've questioned me and attempted to ease my anxiety and intentions to set them and the boat on fire.

Needless to say, I passed this "test" and made my way to Ghana but not before being tested several more times. On my way to the airport, driven by the same brother that was steering the boat (yup, he was a cab driver too…that's actually how I first met him), we were pulled over by a police officer on the road leading to the airport. The driver was nervous, but I later understood this to be a message for the two of us: for me, my protection was being guaranteed, for him, my protection was being guaranteed. I got to the airport and upon entrance I learned that my flight had actually left early!!!! Initially I was supposed to fly to Senegal, lay over for eight hours then fly out to Ghana.

The people who were shocked to see me asked about my flight plans and told me there would be someone at the airport in Senegal to meet me so that I "wouldn't have to sit for hours in the airport." I was uneasy about the offer and fully intended to avoid this person once I arrived in Dakar. Now that my flight had literally left me, I wouldn't have to worry about that. Instead, a lady working at the next counter, for an entirely different airline, said they would honor my ticket and send me to Ghana on a more direct flight; stopping first in the Ivory Coast for 30 minutes then on to Accra!!!! No additional charge, no hassle, just clean and clear accommodation. It was amazing, and yet seemed to be natural and according to plan.

During the flight from Ivory Coast to Ghana, I prayed that I may find a guide that would get me to where I needed to be, and who could introduce me to my initiator. I was clearly on a mission with no road map, and no direct contacts to get me what I KNEW I was going there to receive, further Light. To add to the test, my bank card was "eaten" by an ATM machine back in the U.S., a few days before my flight departed, so I was literally traveling with only a checkbook, a few dalasi[95] and a few cedis,[96] which I saved from my previous trips to Gambia and Ghana. I figured that I could give

95 Gambian money
96 Ghanaian money

Symbolically Speaking: African Lodge #1

a certain amount to the person that helped me at the airport and the rest to the person who drove me to my guesthouse. When we landed, I went through the standard hustle and bustle of clearing immigrations and eventually made it to my bags. One of the customs officers recognized me from my previous trip to Ghana and struck up a conversation with me and walked with me to my stations. He made my experience a lot easier than it could've been so I tipped him first. This left me with only the money I would give to my driver.

At this point, drivers are bombarding me with offers to drive me for an amount that is beyond what I had to give. I find myself repeating the same response over and over again, "I only have 12 cedis, if you are willing to take me for that we can go…" Everyone was asking for 20 cedis. Then suddenly someone grabbed my bag from behind me and said, "Let's go." I turned and saw a brother with a stern and determined look on his face. I repeated my mantra of only having 12 cedis, he repeated his two word command, "Let's go." So I went. We climbed into his mini bus (trotro) and drove off. Of course we began to dialogue and I discovered his name was Emanuel (God with Us). He would eventually become my guide for the entire time I was in Ghana, just he and I, traveling in this 15 passenger trotro…I think my mid-flight prayer was answered.

On my second day there, Emanuel picked me up so we could go to meet a "Master" in order for me to receive my initiation. As we drove along a dirt road, way back into the bush, I felt a certain level of fear and anxiety starting to build in my gut. I attempted to hide the feelings as I marveled out the window at the majestic trees and animals lining the horizon and landscape, but Emanuel picked up on the vibes. He simply stated, "Sometimes you must have courage to get the things that you are after." To which I replied, "You are right…you must also appreciate that we are the only two people that know where I am on the planet, and between the two of us, only you REALLY know where I am. All I know for sure is that I am in this van, on this road somewhere in the heart of Ghana." He then said, with a tone of being offended, "Do you think I am going to do something to you?" I reassured him that wasn't the

Reclaiming Our Stolen Legacy

case nor my concern, but that it was a sense of extreme power that I was feeling coming from deep within myself that made me more nervous than anything[97].

We arrived at our destination after a long drive off the main road between Accra and Kumasi. It was a mystical village outside of Pokuase. There I met my initiator, Eshaka. I can't detail what occurred here but can say that I gained a new appreciation for Malidoma Patrice Some's book *Of Water and the Spirit* by the time we were finished. This initiation was more in-depth and detailed than what I experienced amongst the Jolla in Gambia. Eshaka spoke no English yet we fully understood each other and communicated freely. The one word I could understand that he spoke was "Mami-Wata." I experienced a form of divination that was unlike any I had previously observed. We did our "works" and I was told to come back in two days to pick up what I would need to travel with on my way back to the U.S. After returning and finishing our initial processes, a random Ewe man on the streets recognized me as having done something "powerful." He could see that I was an initiate of his culture, although there were no external or apparent signs.

Since then, I have been visited only once by Eshaka, and this occurred within the first week of my return to the United States. I was laying on my living room floor sleeping when I entered a "dream-state" wherein Eshaka and I were standing on a dirt road next to train tracks. He asked me "Are you a Muslim?" To which I replied, "I submit to the Will of God." Just then he disappeared and a train came blasting down the tracks. I instinctively knew that my task was to catch up to the last car of the train. I began running with no success. As the train got farther and farther away, I realized that I couldn't physically run fast enough, so it couldn't be about my physical abilities. Just then, I began to breath in a certain regulated pattern and simultaneously began to get closer and closer to the train. My breathing in the "dream" became so deep that it startled me "awake." I looked around my living room with great surprise, then immediately laid back down and was again right back along the train tracks running down the train. I caught the caboose, was congratulated by Eshaka, and then "woke up."

---

97   I didn't tell him of my recent experiences in Gambia which was probably contributing to my anxiety at the time.

Symbolically Speaking: African Lodge #1

The above examples serve to illustrate how each of us has a "Master" teacher within, and that our external teachers are tasked with directing us to the internal. Every human being has an internal voice that whispers guidance, insight, wisdom, and direction; all of which is designed to assist us in achieving our greatest and highest good. It is this voice that we stand to gain the most from following. Yet, it is this voice that is most likely to be ignored, drowned out by confusion, discounted, discredited, or undervalued. People are generally taught to submit to and praise an external teacher and/or Master, and are actually rewarded or punished based on their submission to the same. This often sets up a tricky and detrimental situation because most aren't taught how to discern between a worthy external teacher and a corrupt one with authority. This overemphasis and dependence on external teachers, at the expense of developing confidence in our internal Master, is what leaves our youth vulnerable to the predators lurking in youth organizations, religious institutions, the streets, and schools.

As babies, we are fully capable of distinguishing between "bad energy" and "good energy." We have all seen a baby refuse to embrace someone or pull away from an advance by another. We've seen the happy baby burst into tears of protest when a particular person attempts to touch, hold, or even engage them in a conversation. We have also witnessed the parent force the child to go with that person, despite their obvious angst and desire to avoid the individual. Perhaps the parent's own discomfort is the issue. Maybe they are embarrassed that their child is possibly shaming the person being rejected.

Whatever the reason, what is being reinforced for the child, in such a situation, is the devaluing of their internal feelings and desires, and over-valuing the perspective of those in authority. As an initiate, I have found the most valuable teacher of all to be that internal Master, the higher self that dwells at the core of our being. It is the goal of many initiation processes to gain full and consistent access to this Master, in order that the initiate may live as a spiritually evolved human, a God-man/God-woman, amongst the masses. Again, Jesus the Christ, and the earlier example of Heru are the perfect illustrations of this concept.

Reclaiming Our Stolen Legacy

Our ninth virtue, "confidence in one's own ability to learn," is the direct compliment to the eighth virtue. For without a confident disposition, an individual is less likely to attempt mastery of difficult subjects, and is less likely to engage in any prolonged attempts at a challenging and difficult task. Without confidence, no matter the skill level of the individual, they will be hesitant and less likely to initiate (begin) a task. Social and behavioral psychologists have studied this process for decades and have even developed protocols for both developing self-confidence as well as hindering it[98].

When we look into our recent history, we see that over the past 400 + years African descendants have been bombarded with self-esteem depleting experiences, examples, and images; all designed to create, instill, and reinforce a certain inferior identity. This consistent and constant portrayal of negative imagery, the examples of pure and rewarded ignorance, as well as the plethora of demeaning and self-hating characters and role models, have built a paradigm defining how people will begin to view themselves and others like them; in this case, the view is subhuman and unworthy of justice.

It is within this narrowly contrived world that people also develop their expectations of self and others, and from which they map out their own life trajectory. If, for example, children only receive messages that describe their potential in life as limited to lower standards of education, a lower economic status, and lower professional accomplishments, then they are likely to believe these to be the limits of their possibilities. Thus a teacher, no matter how gifted and profound, will run up against this barrier, and the child themselves will serve as the main enforcer, literally working against the attempts to assist and develop their character beyond the preconceived and programmed limitations.

The success of oppression is found in this very virtue. Oppressive systems and people are able to maintain their advantage by thwarting the confidence of the oppressed. To render one helpless by instilling a sense of hopelessness, almost always breeds a stagnant mentality and thus, makes healthy growth and development less likely. The reason this particular attribute is included amongst the ten virtues is because of its positive relationship to achievement,

---

98   See B. F. Skinner's *Beyond Freedom and Dignity*.

and how confidence gives permission to break through barriers that may otherwise seem insurmountable.

During initiation, the sojourner will be faced with a plethora of trials and tribulations, many of which seem impossible to figure out, remedy, and overcome. Some tasks will even defy what many believe to be the limits of human ability; in these cases, the initiate will find themselves having to overcome or risk death in their failure. There is no room for questioning one's abilities. Similar to a lion tamer in the cage with ten lions, they must, at all times and in all ways, be sure of their dominance and confident in their ability to control these beasts. Even when the lions attempt to rebel, the tamer must maintain their disposition of superiority or die.

Similarly, initiates are given opportunities to prove their level by overcoming or preventing dangerous experiences. There are countless stories of how an individual, who recently initiated, is faced with a life or death situation and must call upon something other than the obvious external resources to successfully navigate the situation. There are times when the deck seems totally stacked against the aspirant and yet, their confidence and trust in what they have learned and experienced, puts the situation in its proper place: inferior to the gifts and powers they have developed. Without this confidence, they will surely fail or haphazardly get through the situation, risking loss and injury in the process.

Continuing with the story of my return from Ghana, I will further illustrate this virtue in a real life situation. There was a point in my return trip that I was threatened with being detained in the Ghana airport unless I paid a certain amount of money. I had spent all of the cedis I had, and only retained twenty U.S. dollars for my train ride once I got back to NYC. As I approached the immigrations officer at the Accra airport, I noticed a strange feeling and immediately acknowledged the fact that my tests were continuing. Not knowing what to expect, I cautiously approached the booth and handed the officer my passport. He inspected it and feigned some sort of discrepancy with my last entry into, and departure from, Ghana. He said I would have to pay $100 US dollars in order to leave. I told him I did not have that much money so I couldn't pay.

Reclaiming Our Stolen Legacy

After a small exchange of words, he told me to stand off to the side, keeping my passport. I was commanded to wait for the police officers to come and take me to jail. Others standing in line witnessing this drama all looked concerned for me and my well-being. I momentarily gave in to the vibes of pending doom but immediately snapped myself back into my confident and superior stance. I began to meditate and visualize myself getting onto the plane and arriving safely back in the U.S. After a few minutes I hear the immigrations officer call out "Boy!" I open my eyes and he gestures to me to come over to the booth. I walk over, he stamps my passport and hands it to me and said get on your plane. I smiled, thanked him and went on my way.

Once I arrived in NYC, I was scheduled to stay with my South African "Mother," Mama Zandi, who I met at Fisk University. She let me spend the night with her because my flight back to Tennessee was scheduled for the next day. I got to her apartment, ate, slept and woke up the next morning ready to go. My flight left from ISLIP on Long Island, so I had to take a train from Manhattan to Long Island, using the last bit of my money. I somehow got on the wrong train and ended up on Long Island but on a track that did not lead to the airport.

Upon realizing this, I rode for a while until I got the impulse to get off the train. When I got off, it was a pretty much deserted station with a few cars parked in the lot. I had all of my luggage (including a super heavy duffle bag) dragging behind me and decided to walk down amongst the cars, one of which was a black Lincoln Town Car with black tinted windows, which looked like a car for hire. I approached the driver's door, tapped on the window and asked if he was a "driver." He hesitated and said "Yeah, where you going?" I explained what happened and told him my flight was leaving in about an hour…he looked as if he just received a challenge and told me to get in.

As we are driving along, we struck up small talk. After about 20 minutes into the drive, I finally get up the nerve to tell him I had to pay with a check because I literally didn't have any money nor did I have my ATM card. He glared at me in his rearview mirror with a look that I will never forget. I ensured him the check would be good. He placed his right hand over the seat and I saw his Masonic ring and realized he was checking to see if I was a member of the Craft[99]; at the time I wasn't, but he recognized that I "was." We arrived at the airport, I gave him the check and as I am exiting the car, I look down and find a train token on the ground between the car and the curb. To me, this was a sign that my efforts have been successful and rewarded.

My confidence in my Master as well as my confidence in my own abilities to follow the instructions and implement what I had learned, is what kept me moving in the above examples. One without the other can lead to failure or at least a rough time. Not all tests are this mystical, nor are they all dangerous. In fact, most of our tests are subtle and come via everyday situations like losing keys, missing a call, responding to others and their attitudes, etc. The key is to remain ever aware that you are on a journey towards enlightenment and have consciously decided to improve upon your natural gifts and talents; desiring to maximize your God-given gifts and talents.

The tenth and final virtue for initiates to demonstrate is the "readiness or preparedness for initiation." This virtue seems to be simple and self-explanatory, however, it is equally as powerful and equally as guarded as the other nine. Nowadays, one equates their readiness and/or preparedness with being able to pay financial dues and having the right "connections" for being able to get into the ranks. This is a bastardization of what this virtue truly represents. On the deepest and highest levels, an individual's preparedness is based upon their internal courage and willingness to commit to a life of no longer having the excuse of being ignorant about things. It points to the person's willingness to commit to a life where they are constantly and consistently striving to improve themselves, specifically their character, as well as their physical, mental, and spiritual abilities. A person that is truly ready for initiation is one who is willing to "die" to the world, in order to become superior to the world; as stated in the Book of Genesis, they are truly prepared to have "dominion over all things."

The truly prepared initiate has sought mastery over their

---

[99] One of the many interesting "coincidental" associations of Freemasonry with Africa during my travels.

own person: emotions, thoughts, behaviors, etc. They have imposed upon themselves certain restrictions and limitations for the sole purpose of improving themselves. They are receptive to external guidance, but not dependent on it, as they continue their journey towards Light. These individuals have a sincere and almost obsessive desire to be better, to maximize their potential, and to learn truly who they are, why they are, where they are, what they are and how they came to be. The "who" delves deeply into their identity and spans the mind, body, and spiritual aspects of the person. The "why" speaks directly to the individual's purpose for being alive and serves as a guide for understanding their overall disposition. The "where" refers to the individual's location in space and time, including the era in which they were born, the parents they were born through, the community, race, society, and culture as well as the location on the planet where they find themselves. The "what" is a question about human beingness in general, and the construction of the individual specifically. Knowledge of what we are, and how we relate to all other things, is perhaps the most important knowledge one can pursue and obtain. The "how" of being is the scientific process behind all of creation; its literally what the Book of Genesis is designed to teach, albeit in a highly codified manner.

 An active pursuit along these lines is what demonstrates to the ever-watchful eyes of the initiators, the preparedness of the individual seeker. Astute parents and teachers are capable of identifying potential candidates based on the types of questions they ask, the type of personality they display, the responses they have in times of adversity, as well as their response to others in need. One's preparedness for initiation is an ever evolving state, meaning a person may become ready for various levels of initiation at various points in their development; and this can plateau at any given stage. Thus, it is seen that initiation is a very dynamic and fluid process, and is naturally unique for each and every individual found on the path.

 The practical manifestation of the ten virtues listed above, is tantamount to one's success as an initiate. The discipline necessary to bring forth these attributes is what separates initiates from non-initiates. Be not confused, initiatory success has nothing to do with physical or genetic capability, but is a matter of devotion and perseverance. Each individual has their own innate gifts and talents and is fully capable of producing the ten attributes in their own unique way.

To view Prince Hall Freemasonry in light of what has been detailed above, as descendants from the African Lodge, and with the understanding that the chosen name may have been a codified message for those of us to come later, we open up a world of opportunity to grow and expand ourselves as individuals and as a collective Lodge. The greatness of an African worldview in regards to it's ontology, epistemology, and axiology has been presented narratively throughout this book, but will be explored in greater detail in volume 2 of this work. We will also explore the psychology and practical use of symbolism, as well as reinterpret many of our Masonic symbols through the lens of an African initiate.

The coming volume promises to deepen our understanding of our Craft and will equally challenge our current paradigm, worldview, and understanding of our potential to usher in change. As Universal Men and Women[100], we stand superior to our former uninitiated selves. We have opportunities to improve the human condition beyond its current ever-declining state. The mysteries of today will become the common-knowledge of tomorrow, if we make the necessary sacrifices and devote ourselves to uplifting our status, through commitment and focus, and perhaps most importantly, a shift in paradigm. We can't afford to arbitrarily separate the historical and esoteric parts of Freemasonry. As descendants of the African Lodge, it is our nature to keep them together. To see all of our actions as Ritual, to see ourselves as Divinely Human, and to understand our Craft to be a powerful and ancient tool for self-mastery, we take the necessary first step towards reclaiming our greatness, and we begin to knock the rough edges off the Ashlar. These are exciting times we are blessed to live in. Let's act accordingly.

---

100   A term coined by Mr. Neely Fuller, Jr. in reference to "any male, and/or female, person, who knows and understands truth, and, who has used that knowledge and understanding in a manner that has produced justice and correctness, in all places, in all areas of activity, including Economics, Education, Entertainment, Labor, Law, Politics, Religion, Sex, and War."

APPENDIX A

The Charter Issued to Prince Hall and Members of African Lodge #1 by The Grand Lodge of England

To all and every our right Worshipful and loving Brethren, we, Thomas Howard, Earl of Effingham, Lord Howard, &c, &c, &c, Acting Grand Master, under the authority of His Royal Highness, Henry Frederick, Duke of Cumberland, &c, &c, &c, Grand Master of the Most Ancient and Honorable Society of Free and Accepted Masons, send greetings:

"KNOW YE THAT WE, at humble petition of our right trusty and well beloved Brethren, PRINCE HALL, BOSTON SMITH, THOMAS SANDERSON, and several other Brethren, residing in Boston, New England, in North America, do hereby constitute the said Brethren into a regular LODGE OF FREE AND ACCEPTED MASONS, under the title or denomination of the AFRICAN LODGE, to be opened in Boston, aforesaid, and do further, at their said petition, hereby appoint the said PRINCE HALL to be Master, BOSTON SMITH, Senior Warden, and THOMAS SANDERSON, Junior Warden, for the opening of the said LODGE, and for such further time only as shall be thought proper by the Brethren thereof, it being our will that this our appointment of the above officers shall in no wise affect any future election of officers of the LODGE, but that such elections shall be regulated agreeable to such by-laws of the society, contained in the Book of Constitutions; and we hereby will require you, the said PRINCE HALL, to take especial care that all and every one of said Brethren are, or have been legally made Masons, and that they do observe, perform and keep all the rules and orders contained in the Book of Constitutions; and further, that you do from time to time, cause to be entered in a book kept for that purpose, an account of your proceedings as a

LODGE, together with such rules, orders and regulations, as shall be made for the good government of the same; that in no wise you omit once in every year to send us, or our successors, Grand Master, or Rowland Holt, Esq., our Deputy Grand Master, for the time being, an account in writing of your said proceedings, and copies of all such rules, orders and regulations, as shall be made as aforesaid, together with the list of the members of the LODGE, and such a sum of money as may suit the circumstances of the Lodge and reasonably be expected toward the Grand Charity. Moreover, we hereby will and require you, the said PRINCE HALL, as soon as conveniently may be, to send an account in writing, of what may be done by virtue of these presents.

Given at London, under our hands and seal of Masonry, this 29th day of September, A. L. 5784, A. D. 1784.

"By the Grand Master's command.

Witness:	WM. WHITE, G. S.
(Seal)	R. HOLT, D. G. M."

APPENDIX B

Prince Hall Speech 1792

"A Charge Delivered to the Brethren of the African Lodge"

Dearly and well beloved Brethren of the African Lodge, as through the goodness and mercy of God, we are once more met together, in order to celebrate the Festival of St. John the Baptist; it is requisite that we should on these public days, and when we appear in form, give some reason as a foundation for our so doing, but as this has been already done, in a discourse delivered in substance by our late Reverend Brother John Marrant, and now in print, I shall at this time endeavour to raise part of the superstructure, for howsoever good the foundation may be, yet without this it will only prove a Babel. I shall therefore endeavour to shew the duty of a Mason; and the first thing is, that he believes in one Supreme Being, that he is the great Architect of this visible world, and that he governs all things here below by his almighty power, and his watchful eye is over all our works. Again we must be good subjects to the laws of the land in which we dwell, giving honour to our lawful Governors and Magistrates, giving honour to whom honour is due; and that we have no hand in any plots or conspiracies or rebellion, or side or assist in them: for when we consider the blood shed, the devastation of towns and cities that hath been done by them, what heart can be so hard as not to pity those our distrest brethren, and keep at the greatest distance from them. However just it may be on the side of the opprest, yet it doth not in the least, or rather ought not, abate that love and fellow-feeling which we ought to have for our brother fellow men.

    The next thing is love and benevolence to all the whole family of mankind, as God's make and creation, therefore we ought to love them all, for love or hatred is of the whole kind, for if I love a man for the sake of the image of God which is on him, I must love all, for he made all, and upholds all, and we are dependant upon him for all we do enjoy and expect to enjoy in this world and that which is to come.—Therefore he will help and assist all his fellow-men in distress, let them be of what colour or nation they may, yea even our very enemies, much more a brother Mason. I shall therefore give you a few instances of this from Holy Writ, and first, how did Abraham prevent the storm, or rebellion that was rising between Lot's servants and his? Saith Abraham to Lot, let there be no strife I pray thee between me and thee, for the land is before us, if you will go to the left, then I will go to the right, and if you will go to the right, then I will go to the left. They divided and peace was restored. I will mention the compassion of a blackman to a Prophet of the Lord, Ebedmelech, when he heard that Jeremiah was cast into the dungeon, he made intercession for him to the King, and got liberty to take him out from the jaws of death. See Jer. xxxviii, 7-13.

Also the prophet Elisha after he had led the army of the Eramites blindfold into Samaria, when the King in a deriding manner said, my Father (not considering that he was as much their Father as his) shall I smite, or rather kill them out of the way, as not worthy to live on the same earth, or draw the same air with himself; so eager was he to shed his brethren's blood, that he repeats his blood-thirsty demand, but the Prophet after reproaching him therefore, answers him no, but set bread and water before them; or in other words, give them a feast and let them go home in peace. See 2 Kings vi, 22-23.

I shall just mention the good deeds of the Samaritan, though at that time they were looked upon as unworthy to eat, drink or trade with their fellowmen, at least by the Jews; see the pity and compassion he had on a poor distrest and half dead stranger, see Luke x. from 30 to 37. See that you endeavour to do so likewise.—But when we consider the amazing condescending love and pity our blessed Lord had on such poor worms as we are, as not only to call us his friends, but his brothers, we are lost and can go no further in holy writ for examples to excite us to the love of our fellow-men.—But I am aware of an objection that may arise (for some men will catch at any thing) that is that they were not all Masons; we allow it, and I say that they were not all Christians, and

Appendix B

their benevolence to strangers ought to shame us both, that there is so little, so very little of it to be seen in these enlightened days.

Another thing which is the duty of a Mason is, that he pays a strict regard to the stated meetings of the Lodge, for masonry is of a progressive nature, and must be attended to if ever he intends to be a good Mason; for the man that thinks that because he hath been made a Mason, and is called so, and at the same time will willfully neglect to attend his Lodge, he may be assured he will never make a good Mason, nor ought he to be looked upon as a good member of the Craft. For if his example was followed, where would be the Lodge; and besides what a disgrace is it, when we are at our set meetings, to hear that one of our members is at a drinking house, or at a card table, or in some worse company, this brings disgrace on the Craft: Again there are some that attend the Lodge in such a manner that sometimes their absence would be better than their Company (I would not here be understood a brother in disguise, for such an one hath no business on a level floor) for if he hath been displeased abroad or at home, the least thing that is spoken that he thinks not right, or in the least offends him, he will raise his temper to such a height as to destroy the harmony of the whole Lodge; but we have a remedy and every officer ought to see it put in execution. Another thing a Mason ought to observe, is that he should lend his helping hand to a brother in distress, and relieve him; this we may do various ways—for we may sometimes help him to a cup of cold water, and it may be better to him than a cup of wine. Good advice may be sometimes better than feeding his body, helping him to some lawful employment, better than giving him money; so defending his case and standing by him when wrongfully accused, may be better than clothing him; better to save a brother's house when on fire, than to give him one. Thus much may suffice.

I shall now cite some of our fore-fathers, for our imitation: and the first shall be Tertullian, who defended the Christians against their heathen false accusations, whom they charged with treason against the empire and the Emperor, because of their silent meetings: he proved that to be false for this reason, for in their meetings, they were wont to pray for the prosperity of the Empire, of Rome, and him also; and they were accused of being enemies to mankind, how can that be, said he, when their office is to love and pray for all mankind. When they were charged with worshipping the Sun, because they looked towards the East when they prayed; he defended them against this slander also, and proved that they were slandered, slighted and ill-treated, not for any desert of theirs, but only out of hatred of them and their profession. This friend of the distrest was born in Carthage in Africa, and died Anno Christi 202.

Take another of the same city, Cyprian, for his fidelity to his profession was such, that he would rather suffer death than betray his trust and the truth of the gospel, or approve of the impious worship of the Gentiles: He was not only Bishop of Carthage, but of Spain and the east, west and northern churches, who died Anno Christi 259.

But I have not time to cite but one more (out of hundreds that I could count of our Fathers, who were not only examples to us, but to many of their nobles and learned); that is, Augustine, who had engraven on his table these words:

He that doth love an absent Friend to jeer, May hence depart, no room is for him here.

His saying was that sincere and upright Prayer pierceth heaven, and returns not empty. That it was a shelter to the soul. A sacrifice to God and a scourge to the Devil. There is nothing, said he, more abateth pride and sin than the frequent meditation on death; he cannot die ill, that lives well, and seldom doth he die well, that lives ill: Again, if men want wealth, it is not to be unjustly gotten, if they have it they ought by good works to lay it up in heaven: And again he that hath tasted the sweetness of divine love will not care for temporal sweetness. The reasonable soul made in the likeness of God may here find much distraction, but no full satisfaction; not to be without afflictions, but to overcome them, is blessedness. Love is as strong as death; as death kills the body, so love of eternal life kills worldly desires and affections. He called Ingratitude the Devil's sponge, wherewith he wipes out all the favours of the Almighty. His prayer was: Lord give first what thou requirest,

Appendix B

and then require of me what thou wilt. This good man died Anno Christi 430.

The next is Fulgentius, his speech was, why travel I in the world which can yield me no future, nor durable reward answerable to my pains? Thought it better to weep well, than to rejoice ill, yet if joy be our desire, how much more excellent is their joy, who have a good conscience before God, who dread nothing but sin, study to do nothing but to accomplish the precepts of Christ. Now therefore let me change my course, and as before I endeavoured amongst my noble friends to prove more noble, so now let my care and employment be among the humble and poor servants of Christ, and become more humble that I may help and instruct my poor and distrest brethren.

Thus, my brethren, I have quoted a few of your reverend fathers for your imitation, which I hope you will endeavour to follow, so far as your abilities will permit in your present situation and the disadvantages you labour under on account of your being deprived of the means of education in your younger days, as you see it is at this day with our children, for we see notwithstanding we are rated for that, and other Town charges, we are deprived of that blessing. But be not discouraged, have patience, and look forward to a better day; Hear what the great Architect of the universal world saith, Aethiopia shall stretch forth her hands unto me. Hear also the strange but bold and confident language of J. Husk, who just before the executioner gave the last stroke, said, I challenge you to meet me an hundred years hence. But in the mean time let us lay by our recreations, and all superfluities, so that we may have that to educate our rising generation, which was spent in those follies. Make you this beginning, and who knows but God may raise up some friend or body of friends, as he did in Philadelphia, to open a School for the blacks here, as that friendly city has done there.

I shall now shew you what progress Masonry hath made since the siege and taking of Jerusalem in the year 70, by Titus Vespasian; after a long and bloody siege, a million of souls having been slain or had perished in the city, it was taken by storm and the city set on fire. There was an order of men called the order of St. John, who besides their other engagements, subscribed to another, by which they bound themselves to keep up the war against the Turks. These men defended the temple when on fire, in order to save it, so long, that Titus was amazed and went to see the reason of it; but when be came so near as to behold the Sanctum Sanctorum, he was amazed, and shed tears, and said, no wonder these men should so long to save it. He honored them with many honors, and large contributions were made to that order from many kingdoms; and were also knighted. They continued 88 years in Jerusalem, till that city was again retaken by the Turks, after which they resided 104 years in the Cyrean city of Ptolemy, till the remains of the Holy Conquest were lost. Whereupon they settled on the Island of Cyprus, where they continued 18 years, till they found an opportunity to take the Island Rhodes; being masters of that, they maintained it for 213 years, and from thence they were called Knights of Rhodes, till in the year 1530 they took their residence in the Island of Malta, where they have continued to this day, and are distinguished by the name of the Knights of Malta. Their first Master was Villaret in the year 1099. Fulco Villaret in the year 1322, took the Island of Rhodes, and was after that distinguished by the title of Grand Master, which hath devolved to his Successors to this day.

    Query, whether at that day, when there was an African church, and perhaps the largest Christian church on earth, whether there was no African of that order; or whether, if they were all Whites, they would refuse to accept them as their fellow Christians and brother Masons; or whether there were any so weak, or rather so foolish, as to say, because they were Blacks, that would make their lodge or army too common or too cheap? Sure this was not our conduct in the late war; for then they marched shoulder to shoulder, brother soldier and brother soldier, to the field of battle; let who will answer; he that despises a Black man for the sake of his colour, reproacheth his Maker, and he hath resented it, in the case of Aaron and Miriam. See for this Numbers xii.

    But to return: In the year 1787 (the year in which we received our charter) there were 489 lodges under charge of his late Royal Highness the Duke of Cumberland; whose memory will always be esteemed by every good Mason.

    And now, my African brethren, you see what a noble order

Appendix B

you are members of. My charge to you is, that you make it your study to live up to the precepts of it, as you know that they are all good; and let it be known this day to the spectators that you have not been to a feast of Bacchus, but to a refreshment with Masons; and see to it that you behave as such, as well at home as abroad; always to keep in your minds the obligations you are under, both to God and your fellow men. And more so, you my dear brethren of Providence, who are at a distance from, and cannot attend the Lodge here but seldom; yet I hope you will endeavour to communicate to us by letters of your welfare; and remember your obligations to each other, and live in peace and love as brethren.—We thank you for your attendance with us this day, and wish you a safe return.

    If thus, we by the grace of God, live up to this our Profession; we may cheerfully go the rounds of the compass of this life, having lived according to the plumb line of uprightness, the square of justice, the level of truth and sincerity. And when we are come to the end of time, we may then bid farewell to that delightful Sun and Moon, and the other planets, that move so beautifully round her in their orbits, and all things here below, and ascend to that new Jerusalem, where we shall not want these tapers, for God is the Light thereof; where the Wicked cease from troubling, and where the weary are at rest.

> Then shall we hear and see and know,
> All we desir'd and wish'd below,
> And every power find sweet employ,
> In that eternal world of joy.
> Our flesh shall slumber in the ground,
> Till the last trumpet's joyful sound,
> Then burst the chains with sweet surprize,
> And in our Saviour's image rise.

Symbolically Speaking: African Lodge #1

APPENDIX C

Prince Hall's Speech, 1797

Prince Hall Speaks To The African Lodge, Cambridge, Massachusetts

Beloved Brethren of the African Lodge: It is now five years since I delivered a charge to you on some parts and points of masonry. As one branch or superstructure of the foundation, I endeavored to show you the duty of a mason to a mason, and of charity and love to all mankind, as the work and image of the great God and the Father of the human race. I shall now attempt to show you that it is our duty to sympathise with our fellow-men under their troubles, and with the families of our brethren who are gone, we hope, to the Grand Lodge above.

We are to have sympathy, but this, after all, is not to be confined to parties or colors, nor to towns or states, nor to a kingdom, but to the kingdoms of the whole earth, over whom Christ the King is head and grand master for all in distress.

Among these numerous sons and daughters of distress, let us see our friends and brethren; and first let us see them dragged from their native country, by the iron hand of tyranny and oppression, from their dear friends and connections, with weeping eyes and aching hearts, to a strange land, and among a strange people, whose tender mercies are cruel,—and there to bear the iron yoke of slavery and cruelty, till death, as a friend, shall relieve them. And must not the unhappy condition of these, our fellow-men, draw forth our hearty prayers and wishes for their deliverance from those merchants and traders, whose characters you have described in Revelation xviii. 11-13? And who knows but these same sort of traders may, in a short time, in like manner bewail the loss of the African traffic, to their shame and confusion? The day dawns now in some of the West India Islands. God can and will change their

Symbolically Speaking: African Lodge #1

condition and their hearts, too, and let Boston and the world know that He hath no respect of persons, and that bulwark of envy, pride, scorn and contempt, which is so visible in some, shall fall.

Now, my brethren, nothing is stable; all things are changeable. Let us seek those things which are sure and steadfast, and let us pray God that, while we remain here, he would give us the grace of patience, and strength to bear up under all our troubles, which, at this day, God knows, we have our share of. Patience, I say; for were we not possessed of a great measure of it, we could not bear up under the daily insults we meet with in the streets of Boston, much more on public days of recreation. How, at such times, are we shamefully abused, and that to such a degree, that we may truly be said to carry our lives in our hands, and the arrows of death are flying about our heads.

My brethren, let us not be cast down under these and many other abuses we at present are laboring under,—for the darkest hour is just before the break of day. My brethren, let us remember what a dark day it was with our African brethren, six years ago, in the French West Indies. Nothing but the snap of the whip was heard, from morning to evening. Hanging, breaking on the wheel, burning, and all manner of tortures, were inflicted on those unhappy people. But, blessed be God, the scene is changed. They now confess that God hath no respect of persons, and therefore, receive them as their friends, and treat them as brothers. Thus doth Ethiopia stretch forth her hand from slavery, to freedom and equality.

APPENDIX D

John Marrant Sermon of 1789

A Sermon Preached on the 24th Day of June 1789, being the Festival of St. John the Baptist at the Request of the Right Worshipful the Grand Master Prince Hall, and the Rest of the Brethren of the African Lodge of the Honorable Society of Free and Accepted Masons, in Boston, by the Reverend Brother Marrant, Chaplain.

ROMANS xii. 10.
"Be kindly affectioned one to another, with brotherly love, in honour preferring one another."

In this chapter, from whence my text is taken, we find the Apostle Paul labouring with the Romans to press on them the great duties of Brotherly Love.

By an entire submission and conformity to the will of God, whereby are given to us exceeding great and precious promises, that by these we might be made partakers of the divine nature, having escaped the corruption that is in the world through lust—That being all members of the body of Christ with the Church, we ought to apply the gifts we have received to the advantage of our brethren, those of us especially who are called to any office in the church, by discharging it with zeal and integrity and benevolence, which is the most important duty, and comprehends all the rest, and particularly the following—which the apostle here sets down—which are to love one another sincerely, to be ready to all good offices—to sympathize in the good or evil that befalls our brethren, to comfort and assist those that are in affliction, and to live together in a spirit of humility, peace and unity. Benevolence does yet further oblige Christians to love and bless those who hate them and injure them, to endeavour to have peace with all men, to abstain from revenge, and to render them good for evil; these are the most essential duties of the religion we profess; and we deserve the name of Christians no further than we sincerely practice them to the glory of God and the good of our own souls and bodies, and the good of all mankind.

But first, my Brethren, let us learn to pray to God through our Lord Jesus Christ for understanding, that we may know ourselves; for without this we can never be fit for the society of man, we must learn to guide ourselves before we can guide others, and when we have done this we shall understand the apostle, Romans xii. 16. "Be not wise in your own conceits," for when we get wise in ourselves we are then too wise for God, and consequently not fit for the society of man—I mean the Christian part of mankind—Let all my brethren Masons consider what they are called to—May God grant you an humble heart to fear God and love his commandments; then and only then you will in sincerity love your brethren: And you will be enabled, as in the words of my text, to be kindly affectioned one to another, with brotherly love in honour preferring one another. Therefore, with the apostle Paul, I beseech you therefore brethren, by the mercies of God, that ye present your bodies a living sacrifice, holy, acceptable unto God, which is your reasonable service—let love be without dissimulation, abhor that which is evil, cleave to that which is good. These and many other duties are required of us as Christians, every one of which are like so many links of a chain, which when joined together make one complete member of Christ; this we profess to believe as Christians and Masons.— I shall stop here with the introduction, which brings me to the points I shall endeavour to prove.— First, the anciency of Masonry, that being done, will endeavour to prove all other titles we have a just right as Masons to claim—namely, honourable, free and accepted: To do this I must have recourse to the creation of this our world.—After the Grand Architect of the Universe had framed the heavens for beauty and delight for the beings he was then about to make, he then called the earth to appear out of darkness, saying, let there be light, and it was so; he also set the sun, moon and stars in the firmament of heaven, for the delight of his creatures—he then created the fishes of the sea, the fowls of the air, then the beasts of the earth after their various kinds, and God blessed them.

Thus all things were in their order prepared for the most

Appendix D

excellent accomplished piece of the visible creation, Man.—The forming [of] this most excellent creature Man, was the close of the creation, so it was peculiar to him to have a solemn consultation and decree about his making, and God said, let us make Man.—Seneca says, that man is not a work huddled over in haste, and done without fore-thinking and great consideration, for man is the greatest and most stupendous work of God.—Man hath not only a body in common with all inferior animals, but into his body was infused a soul of a far more noble nature and make—a rational principle to act according to the designs of his creation; that is, to contemplated the works of God, to admire his perfections, to worship him, to live as becomes one who received his excellent being from him, to converse with his fellow creatures that are of his own order, to maintain mutual love and society, and to serve God in consort.

Man is a wonderful creature, and not undeservedly said to be a little world, a world within himself, and containing whatever is found in the Creator.—In him is the spiritual and immaterial nature of God, the reasonableness of Angels, the sensitive power of brutes, the vegetative life of plants, and the virtue of all the elements he holds converse with in both worlds.—Thus man is crowned with glory and honour, he is the most remarkable workmanship of God.

And is man such a noble creature and made to converse with his fellow men that are of his own order, to maintain mutual love and society, and to serve God in consort with each other?—then what can these God-provoking wretches think, who despise their fellow men, as tho' they were not of the same species with themselves, and would if in their power deprive them of the blessings and comforts of this life, which God in his bountiful goodness, hath freely given to all his creatures to improve and enjoy?

Surely such monsters never came out of the hand of God in such a forlorn condition.—Which brings me to consider the fall of man; and the Lord God took the man and put him into the garden of Eden, to dress it and keep it, and freely to eat of every tree of the garden; here was his delightful employ and bountiful wages, and but one tree out of all that vast number he was forbidden to eat of. Concerning this garden, there have been different opinions about it by the learned, where it was, but the most of them agree that it was about the center of the earth, and that the four rivers parted or divided the four quarters of the world. The first was Pison, that was it which compassed the land of Havilah; this river Pison is called by some Phasis, or Phasis Tigris, it runs (they say) by that Havilah whither the Amelekites fled, see I Sam. xv. 7. and divides it from the country of Susianna, and at last falls into the Persian Gulf, saith Galtruchius and others; but from the opinions of Christian writers, who hold, that Havilah is India, and Pison the river Ganges. This was first asserted by Josephus, and from him Eustubius, Jerome, and most of the fathers received it, and not without good reason; for Moses here adds, as a mark to know the place by, that there is gold and the gold of that land is good; now it is confessed by all, that India is the most noted for gold, and of the best sort. It is added again, a note whereby to discover that place, that there is bdellium and the onyx stone—and India is famous for precious stones and pearls.—The name of the second river is Gihon, the same is it which compasseth the whole land of Ethiopia (or Cush as it is in the original) there is reason to believe that this Gihon is the river Nile, as the forenamed Josephus and most of the ancient writers of the church hold, and by the help of the river Nile, Paradise did as it were border upon Egypt, which is the principal part of the African Ethiopia, which the ancient writers hold is meant there: The name of the third river is Hiddekel, that is it which goeth toward the east of Assyria, ver. 14. That it was a river belonging to Babylon is clear from Dan. x.4; this is concluded to be the river Tygris, which divides Mesopotamia from Assyria, and goeth along with Euphrates, this being the great middle channel that ran through Edom or Babylon, and may be thought to take its name from its fructifying quality.

These are the four grand land marks which the all-wise and gracious God was pleased to draw as the bounds and habitation of all nations which he was about to settle in this world; if so, what nation or people dare, without highly displeasing and provoking that God to pour down his judgments upon them.—I say to despise or tyrannize over the lives or liberties, or encroach on their lands, or to enslave their bodies? God hath and ever will visit such a nation or people as this.—Envy and pride are the leading lines to

Appendix D

all the miseries that mankind have suffered from the beginning of the world to this present day. What was it but these that turned the devil out of heaven into a hell of misery, but envy and pride?—Was it not the same spirit that moved him to tempt our first parents to sin against so holy and just a God, who had but just (if I may use the expression) turned his back from crowning Adam with honour and glory?—But envy at his prosperity hath taken the crown of glory from his head, and hath made us his posterity miserable.—

What was it but this that made Cain murder his brother, whence is it but from these that our modern Cains call us Africans the sons of Cain? (We admit it if you please) and we will find from him and his sons Masonry began, after the fall of his father. Altho' Adam, when placed in the garden, God would not suffer him to be idle and unemployed in that happy state of innocence, but set him to dress and to keep that choice piece of earth; here he was to employ his mind as well as exercise his body; here he was to contemplate and study God's works; here he was to enjoy God, himself and the whole world, to submit himself wholly to his divine conduct, to conform all his actions to the will of his Maker; but by his sudden fall he lost that good will that he owed to his God, and for some time lost the study of God's works; but no doubt he afterwards taught his sons the art of Masonry; for how else could Cain after so much trouble and perplexity have time to study the art of building a city, as he did on the east of Eden, Gen. iv. 17. and without doubt he teached his sons the art, ver. 20, 21.—

But to return, bad as Cain was, yet God took not from him his faculty of studying architecture, arts and sciences—his sons also were endued with the same spirit, and in some convenient place no doubt they met and communed with each other for instruction. It seems that the allwise God put this into the hearts of Cain's family thus to employ themselves, to divert their minds from musing on their father's murder and the woeful curse God had pronounced on him, as we don't find any more of Cain's complaints after this. Similar to this we have in the 6 Gen. 12 & 13, that God saw that all men had corrupted their way, and that their hearts were only evil continually; and 14, 15, 16 verses, the great Architect of the universe gives Noah a complete plan of the ark and sets him to work, and his sons as assistants, like deputy and two grand wardens. One thing is well known, our enemies themselves being judges, that in whatsoever nation or kingdom in the whole world where Masonry abounds most, there hath been and still are the most peaceable subjects, cheerfully conforming to the laws of that country in which they reside, always willing to submit to their magistrates and rulers, and where Masonry most abounds, arts and sciences, whether mechanical or liberal, all of them have a mighty tendency to the delight and benefit of mankind; therefore we need not question but the allwise God by putting this into our hearts intended, as another end of our creation, that we should not only live happily ourselves, but be likewise mutually assisting to each other.

Again, it is not only good and beneficial in a time of peace, in a nation or kingdom, but in a time of war, for that brotherly love that cements us together by the bonds of friendship, no wars or tumults can separate; for in the heat of war if a brother sees another in distress he will relieve him some way or other, and kindly receive him as a brother, preferring him before all others, according to the Apostle's exhortation in my text, as also a similar instance you have I Kings, x. from 31st to 38th verse, where you find Ben-hadad in great distress, having lost a numerous army in two battles, after his great boasting, and he himself forced to hide himself in a chamber, and sends a message to Ahab king of Israel to request only his life as a captive; but behold the brotherly love of a Mason! No sooner was the message delivered, but he cries out in a rapture—is he alive—he is my brother!

Every Mason knows that they were both of the craft, and also the messengers. Thus far may suffice for the anciency of this grand art; as for the honour of it—it is a society which God himself has been pleased to honour ever since he breathed into Adam the breath of life, and hath from generation to generation inspired men with wisdom, and planned out and given directions how they should build, and with what materials. And first, Noah in building the ark wherein he was saved, while God in his justice was pleased to destroy the unbelieving world of mankind. The first thing Noah did upon his landing was to build an altar to offer sacrifice to that great God which had delivered him out of so great a deluge; God

Appendix D

accepted the sacrifice and blessed him, and as they journeyed from the east towards the west, they found a plain in the land of Shinar and dwelt there, and his sons.

Nimrod the son of Cush, the son of Ham, first founded the Babylonian monarchy, and kept possession of the plains, and founded the first great empire at Babylon, and became grand master of all Masons, he built many splendid cities in Shinar, and under him flourished those learned Mathematicians, whose successors were styled in the book of Daniel, Magi, or wise men, for their superior knowledge. The migration from Shinar commenced fifty three years after they began to build the tower, and one hundred and fifty four years after the flood, and they went off at various times and travelled east, west, north and south, with their mighty skill, and found the use of it in settling their colonies; and from Shinar the arts were carried to distant parts of the earth, notwithstanding the confusion of languages, which gave rise to Masons' faculty and universal practice of conversing without speaking, and of knowing each other by signs and tokens; they settled the dispersion in case any of them should meet in distant parts of the world who had been before in Shinar.

Thus the earth was again planted and replenished with Masons the second son of Ham carried into Egypt; there he built the city of Heliopolis—Thebes with an hundred gates—they built also the statue of Sphinx, whose head was 120 feet round, being reckoned the first or earliest of the seven wonders of arts. Shem the second son of Noah remained at Ur of the Chaldeans in Shinar, with his father and his great grandson Heber, where they lived in private and died in peace: But Shem's offspring travelled into the south and east of Asia, and their offspring propagated the science and the art as far as China and Japan.

While Noah, Shem and Heber diverted themselves at Ur in mathematical studies, teaching Peleg the father of Rehu, of Sereg, Nachor, and Terah, father of Abram, a learned race of mathematicians and geometricians; thus Abram, born two years after the death of Noah, had learned well the science and the art before the God of glory called him to travel from Ur of the Chaldeans, but a famine soon forced him down to Egypt; the descendants of Abram sojourned in Egypt, as shepherds still lived in tents, practiced very little of the art of architecture till about eighty years before their Exodus, when by the overruling hand of providence they were trained up to the building with stone and brick, in order to make them expert Masons before they possessed the promised land; after Abram left Charran 430 years, Moses marched out of Egypt at the head of 600,000 Hebrews, males, for whose sakes God divided the red sea to let them pass through Arabia to Canaan, God was pleased to inspire their grand master Moses, and Joshua his deputy, with wisdom of heart; so the next year they raised the curious tabernacle or tent; God having called Moses up into the mount and gave him an exact pattern of it, and charges him to make it exactly to that pattern, and withal gave him the two tables of stone; these he broke at the foot of the mount; God gave him orders to hew two more himself, after the likeness of the former.

God did not only inspire Moses with wisdom to undertake the oversight of the great work, but he also inspired Bezalel with knowledge to do all manner of cunning workmanship for it.—Having entered upon the Jewish dispensation, I must beg leave still to take a little notice of the Gentile nations, for we have but these two nations now to speak upon, namely, the Gentiles and the Jews, till I come to the Christian area.

The Canaanites, Phoenicians and Sidonians, were very expert in the sacred architecture of stone, who being a people of a happy genius and frame of mind, made many great discoveries and improvements of the sciences, as well as in point of learning. The glass of Sidon, the purple of Tyre, and the exceeding fine linen they wove, were the product of their own country and their own invention; and for their extraordinary skill in working of metals, in hewing of timber and stone; in a word, for their perfect knowledge of what was solid in architecture, it need but be remembered that they had in erecting and decorating of the temple at Jerusalem, than which nothing can more redound to their honour, or give a clearer idea of what this one building must have been.—

Their fame was such for their just taste, design, and ingenious inventions, that whatever was elegant, great or pleasing, was distinguished by way of excellence with the epithet of Sidonian.—

Appendix D

The famous temple of Jupiter Hammon, in Libyan Africa, was erected, that stood till demolished by the first Christians in those parts; but I must pass over many other cities and temples built by the Gentiles.

God having inspired Solomon with wisdom and understanding, he as grand master and undertaker, under God the great architect, sends to Hiram King of Tyre, and after acquainting him of his purpose of building a house unto the name of the Lord his God, he sends to him for some of his people to go with some of his, to Mount Lebanon, to cut down and hew cedar trees, as his servants understood it better than his own, and moreover he requested him to send him a man that was cunning, to work in gold and in silver, and in brass, iron, purple, crimson and in blue, and that had skill to engrave with the cunning men, and he sent him Hiram, his name-sake this Hiram, God was pleased to inspire with wisdom and understanding to undertake, and strength to go through the most curious piece of workmanship that was ever done on earth.—

Thus Solomon as grand master, and Hiram as his deputy, carried on and finished that great work of the temple of the living God, the inside work of which, in many instances as well as the tabernacle, resembles men's bodies; but this is better explained in a well filled lodge; but this much I may venture to say, that our blessed Saviour compared his sacred body to a temple, when he said, John ii. 19. Destroy this temple and I will raise it up again in three days; and the Apostle, I Peter, i. 14 says, that shortly he should put off this tabernacle. I could show also that one grand end and design of Masonry is to build up the temple that Adam destroyed in Paradise—but I forbear. Thus hath God honoured the Craft, or Masons, by inspiring men with wisdom to carry on his stupendous works.

It is worthy our notice to consider the number of Masons employed in the work of the Temple: Exclusive of the two Grand Masters, there were 300 princes, or rulers, 3,300 overseers of the work, 80,000 stone squarers, setters, layers or builders, being able and ingenious Crafts, and 30,000 appointed to work in Lebanon, 10,000 of which every month, under Adoniram, who was the Grand Warden; all the free Masons employed in the work of the

Symbolically Speaking: African Lodge #1

Temple was 119,600, besides 70,000 men who carried burdens, who were not numbered among Masons; these were partitioned into certain Lodges, although they were of different nations and different colours, yet were they in perfect harmony among themselves, and strongly cemented in brotherly love and friendship, till the glorious Temple of Jehovah was finished, and the cap-stone was celebrated with great joy—Having finished all that Solomon had to do, they departed unto their several homes, and carried with them the high taste of architecture to the different parts of the world, and built many other temples and cities in the Gentile nations, under the direction of many wise and learned and royal Grand Masters, as Nebuchadnezzar over Babylon—Cyrus over the Medes and Persians—Alexander over the Macedonians—Julius Cæsar over Rome, and a great number more I might mention of crowned heads of the Gentile nations who were of the Craft, but this may suffice.—

    I must just mention Herod the Great, before I come to the state of Masonry from the birth of our Saviour Jesus Christ.— This Herod was the greatest builder of his day, the patron and Grand Master of many Lodges; he being in the full enjoyment of peace and plenty, formed a design of new building the Temple of Jerusalem. The Temple built by the Jews after the captivity was greatly decayed, being 500 years standing, he proposed to the people that he would not take it down till he had all the materials ready for the new, and accordingly he did so, then he took down the old one and built a new one.—Josephus describes this Temple as a most admirable and magnificent fabric of marble, and the finest building upon earth—Tiberius having attained the imperial throne, became an encourager of the fraternity.

    Which brings me to consider their freedom, and that will appear not only from their being free when accepted, but they have a free intercourse with all Lodges over the whole terrestrial globe; wherever arts flourish, a man hath a free right (having a recommendation) to visit his brethren, and they are bound to accept him; these are the laudable bonds that unite Free Masons together in one indissoluble fraternity—thus in every nation he finds a friend, and in every climate he may find a house—this it is to be kindly affectioned one to another, with brotherly love, in honour preferring one

Appendix D

another.

Which brings me to answer some objections which are raised against the Masons, and the first is the irregular lives of the professors of it.—It must be admitted there are some persons who, careless of their own reputation, will consequently disregard the most instructive lessons.—Some, I am sorry to say, are sometimes to be found among us; many by yielding to vice and intemperance, frequently not only disgrace themselves, but reflect dishonour on Masonry in general; but let it be known that these apostates are unworthy of their trust, and that whatever name or designation they assume, they are in reality no Masons: But if the wicked lives of men were admitted as an argument against the religion which they profess, Christianity itself, with all its divine beauties, would be exposed to censure; but they say there can be no good in Masonry because we keep it a secret, and at the same time these very men themselves will not admit an apprentice into their craft whatever, without enjoining secrecy on him, before they receive him as an apprentice; and yet blame us for not revealing our's—Solomon says, Prov. xi. 12, 13. He that is void of wisdom despiseth his neighbour, but a man of understanding holdeth his peace; a tale-bearer revealeth secrets, but he that is of a faithful spirit concealeth the matter.

Thus I think I have answered these objections. I shall conclude the whole by addressing the Brethren of the African Lodge. Dear and beloved brethren, I don't know how I can address you better than in the words of Nehemiah (who had just received liberty from the king Artaxerxes, letters and a commission, or charter, to return to Jerusalem) that thro' the good hand of our God upon us we are here this day to celebrate the festival of St. John—as members of that honorable society of free and accepted Masons—as by charter we have a right to do—remember your obligations you are under to the great God, and to the whole family of mankind in the world—do all that in you lies to relieve the needy, support the weak, mourn with your fellow men in distress, do good to all men as far as God shall give you ability, for they are all your brethren, and stand in need of your help more or less—for he that loves every body need fear nobody: But you must remember you an under a double obligation to the brethren of the craft of all nations on the face of the earth, for there is no party spirit in Masonry; let them make parties who will, and despise those they would make, if they could, a species below them, and as not made of the same clay with themselves; but if you study the holy book of God, you will there find that you stand on the level not only with them, but with the greatest kings on the earth, as Men and as Masons, and these truly great men are not ashamed of the meanest of their brethren.

    Ancient history will produce some of the Africans who were truly good, wise, and learned men, and as eloquent as any other nation whatever, though at present many of them in slavery, which is not a just cause of our being despised; for if we search history, we shall not find a nation on earth but has at some period or other of their existence been in slavery, from the Jews down to the English Nation, under many Emperors, Kings and Princes; for we find in the life of Gregory, about the year 580, a man famous for his charity, that on a time when many merchants were met to sell their commodities at Rome, it happened that he passing by saw many young boys with white bodies, fair faces, beautiful countenances and lovely hair, set forth for sale; he went to the merchant their owner and asked him from what country he brought them; he answered from Britain, where the inhabitants were generally so beautiful. Gregory (sighing) said, alas! for grief, that such fair faces should be under the power of the prince of darkness, and that such bodies should have their souls void of the grace of God.

    I shall endeavour to draw a few inferences on this discourse by way of application.— My dear Brethren, let us pray to God for a benevolent heart, that we may be enabled to pass through the various stages of this life with reputation, and that great and infinite Jehovah, who overrules the grand fabric of nature, will enable us to look backward with pleasure, and forward with confidence—and in the hour of death, and in the day of judgment, the well grounded hope of meeting with that mercy from our Maker which we have ever been ready to shew to others, will refresh us with the most solid comfort, and fill us with the most unspeakable joy. Such as Tertullian, Cyprian, Origen, Augustine, [illegible].

    And should not this learn us that new and glorious com-

Appendix D

mandment of our Lord Jesus Christ to his disciples, when he urges it to them in these words—Love the Lord thy God with all thy heart, and thy neighbour as thyself—Our Lord repeats and recommends this as the most indispensable duty and necessary qualification of his disciples, saying, hereby shall all men know that ye are my disciples, if ye have love one to another.—And we are expressly told by the Apostle, that charity, or universal love and friendship, is the end of the commandment.

Shall this noble and unparalleled example fail of its due influence upon us—shall it not animate our hearts with a like disposition of benevolence and mercy, shall it not raise our emulation and provoke our ambition—to go and do likewise.

Let us then beware of such a selfishness as pursues pleasure at the expense of our neighbour's happiness, and renders us indifferent to his peace and welfare; and such a self-love is the parent of disorder and the source of all those evils that divide the world and destroy the peace of mankind; whereas Christian charity—universal love and friendship— benevolent affections and social feelings, unite and knit men together, render them happy in themselves and useful to one another, and recommend them to the esteem of a gracious God, through our Lord Jesus Christ.

The few inferences that have been made on this head must be to you, my worthy brethren, of great comfort, that every one may see the propriety of a discourse on brotherly love before a society of free Masons—who knows their engagements as men and as Christians, have superadded the bonds of this ancient and honourable society—a society founded upon such friendly and comprehensive principles, that men of all nations and languages, or sects of religion, are and may be admitted and received as members, being recommended as persons of a virtuous character.

Religion and virtue, and the continuance and standing of this excellent society in the world—its proof of the wisdom of its plan—and the force of its principles and conduct has, on many occasions, been not, a little remarkable—as well among persons of this, as among those of different countries, who go down to the sea and occupy their business in the great waters, they know how readily people of this institution can open a passage to the heart of a brother; and in the midst of war, like a universal language, is understood by men of all countries—and no wonder.—If the foundation has been thus laid in wisdom by the great God, then let us go on with united hearts and hands to build, and improve upon this noble foundation—let love and sincere friendship in necessity instruct our ignorance, conceal our infirmities, reprove our errors, reclaim us from our faults—let us rejoice with them that rejoice, and weep with those that weep—share with each other in our joys, and sympathize in our troubles.

And let the character of our enemies be to resent affronts—but our's to generously remit and forgive the greatest; their's to blacken the reputation and blast the credit of their brethren—but our's to be tender of their good name, and to cast a veil over all their failings; their's to blow the coals of contention and sow the seeds of strife among men—but our's to compose their differences and heal up their breaches.

In a word, let us join with the words of the Apostle John in the 19th chapter of Revelations, and after these things I heard a great voice of much people in heaven, saying, Alleluia, salvation and glory, and honour, and power, unto the Lord our God; for true and righteous are his judgments—and the four and twenty elders, and the four beasts, fell down and worshipped God that sat on the throne, saying, Amen; Alleluia; and a voice came out of the throne, saying, praise our God, all ye his servants, and ye that fear him, both small and great.

To conclude the whole, let it be remembered, that all that is outward, whether opinions, rites or ceremonies, cannot be of importance in regard to eternal salvation, any further than they have a tendency to produce inward righteousness and goodness—pure, holy, spiritual and benevolent affections can only fit us for the kingdom of heaven; and therefore the cultivation of such must needs be the essence of Christ's religion.—God of his infinite mercy grant that we may make this true use of it. Unhappily, too many Christians, so called, take their religion not from the declarations of Christ and his apostles, but from the writings of those they esteem learned.—But, I am to say, it is from the New Testament only, not from any books whatsoever, however piously wrote, that we ought

Appendix D

to seek what is the essence of Christ's religion; and it is from this fountain I have endeavoured to give my hearers the idea of Christianity in its spiritual dress, free from any human mixtures—if we have done this wisely we may expect to enjoy our God in the world that is above—in which happy place, my dear brethren, we shall all, I hope, meet at that great day, when our great Grand Master shall sit at the head of the great and glorious Lodge in heaven—where we shall all meet to part no more for ever and ever—Amen.

Symbolically Speaking: African Lodge #1

APPENDIX E

The Origin and Objects of Ancient Freemasonry Its Introduction into the United States, and Legitimacy Among Colored Men. A Treatise Delivered Before St. Cyprian Lodge, No. 13, June 24th, A. D. 1853—A. L. 5853.

By M. R. Delany, K. M., D. D. G. H. P.

PITTSBURGH, JUNE 30, A. D. 1853, A. L. 5853.

Gentlemen, Brethren, Companions and Sir Knights:
    I have received a note jointly from a Committee appointed by St. Cyprian Lodge, No. 13, and a Communication held by the District Deputy Grand Master, desiring that the Treatise delivered by me before the public, on the 24th day of June (the Annual Festival of our Patron, St. John the Baptist) be published in pamphlet form. With this request, I readily and cheerfully comply.
    Permit me to say, in this connection, that whatever undue and unwarrantable obstructions may be thrown in our way by American Masons; and they are many—though there are some honorable exceptions—it is within the power of the Grand Lodge of England to decide in the matter, and at once establish our validity. For this purpose, I now suggest, through you, that all of our Subordinate Lodges throughout the United States at once petition their respective Grand Lodges, and the Grand Lodges respectively agree, and, together with the National Grand Lodge, meet by delegated representatives of Past Masters—not to exceed three from each Grand Lodge, and the same number from each District over which there may be a District Deputy Grand Master; the National Grand Lodge sending one for each State Grand Lodge—in a National Grand Masonic Convention, for the single purpose of petitioning the Grand Lodge of England for a settlement of the question of the legality of Colored Masons in the United States, claiming to have originated from the warrant granted to Prince Hall, of Boston. This should at once be done, to settle the controversy, as it would to us

be a great point gained, because it would be the acknowledgement and establishment of a right among us as a people, which is now disputed, but which legitimately belongs to us.

We have for years been fraternally outraged, simply for the want of a proper and judicious course being pursued on the part of our Masonic authorities, and the present loudly calls upon us for action in this matter. We are either Masons or not Masons, legitimate or illegitimate; if the affirmative, then we must be so acknowledged and accepted—if the negative, we should be rejected. We never will relinquish a claim to an everlasting inheritance, but by the force of stern necessity; and there is not that Masonic power in existence, with the exception of the Grand Lodge of England, to which we will yield in a decision on this point. Our rights are equal to those of other American Masons, if not better than some; and it comes not with the best grace for them to deny us.

The suggested Convention should be held in some central place, during the ensuing three years of the National Grand Lodge administration, and in not less than one year from this date, so that full time may be given, for reflection and action, on the part of the various Subordinate and Grand Lodges.

Let not the hopes of our brethren languish, though calumny and slander may have done their work.

> O, Slander! Foulest imp of hell!
> Thy tongue is like the scorpion's sting!
> Nor peace nor hope can near thee dwell;
> Thy breath can blast the fairest thing!
> O, could I grasp the thunderbolt!
> I'd crush thee, limping fiend of hell!
> From earth I'd chase thy serpent soul,
> And chain thee where the furies dwell!
> —Bishop Payne.

Fraternally Yours,
    In the bonds of Union and Fellowship,

                      M. R. DELANY
To Elias Edmonds, Wm. B. Austin, &c. Committees.

Appendix E
A TREATISE.

"Great is Truth, and must prevail."

To introduce the subject of Ancient Freemasonry at this period, with a design to adduce anything new, at least to the enlightened, would be a work of supererogation, having the semblance of assumption, more than an effort to impart information.

Summoned by your invitation to deliver a Treatise, I have chosen for my subject, THE ORIGIN, OBJECTS, AND INTRODUCTION OF FREEMASONRY INTO THE UNITED STATES— and also its introduction among colored men in this country. I shall, therefore, proceed at once to the discharge of my duty, doing the best I can according to the opportunity and means at hand for the accomplishment of this end.

Masonry was originally intended for the better government of man—for the purpose of restraining him from a breach of the established ordinances. The first law given to man was by God himself—that given in the Garden of Eden, forbidding the eating of the reserved fruit. (Gen. 2:17.) The first institution was that of marriage. (Gen. 2:21, 24.) The first breach of the law was committed by eating the forbidden fruit. (Gen. 3:6.) The first punishment inflicted on man was by God himself, for a breach of the law. (Gen. 3:16-19.) The first city was built by Cain, and named after his first-born, son, Enoch.

MAN FROM ADAM TO NOAH

During the period from Adam to Noah, the life of man was of long duration, each individual living through several hundred years of time. His habits, customs and manner of living were simple; residing in thinly peopled localities, for there were then no densely populated cities, and relying mainly on husbandry as a means of support.

MAN FROM NOAH TO SOLOMON

From Noah to Solomon, the character of man underwent an entire and important change. Noah's three sons, scattering abroad over the earth, built great cities, and established many and various policies, habits, manners and customs, for the government of their people. At this period, it will be remembered, a general separation in interests and sympathies took place among these brethren, (the children of one household parentage,) which continued to manifest itself in hostile array until the building of the temple by Solomon, king of Israel. I do not pretend to assert that hostilities then entirely ceased, but that mankind were better governed after that period, will not be denied.

In the earliest period of the Egyptian and Ethiopian dynasties, the institution of Masonry was first established. Discovering a defect in the government of man, first suggested an inquiry into his true state and condition. Being a people of a high order of intellect, and subject to erudite and profound thought, the Egyptians and Ethiopians were the first who came to the conclusion that man was created in the similitude of God. This, it will be remembered was anterior to the Bible record, because Moses was the recorder of the Bible, subsequent to his exodus from Egypt, all his wisdom and ability having been acquired there; as a proof of which, the greatest recommendation to his fitness for so high and holy an office, and the best encomium which that book can possibly bestow upon him in testimony of his qualifications as its scriptor, the Bible itself tells us that "Moses was learned in all the wisdom of the Egyptians."

The Ethiopians early adduced the doctrine and believed in a trinity of the Godhead. Though heathens, their mythology was of a high and pure order, agreeing in regard to the attributes of the Deity with the doctrine of Christians in after ages, as is beautifully illustrated in the person of Jupiter Ammon, the great god of Egypt and Ethiopia, who was assigned a power over heaven, earth and hell, as well as over all the other gods, thereby acknowledging his omnipotence—all other gods possessing but one divine attribute or function, which could only be exercised in his particular department of divinity.*

[*Jupiter was represented as seated on a throne of gold and ivory—figurative of heaven, as the "pearly gates and golden streets."—holding in his left hand a scepter, figurative of his earthly power; his right hand grasping a thunder-bolt, the ancient idea of the power and *terrors of hell.*]

MAN THE LIKENESS OF GOD

What is God, that man should be his image, and what knowledge should man obtain in order to be like God? This wisdom was possessed in the remotest period by the wise men of Egypt and Ethiopia, and handed down only through the priesthood to the recipients of their favors, the mass of mankind being ignorant of their own nature, and consequently prone to rebel against their greatest and best interests.

God is a being possessing various attributes: and all Masons, whether Unitarian, Trinitarian, Greek, Jew or Mohammedan, agree upon this point, at least without controversy. Where there are various functions, there must be an organ for the exercise of each function,—and this conclusion most naturally led man to inquire into his own nature, to discover the similitude between himself and his Creator.

The three great attributes of Deity—all-wise, omnipotence, and omnipresence—were recognized by the ancients, and represented in the character given to their ruling god—as above mentioned—as presiding over the universe of eternal space—of celum, terra, and tartarus—answering to the Christian doctrine of three persons in one—Father, Son and Holy Ghost.*

[*One of the old doctrines of the priesthood was, that God the Father presided over heaven, the Holy Ghost on earth, and Christ the Son in hell; hence, his descent into the grave, is called a descent into hell, where some believe, or affect to believe, he ever remains: and this is the foundation of the belief of that Christian sect whose doctrines teach a purification and redemption in the grave,—purgatory, a place of purging or purification—or hell.]

Man, then, to assimilate God, must, in his nature, be a trinity of systems—morally, intellectually and physically. This great truth appears to have been known to King David, who, with emotion, exclaims, "We are wonderfully and fearfully made."

To convince man of the importance of his own being, and

impress him with a proper sense of his duty to his Creator, were what was desired, and to effect this, would also impress him with a sense of his duty and obligations to society and the laws intended for his government. For this purpose, was the beautiful fabric of Masonry established, and illustrated in the structure of man's person.

Man, scientifically developed, is a moral, intellectual and physical being—composed of an osseous, muscular and vital structure; of solid, flexible and liquid parts. With an intellect—a mind, the constituent principles of which he is incapable of analyzing or comprehending; which rises superior to its earthy tenement; with the velocity of lightning, soars to the summit of altitude, descends to the depth of profundity, and flies to the wide-spread expanse of eternal space. What can be more God-like than this, to understand which is to give man a proper sense of his own importance, and consequently his duty to his fellows, by which alone, he fulfills the high mission for which he was sent on his temporary pilgrimage.

While the Africans, who were the authors of this mysterious and beautiful Order, did much to bring it to perfection by the establishment of the great principles of man's likeness to Jehovah in a triune existence; yet, until the time of King Solomon, there was a great deficiency in his government, in consequence of the policy being monopolized by the priesthood and certain privileged classes or families.

FROM SOLOMON DOWN.

For the purpose of remedying what was now conceived to be a great evil in the policy of the world, and for their better government to place wisdom within the acquirement of all men, King Solomon summoned together the united wisdom of the world,—men of all nations and races—to consider the great project of reducing the mystic ties to a more practical and systematic principle, and stereotyping it with physical science, by rearing the stupendous and magnificent temple at Jerusalem.* For the accomplishment of this masterpiece of all human projects, there were laborers or attendants, mechanics or workmen, and overseers or master-builders. Added to these, there was a designer or originator of all the

Appendix E

schemes, an architect or draughtsman, and a furnisher of all the materials for the building—all and every thing of which was classified and arranged after the order of trinity, the building itself, when finished, being composed of an outer, an inner, and a central court.

Previous to the building of the temple, Masonry was only allegorical, consisting in a scientific system of theories, taught through the medium of Egyptian, Ethiopian, Assyrian, and other oriental hieroglyphics, understood only by the priesthood and a chosen few. All the sovereigns and members of the royal families were Masons, because each member of the royal household had of necessity to be educated in the rituals of the priesthood. And it was not until after Masonry was introduced into Asia by the Jews—it being strictly forbidden by the Jewish laws for women to be priests—that females were prohibited from being Masons. Among other nations of the ancients, priestesses were common, as is known to the erudite in history; and Candace, queen of Sheba, was a high-priestess in her realm—hence her ability to meet King Solomon in the temple, having passed the guards, by words of wisdom, from the outer to the inner court, where she met the king in all his wisdom, power and glory.

After the completion of this great work, the implements of labor having been laid aside, there were scattered to the utmost parts of the earth, seventy thousand laborers, eighty thousand workmen, and three thousand and three hundred master-builders, making one hundred and fifty-three thousand and three hundred artizans*, each of whom having been instructed in all the mysteries of the temple, was fully competent to teach all the arts and sciences acquired at Jerusalem in as many different cities, provinces, states or tribes. At this period, the mysteries assumed the name of Masonry, induced from the building of the temple; and at this time, also, commenced the universality of the Order, arising from the going forth of the builders into all parts of the world. This, then, was the establishment of Masonry, which has been handed down through all succeeding ages.

[*Here the Trinity is again typified: three times fifty thousand, three times one thousand, and three times one hundred.]

Symbolically Speaking: African Lodge #1

For a period of years after the destruction of the temple and the sacred mystic records, there was some slight derangement in the Craft; men were becoming ungovernable both in church and state, owing to the want of proper instruction, and their consequent ignorance of the relation they bore to their Creator and society. Or the purpose of again bringing back the "prodigal son" to the household of his father, the "stray sheep" to the rich pastures of the fold of Israel, and repairing the somewhat defaced honored monument of time, Prince Edwin of England, in 930 of the Christian era, being nine hundred and twenty-two years ago, summoned together at York, all the wise men of the order, where the rites were again scientifically systematized, and preserved for coming time. At this point, the Order, in honor to Prince Edwin, assigned to itself the title of York Masonry.

THE STAGES OF MAN'S HISTORY.

We have here the history of man's existence from Adam to Solomon, showing three distinct periods, fraught with more mystery than all things else, save the ushering in of the Christian era by the birth of the adorable Son of God: his origin in Adam's creation, his preservation in Noah's ark, and his prospects of redemption from the curse of God's broken laws by the promises held out in that mysteriously incomprehensible work of building the temple by Solomon. Adam, Noah and Solomon, then, are the three types of the condition of man—his sojourn here on earth, and his prospectus of a future bliss.

Founded upon the similitude and consequent responsibility to his Creator, the ancients taught the doctrine of a rectitude of conduct and purpose of heart, as the only surety for the successful government of man, and the regulations of society around him. Whether Gentiles, Greeks or Jews, all taught the same as necessary to is government on earth—his responsibility to a Supreme Being, the author and creator of himself. But the mythology of those days, not unlike the scientific theology of the days in which we live, consisted of a sea of such metaphysical depth, that the mass of mankind was unable to fathom it. Instead, then, of accomplishing the object for which this wise policy was established, the design was

Appendix E

thwarted by the manner in which it was propagated. Man adhered but little, and cared less, for that in which he could never be fully instructed, nor be made to understand, in consequence of his deficiency in a thorough literary education—this being the exclusive privilege of those in affluent circumstances. All these imperfections have been remedied, in the practical workings of the comprehensive system of Free and Accepted Masonry, as handed down to us from the archives at Jerusalem. All men, of every country, clime, color and condition, (when morally worthy,) are acceptable to the portals of Masonic jurisprudence.

In many parts of the world, the people of various nations were subject to lose their liberty in several ways. A forfeiture by crime, as in our country; by voluntary servitude for a stipulated sum or reward, as among the Hindoos; and by capture in battle and being sold into slavery, as in Algiers. Against these Masonry found it necessary to provide, and accordingly, the first two classes were positively proscribed as utterly unworthy of its benefits, as they were equally unworthy of the respectful consideration of the good among mankind. In this, however, was never contemplated the third class of bondees; for none but he who voluntarily compromised his liberty was recognized as a slave by Masons. As there must be a criminal intention in the commission of a crime, so must the act of the criminal be voluntary; hence the criminal and the voluntary bondsman have both forfeited their Masonic rights by willing degradation. In the case of the captive, an entirely different person is presented before us, who has greater claims upon our sympathies than the untrammeled freeman. Instead of the degraded vassal and voluntary slave, whose prostrate position only facilitates the aspect of his horrible deformity, you have the bold, the brave, the high-minded, the independent-spirited, and manly form of a kindred brother in humanity, whose heart is burning, whose breast is heaving, and whose soul is wrung with panting aspirations for liberty—a commander, a chieftain, a knight, or a prince, it may be—still he is a captive, and by the laws of captivity a slave. Does Masonry, then, contemplate the withholding of its privileges from such applicants as these? Certainly not; since Moses, (to whom our great Grand Master Solomon, the founder of the temple, is indebted for his Masonic wisdom,) was born and lived in captivity eighty years, and by the laws of his captors a slave. It matters not whether captured in actual conflict, sleeping by the wayside, or in a cradle of bulrushes, after birth; so that there be a longing aspiration for liberty, and a manly determination to be free. Policy alone will not permit of the order to confer Masonic privileges on one while yet in captivity; but the fact of his former condition as such, or that of his parents, can have no bearing whatever on him. The mind and desires of the recipient must be free; and at the time of his endowment with these privileges, his person and mind must be unencumbered with all earthly trammels or fetters. This is what is meant by Free and Accepted Masonry, to distinguish it from the order when formerly conferred upon the few, like the order of nobility, taking precedence by rank and birth, whether the inheritor was worthy or not of so high and precious privileges.

In the three great periods as presented to view, you have the three great stages of man's existence—Adam, with child-like innocence in the Garden of Eden, turned out for disobedience, as a youth upon the world without the protecting hand of his Omnipotent Parent—Noah, as in adventurous manhood, in constructing and launching his great vessel (the Ark) upon the "face of the great deep;" and Solomon, as in old age, in devising, planning and counseling, and heaping up treasures in building the Temple of Jerusalem; all of which is impressively typified in the cardinal Degrees of Masonry. The Entered Apprentice as a child, and as in youth the Fellow Craft; the Master Mason, as in mature and thinking manhood; and as an old and reflective man of years and wisdom, the Royal Arch completes the history of his journey of life.

ITS INTRODUCTION INTO THE UNITED STATES

Masonry was introduced into the United States by grant of warrant to Henry Price, Esq. of Boston, on the 30th of July, 1733, as Right Worshipful Grand Master of North America, "with full power and authority to appoint his Deputy," by the Right Honorable and Most Worshipful Anthony Lord Viscount Montague, "Grand Master of Masons in England." (Cole's Lib. P. 332) I do not conceive it necessary to prosecute the history of Masonry farther in this

Appendix E

country; but let it suffice to say that hostilities which commenced between Great Britain and America in 1775, absolved all Masonic ties between the two countries, and left American Masons free to act according to the suggestions of the peculiar circumstances in which they were then placed. With the independence of the country, commenced the independence of Masonic jurisdiction in the United States.*

It is said, that at that early period of its existence in this country, entertaining a kind of superstitious idea of its sacredness, the Masonic warrant was kept closely in some secret place, prohibited from the view of all but Masons; consequently when General Warren—who was the Grand Master of Massachusetts—fell in the Revolutionary struggle, the warrant was lost, and with it, Masonry in Massachusetts. All Masons are familiar with the fact, that Grand Master Warren was raised from his grave and a search made, doubtless, supposing that the warrant might have been found concealed about his person.

The Grand Lodge of Massachusetts was formed in 1769; Maine, New Hampshire, 1789; Rhode Island, 1791; Vermont, 1794; New York, 1787; (another being established in 1826, which has recently been denounced by England and all other legal Masonic jurisdictions throughout the world;) New Jersey, 1786; Pennsylvania, 1734, under England, to which she remained attached until September, 1786, when the connection was absolved; Delaware, 1806; Virginia, 1778; N. Carolina, 1787; S. Carolina, 1787; Georgia, 1786; Ohio, 1808; Kentucky, 1800; Louisiana, Mississippi and Tennessee, the data not being given (Cole's Lib. pp. 363 – 375). This gives a fair history of the introduction of Masonry into the United States of America.

[* *This Grand Lodge dissolved in 1847, after an existence of fifteen years, becoming convinced that they had no just nor legal foundation for an independent existence; and none contributed more to the accomplishment of so desirable an end, than the then acting Grand Master of the Hiram Grand Lodge,—Mr. Samuel Van Brakle, an upright, intelligent, and excellent man.*]

AMONG COLORED MEN IN THE UNITED STATES

In the year 1784, a number of colored men in Boston, Massachusetts, applied to the proper source for a grant of Masonic privileges, which being denied them, by force of necessity they went to England, which, at that time not recognizing the Masonic fraternity of America, the then acting Grand Master, (recorded on the warrant as the Right Honorable, Henry Frederick, Duke of Cumberland) granted a warrant to the colored men to make Masons and establish Lodges, subject, of course, to the Grand Lodge of England. In course of time, their ties became absolved; not before it was preceded by the establishment of an independent Grand Lodge in Philadelphia, Pa., by colored men, and subsequently, a general Grand Lodge, known as the First Independent African Grand Lodge of North America.

In the year 1832, another Grand Lodge was established by a party of dissatisfied colored Masons in the city of Philadelphia, known as the "Hiram Grand Lodge of the State of Pennsylvania."* There was, also, for many years, a small faction who rather opposed the F. I. A. G. L. still adhering to what they conceived to be the most legitimate source—the old African Lodge of Boston; among whom was the colored Lodge of Boston, and a very respectable body in New York city, known as the "Boyer Lodge." In December, 1847, by a grand communication of representative body of all the colored Lodges in the United States, held in the city of New York, the differences and wounds which long existed were all settled and healed, a complete union formed, and a National Grand Lodge established, by the choice and election, in due Masonic form, of Past Master, John T. Hilton, of Boston, Mass. Most Worshipful Grand Master of the National Grand Lodge, and William E. Ambush, M. W. N. G. Secretary. This, perhaps, was the most important period in the history of colored Masons in the United States; and had I the power to do so, I would raise my voice in tones of thunder, but with the pathetic affections of a brother, and thrill the cord of every true Masonic heart throughout the country and the world; especially of colored men; in exhortations to stability and to Union. Without it, satisfied am I, that all our efforts, whether as men or Masons, must fail—utterly fail. "A house divided against itself, cannot stand"—

Appendix E

the weak divided among themselves in the midst of the mighty, are thrice vanquished—conquered without a blow from the strong; the sturdy hand of ruthless may shatter in pieces our column guidance, and leave the Virgin of Sympathy to weep through all coming time.

I have thus, as cursorily as possible, given you a faint history of the origin and objects of ancient Free Masonry; its introduction into this country among white and colored men; and he who rejects Masonry as an absurd and irreligious institution, must object to the Scriptures of eternal truth, and spurn the Bible as a book of mummeries.

But there have been serious objections urged against the legitimacy of Ancient Freemasonry among colored men of African descent or affinity in the United States, emanating at various times from different directions, of high Masonic authority in the Republic, and, consequently, received and adopted with a readiness as surprising as it was unkind and unjust by almost all of the Subordinate, and many of the Grand Lodges throughout the country, especially in the non-slaveholding States.*

Among the earliest, and, peradventure, the first of these intended fratricidal assaults, was that of the Grand Lodge of Pennsylvania in the year 18__; a distinguished and talented ex-editor and present member of Congress, and Col. P. an ex-Post Master,

[* A fact worthy of remark, that there is no comparison between the feelings manifested toward colored, by Northern and Southern Masons. Northern Masons, notwithstanding Masonry knows no man by descent, origin, or color, seldom visit colored Masonic Lodges; and when they do, it is frequently done by stealth! While, to the contrary, Southern Masons recognize and fellowship colored men, as such, whenever they meet them as Masons. The writer has more than once sat in Lodge in the city of C_____, with some of the first gentlemen of Kentucky, where there have been present Col. A. a distinguished lawyer, Esquire L. one of the first Aldermen of the place, and Judge M. President of the Judges' Bench. This is a matter of no unfrequent occurrence, and many of our members have done the same.]

Symbolically Speaking: African Lodge #1

if I mistake not, being at the time among the Grand officers, if not the Committee who visited and reported concerning the African Grand Lodge in Eleventh Street, Philadelphia. And I should not at this late day refer to the doings of those distinguished personages in this connection, but for the purpose of —as it never as yet has publicly been done—vindicating the above named First Independent African Grand Lodge of North America, against the aspersions of those multifarious outward forces which have so long been leveled against her Masonic ramparts. Lambparts, perhaps, would be a term far more appropriate; because our Masonic fathers have submitted really with the most lamb-like passiveness to the terrible and disparaging ordeal.

In this wise, the circumstance referred to happened. The question had long been mooted among the white members of the Fraternity, as to the legitimacy and reality of colored Masons; and, consequently, a Committee from the Grand Lodge of Pennsylvania (white) was appointed to visit the colored Grand Lodge then situated in Eleventh Street, (Phila.) to apply the Masonic test, and prove or disprove their capacity as recipients of the ancient and honorable rituals of the mystic order.

A Grand Communication being congregated for the purpose, at the appointed time, the Committee went. A Committee of Examination being sent out, who—instead of as they should have done, had there been in waiting St. John the Baptist, St. John the Evangelist, or St. Paul in his daring attitude as the chief Christian on the Isle of Malt; examined them—on seeing the gentlemen, all men of the first standing in the city of Philadelphia, who had often been seen in Masonic processions, and so far, known—as they thought—to be Masons—an unwise conclusion to be sure; reported them to the Chair; when without question—and entirely through deference—the Chair replied, "Admit them," &c.—They entered; inspected, over-sighted, and examined the work of the colored Masons, applying the scrutiny of a suspicious eye, and the test of plumb, level and square; all of which they pronounced to be good work, square, and just such work as was required to be done; but, for this act of courtesy, and undue deference on their part, they were denounced by the Grand Lodge of Pennsylvania, as being

Appendix E

unworthy of the high privileges they possessed.

Had these gentlemen been half so generous as they were determined on being just, they could and would have readily excused the blunder made by the colored masons, when considering the relative position in community of the two parties who then met as Committees; the one subservient to the other in all the relations of life. In all the social relations in which they had formerly met, the one was domestic and the other superior—the one ignorant and the other intelligent; in a word, the one master and the other servant.

But I come not to plead in extenuation for the blunders—the palpable and reprehensible blunders of our colored Masonic brethren and fathers; may I not say that it served them right, and has done them good, since their too great deference for persons in certain relations of life in this country, has done us much injury in other respects than this. But that time is not now, neither are we those brethren; and they who now stand at the head of our Masonic jurisdiction, are competent and adequate to the task for which they have been selected; so that the same excuse no longer exists for the Grand Lodge of Pennsylvania. Neither would I vindictively censure our fathers, as they did very well for their day and generation; and all that they did, was done for the best: they meant well, and that is all, at least, that I require at their hands. And now, in presence of this vast assemblage, before all the world, in the name of the Holy St. John—calling God to witness, I this day acquit them of all blame in the matter of that which they did, in admitting the Grand Lodge Visiting Committee, promising it will never be done again!

The second, and probably most formidable objection raised to colored Masons was, that they emanated from Grand Lodges, existing contrary to the general regulations of Masonry, in States where there were previously existing Grand Lodges.

This objection will easily be refuted, when it is considered that under the government of England, whence the general regulations of Masonry take their modern rise, for the sake of the craft, prompted by necessity, the establishment of a Grand Lodge was permitted in Scotland and Ireland; and at one time, for a short period, probably Wales; although the Grand Lodge of England extended her jurisdiction over all of these provinces.

Symbolically Speaking: African Lodge #1

At the time, the Scotch, Irish, and Welsh, all had certain domestic, social and political relations which seriously forbade their identity with the Grand Lodge of England; consequently, they severally established their own jurisdictions, all of which, were cordially acknowledged and sanctioned by the Grand Lodge of the British Empire. I may be mistaken about the Welsh; but as to the others I am certain.*

And can there be a greater demand for an independent jurisdiction of Masonry among the Scotch and Irish than among the colored men of the Unite States? Certainly not. Nothing so great; as among them, it was a matter of choice, not wishing, for reasons better known to themselves, to be subordinate to the Grand Lodge of England; while with us it was forced upon our fathers by necessity, they having applied to different Grand Lodges, at different times, in different States—as in Massachusetts and Pennsylvania—for warrants to work under them, and as often spurned and rejected. What could, what should, or what would they do but establish an independent jurisdiction? If they desired to be Masons, they must have done this; indeed, not to have done it, would have been to relinquish their rights as men, and certainly be less than Masons.

[*And even now, in consequence of peculiar position and relations of the two places, there exists in the Canadas a Grand Lodge for the British Provinces of North America, extending over Nova Scotia, New Brunswick, Canada East, Canada West, and the Hudson Bay country; Sir Allen Napier Mac Nab, Knight Baronet, Right Worshipful Grand Master, with full power to grant warrants and establish Subordinate Lodges throughout British America. This Grand Lodge jurisdiction, was established not to suit the conveniency of the Most Worshipful Grand Lodge of England, but the conveniency and peculiar circumstances of the people of British North America, who demanded the right, which was readily conceded by the Most Worshipful Grand Lodge, thereby acknowledging the legality of such separate jurisdictions, all within the same political and Masonic dependencies.]

Appendix E

But we profess to be both men and Masons; and challenge the world, to try us, prove us, and disprove us, if they can.*

In 1847, after the establishment of Star Lodge No. 18, in Carlisle, Pa. a Committee of white Masons from the white Lodge in Carlisle—working under the Grand Lodge of Pennsylvania—with the Worshipful Master at its head, visited a Committee from the colored Lodge; and after a satisfactory conference, decided that they were legal and worthy ancient York Masons, but never, as they promised, made a report. The writer has met with white Masons who have been frank enough to tell him that they had been obligated not to recognize nor fellowship a colored Mason! These were Pennsylvania Masons. But he is frank to say, that while they are timid about visiting, there are hundreds who readily recognize a colored Mason wherever they find him, and consider it contrary to Masonry to act otherwise.

As the ultimum et unicum remedium—the last and only remedy—a resort has been made to prove that colored men in the United States are ineligible to Masonic privileges. And among the many who have made this attack, none stand forth with a bolder front than the honorable Jacob Brinkerhoof, of Ohio, ex-member of Congress, who, in an elaborate oration delivered before the Masonic Fraternity of that State in 1850 or '51, on an occasion of a Communication of the Grand Lodge, declared that no man who ever had been, or the descendant of any who had been a slave, could ever be a Mason. This, coming from such authority, on such an occasion was eagerly seized hold of, and published in the news journals from Baffin's Bay to Behring's Straits. It may have been

[* The late Chief Justice, John Gibson,—as Col. J. S. of this city, a high Mason, will bear witness—when Grand Master of Pennsylvania, was known to acknowledge that the colored Masons of Pennsylvania were as legal as the whites, but intimated that it would be "bad policy" so to decide publicly. Bad policy! Policy in Masonry! and wrong to do right! Cherubim shrink back from the portals of Mercy, drooping their golden pinions in sorrow; and Justice casts down her balance, and cases her sword in despair!]

sport to him, but certainly was intended as death to us; and the honorable ex-member of Congress, may yet learn, that he is much more an adept in legal than Masonic jurisprudence—much better adapted to State than Lodge government. How will this bear the test of intelligent inquiry? Let us examine.

Moses, as before mentioned, of whom the highest encomium given, is said to have been learned in all the wisdom of the Egyptians, was not only the descendant of those who had been slaves, but of slave parents; and himself, at the time that he was so taught and instructed in this WISDOM, was a slave! Will it be denied that the man who appeared before Pharaoh, and was able to perform mystically all that the wisest among the wise men of that mysteriously wise nation were capable of doing, was a Mason? Was not the man who became the Prime Minister and High Priest of Ceremonies among the wise men of Africa, a Mason? If so, will it be disputed that he was legitimately such? Are not we as Masons, and the world of mankind, to him the Egyptian slave—may I not add, the fugitive slave—indebted for a transmission to us of the Masonic Records—the Holy Bible, the Word of God? What says the honorable Jacob Brinkerhoof to this? Let a silent tongue answer the inquiry, and a listening ear give sanction to his condemnation.

But if this doctrine held good, according to the acceptation of the term slave, any one who has been deprived of his liberty, and thereby rendered politically and socially impotent, is a slave; and, consequently, Louis Kossuth, ex-Governor of Hungary, bound by the chains of Austria, in the city of Pateya, was, to all intents and purposes, according to this definition, a slave. And when he effected his escape to the United States, was (like Moses from Egypt) a fugitive slave from his masters in Austria, and, therefore, by the decree of the honorable ex-member of Congress, incapable of ever becoming a Mason.

But Governor Kossuth was made a Mason in Cincinnati, Ohio, the resident State of Mr. Brinkerhoof, and, therefore, according to him, the Governor is not a Mason at all. He has been a slave! Is the Order prepared for this? Is Mr. Brinkerhoof prepared for it? No, he is not. Then what becomes of his vaunting against colored men? For towards such he intended his declarations to have a bear-

Appendix E

ing. Let the deserved rebuke of silence answer.

But was the requisition, that men should be free born, or free at the time of making them Masons, intended, morally and logically, to apply to those who lost their liberty by any force of invasion and unjust superior power?

No such thing. In the days of King Solomon, as mentioned elsewhere, there were two classes of men denied Masonic privileges: he who lost his liberty by crime, and he who, like Esau, "sold his birthright for a mess of pottage"—a class who bartered away their liberty for a term of years, in consideration of a trifling pecuniary gain. These persons were the same in condition as the Coolies (so called) in China, and the Peons of Mexico, both of whom voluntarily surrendered their rights, at discretion, to another. These persons, and these alone, were provided against, in the wise regulations concerning freemen, as Masons.

Did they apply to any others, the patriot, sage, warrior, chieftain and hero—indeed, the only true brave and chivalric, the most worthy and best specimens of mankind—would be denied a privilege, which, it would seem, they should be the most legitimate heirs.

The North American Indians, too, have been enslaved; and yet there has not, to my knowledge, been a syllable spoken or written against their legitimacy; and they, too, are Masons, or have Masonry among them, the facts of which are frequently referred to by white Masonic orators, with pleasurable approbation and pride.

But to deny to black men the privileges of Masonry, is to deny to a child the lineage of its own parentage. From whence sprung Masonry but from Ethiopia, Egypt, and Assyria—all settled and peopled by the children of Ham?

Does any one doubt the wisdom of Ethiopia? I have but to reply, that in the days of King Solomon's renown and splendor, she was capable of sending her daughters to prove him with hard questions. If this be true, what must have been her sons! A striking and important historical fact will be brought to bear, touching the truthfulness of this matter; and, discarding all profane and general, I shall take sacred history as our guide.

Moses was quite a young man—and, consequently, could

not have been endowed with wisdom—when, seeing the maltreatment of an Israelite by the Egyptian, he slew him, burying his body in the sand; when, immediately after, the circumstance having become known to Pharaoh, he fled into Midian, a kingdom of Ethiopia.

He there sought the family of Jethro, the Ethiopian prince and priest of Midian, in whose sight, after short residence, he found favor, and married his daughter Zipporah. Zipporah, being a princess, was a shepherdess and priestess, as all priests were shepherds;* and Moses, consequently, became a shepherd, keeping the flocks of Jethro his father-in law, watching them by day and by night, on hill and in valley. Here Moses continued to dwell, until called by the message of the Lord, to sue before Pharaoh for the deliverance of Israel.

From whence could Moses—he leaving Egypt when young—have derived his wisdom, if not from Ethiopians? Is it not a reasonable, nay, the only just conclusion to infer, that his deep seated knowledge was received from them, and that his learned

[* *It is frequently referred to by modern writers, as an evidence of the reverses of circumstances in the life of man, who, with some degree of surprise, tell us that king David was once a shepherd, and attended flocks. This is no strange matter, when it is remembered that all princes in those days were priests; and all priests, as a necessary part of their education, had to be shepherds. As we may reasonably infer, there were two objects in view in the establishment of this singular mythological ordinance. The first was, that the shepherd, by continually looking out for a change in weather, and thereby gazing up to the heavens, might keep his mind more fixed upon the high calling that awaited him—administering at the altar—and thus assimilate the person of his deity; and the second, that by attending the sheep, he might be impressed with their innocence, and thereby learn the true character that should distinguish him before the gaze of the inquisitive eye. Of the seven daughters of Midian, the children of Jethro, all, as will be seen, were shepherdesses, and, consequently, all priestesses. Ex. 2 c.*]

Appendix E

wife Zipporah, who accompanied him by day and by night, through the hills and vales, contributed not a little to his acquirements? Certainly, this must have been so; for the Egyptians were a colony from Ethiopia, and derived their first training from them; the former, as the country filled up, moving and spreading farther down the Nile, until, at length, becoming very numerous, they separated the kingdom, establishing an independent nation, occupying the delta at the mouths of the river.

Where could there a place, so appropriate be found, for the study of those mysteries as upon the highest hills and in the deepest valleys? Is it not thus that the mysteries originated, the habits of the shepherds with their flocks, leading them to the hills and valleys?

It was also in Ethiopia where God appeared to Moses in a burning bush; and here where he told him, "Put off thy shoes from off thy feet; for the place whereon thou standeth is holy ground." And this "holy ground" was in Ethiopia or Midian, the true ancient Africa. Truly, if the African race have no legitimate claims to Masonry, then is it illegitimate to all the rest of mankind.

Upon this topic I shall not farther descant, as I believe it is a settled and acknowledged fact, conceded by all intelligent writers and speakers, that to Africa is the world indebted for its knowledge of the mysteries of Ancient Freemasonry. Had Moses, nor the Israelites, never lived in Africa, the mysteries of the wise men of the East had never been handed down to us.

Was it not Africa that gave birth to Euclid, the master geometrician of the world? And was it not in consequence of a twenty-five years' residence in Africa that the great Pythagorus was enabled to discover that key problem in geometry—the forty-seventh problem of Euclid—without which Masonry would be incomplete? Must I hesitate to tell the world that, as applied to Masonry, the word—Eureka—was first exclaimed in Africa? But—there! I have revealed the Masonic secret, and must stop!

Masons, Brethren, Companions and Sir Knights, hoping that for this disclosure, by a slip of the tongue, you will forgive me—as I may have made the world much wiser—I now commit you and our cause into the care and keeping of the Grand Master of the Universe.

Symbolically Speaking: African Lodge #1

APPENDIX F

The African Lodge, an Oration:
Delivered Before the Grand Master, Wardens, and Brethren of the Most Ancient and Venerable Lodge of African Masons
(as found in *The Columbian Magazine,* for August 1788. Philadelphia, PA)

ADVERTISEMENT—SOME Readers, perhaps, may need to be informed, that in a certain metropolis, on this continent, there is a fraternity of Negroes, who are formed into a Lodge. They celebrate festivals, walk in processions, and wear aprons: but, it is said, are not readily acknowledged as masons by their white brethren. Their rights and claims are vindicated in this oration, which was spoken in the Mandingo language, at a late meeting of their lodge, by a very learned brother, and is now translated into English doggerel by a gentleman, formerly concerned in the African commerce, who is well versed in that ancient, musical, and sonorous language, but is afraid that he has not been able to express all its beauties in our modern, mixed and imperfect dialect.

SCENE. — A long room, with a table in the midst, elevated on six voluted columns. The grand master, adorned with the jewels of his order, at the upper end, under an arch, painted with all the colours of the rainbow. The wardens on each side with ivory wands. Before the grand master on the table, a model of an Egyptian pyramid in ivory. On one side of the arch, a representation of the antediluvian city built by Cain, and on the other of Noah's Ark in basso-relievo. At the lower end of the table a model of the ruined tower of Babel, in porcelain. The fraternity ranged on each side of the table according to their respective degrees. Trowels, levels, plumb-lines, bottles, bowls, tankards, and other necessary implements of the craft. The orator mounted on a pedestal at the lower end of the table. The grand master strikes with his mallet on the trestle-board, and the orator begins.

MY sable friends, and brethren dear,
To my instruction lend your ear.
While from the purest source I trace,
The ancient story of our race;
And shew by strong and cogent reasons
Our claim to be accepted masons.
I know the vulgar herd of whites
Deny our ancient sacred rights,
And proudly to themselves confine
The honors of the rule and line;
But I intend, before I've done,
To make it clear as noon-day sun,
That ours, tho' bitterly be-curst,
Is justly reckon'd *lodge the first.*
 IMPRIMIS, then, I lay it down,
A sacred truth, which all must own.
That he who reckons farthest back,
(In case he does not miss the track),
Has the most righteous claim to be,
The foremost in antiquity.
This is my major proposition;
Then comes the minor in transition.
As thus—by universal fame
We blacks are call'd *"the seed of CAIN,"*
Because on him a mark was set,
As black as ebony or jet;

Symbolically Speaking: African Lodge #1

A mark indelible no doubt,
For water could not wash it out.
Now it is clear from text of Moses,
(Which every brotherhood supposes
The best of books) that this said Cain
Built the FIRST city*[1] —Ergo, then
This ground we safely rest the case on,
That brother Cain was the first mason.

   T'invalidate our plea from hence,
I know they make a shrewd pretence,
That Adam knew the art and taught it;
But Moses nothing says about it.
Adam, indeed, was somewhat knowing
And fairly catch'd the art of sewing;
A taylor then he might be reckon'd;
But not a mason first nor second,
And the first lodge however odd,
Was held within the land of Nod.
There all the arts and sciences,
Were cultivated with success.
Music was taught by brother Jubal
And smithery by brother Tubal.
And in a word to end the story
Nod was of arts the lab'ratory.

   Brethren 'tis best whene'er we can
Our argument to fairly scan;
And where'tis short to give it length'ning.
Or where'tis weak to give it strength'ning;
Thus, haycock like, we trim it round,
And make it fairly stand its ground.

   There is, I know, a grand objection
Against this stating of the question.
Because this self-same Moses says,
It rain'd for forty nights and days,
Till ev'ry living thing was drown'd
Both in the air and on the ground;
Save those which Noah did embark
On board the good ship call'd,
THE ARK.
Noah did not of Cain proceed,
But sprang from Seth's more favour'd breed;
And none but Noah's sons and daughters
Escaped this worst of all disasters.
Therefore they hastily conclude,
As Cain's seed perish'd in the flood,
That none but white folks kept the art,
Which Noah did to them impart.

   Thus far th'objectors; but I trow,
Their vain presumption we'll o'erthrow.
For not to have recourse to names,
O! Abbe Raynal or Lord Kaimes,
Or others, who have boldly said
Men did not all come from one head;
But other pairs were made beside
Our father Adam and his bride;
Or other folks were fav'd as well
As Noah in his wooden cell;
Setting aside these loose conjectures,
As quite unworthy such grave lectures;
I plump deny there's any force
In th' argument, to say no worse.
For who the deuce has e'er pretended,
That masons, as such are descended
In ordinary course of nature,
Like pumpkin, melon, or potatoe?
What author ever has related,
That mason blood is propagated?
If not,—then surely we may say,
Tho' Cain's seed all were wash'd away,
A sooty lodge might still be found
On Noah's as on Adam's ground.
And who can this belief refuse,
That Ham stood up in Cain's old shoes?
Was cursed Cain of blacks the first?
And was not Ham as sorely curst?
"Servant of servants," was his doom
And turn'd adrift from house and home,
He strait to'fric bent his way,
And pitch'd his tent 'mong beasts of prey;
The plains of Nile he first subdu'd,
And reign'd supreme o'er all his brood.
There mason's art reviv'd as soon,
Or sooner than at Babylon.

---

*1 *Thus far we've safely got I think, so brothers hand about the drink. Here's to the mem'ry of old* CAIN! *Hem, ha.* —*I'll now set off again.*

Appendix F

There cities, pyramids, and tow'rs
Surpassing all the fabled bowr's
Of Adam's ancient paradise,
Or works of fam'd Semiramis,
Have stood the shocks of hary time,
To th' honor of their bricks and lime.
Come brothers toss about the pot;
The weather's surely very hot:
Besides there's something in this ale
That wonderfully helps my tale.
And in my sober way of thinking
Masons ne'er work less for drinking.
Here's to old HAM *our second founder,*
There never was a mason sounder
In wind and limb.—But to proceed
In tracing our Masonic creed.
   Our pert objectors make a plea,
That masons must be always free.
No slaves, said they, are e'er allow'd
To rank among the apron'd crowd'
Therefore the sooty sons of Ham
Are ever barr'd the hallow'd name.
   But, gentlemen, you're all mistaken,
As certainly as eggs are bacon.
For we can prove it firm and true,
That slaves have wrought as well as you.
Here I again call Moses aid,
Who in his Pentateuch[2]* has said,
That Jacob's seed in Egypt's land,
When under Phar'oh's galling hand,
To slav'ry doom'd and hard oppress'd.
With bitter bondage, void of rest,
Did work in brick, and lime, and mortar,
Fetch'd their own straw, and brick, and water.
And built up cities known in story,
Renown'd for treasures and for glory.
   From this account we clearly see
Men may be masons tho' not free;
And masonry will never thrive
Unless its tools be "op'rative,"
For prithee tell me, why the deuce
Should instruments be out of use?
Or why should masons selves lie still,
And to the lodge confine their skill?
Nor Ever benefit their neighbours,
By all their boasted arts and labours?
Why should those speculative drones
Claim the sole rights of Hiram's sons,
Who never move a tool to work
Unless, perhaps, their knife and fork?
I understand not such pretences,
The men are surely void of senses:
Workmen there must be, or I'm certain,
The trade cannot be worth a farthing.
   Come, brothers push about the cann,
For work and drink go hand in hand.
It ought to be a rule I think,
"He that won't work shall never drink."
I'll move to have this resolution
An article in our constitution.
Here's to the right old standard hive
Of busy masons "operative."
   But to the arg'ment from the cup,
'Tis time that I should sum it up.
   You've heard, this noble art began
As far back as the days of Cain.
In the *black* lodge of ancient Nod
Was taught the science of the Hod.
And in the post-diluvian time
This art so "beauteous and sublime,"
Reviv'd in the *black* lodge of Ham;
Where students from all quarters came,
To hear the scientific lecture,
And learn the trade of architecture.
Besides it must not be forgot
That free or slave, it matters not;
For masons labour has been wrought
By those who buy and those who are bought.
We then conclude for weighty reasons
That SLAVES may be ACCEPTED MASONS.
   But *we* have need of no such plea,
Thanks to our country WE ARE FREE.
Slav'ry that curse, that false pretence
By government is banish'd hence.
No slaves in durance here are bound
Save those on Castle William's ground;
But "free and equal" are the terms

---
*   Exodus 1.

Symbolically Speaking: African Lodge #1

By which we hold our lives and farms.
White, brown, and black, and ev'ry shade
Have equal "rights" to them convey'd.
   Besides, we see our rightful claim
Acknowledg'd by great EFFINGHAM,
That noble patriot who disdain'd
To have his well-earn'd laurels stain'd,
By fighting with his brother freemen
Columbia's hardy sons and yeomen.
With noble fortitude of mind
When George commanded, he resign'd;
Nor to America would go,
To gather fame with Gage and Howe;
Nor to the world shew British follies,
Like John Burgoyne and Charles Cornwallis.
From him our charter we derive,
Masons from Afric, operative.
The point being handled thus at large,
I'll close it briefly with a charge.
   We all agree the moral part
Of this sublime, masonic art,
Is to be faithful, just, and kind,
And serve with freedom all mankind.
Let ev'ry one then live by reason
And from the halter keep his weazon.
Let ev'ry man his living get,
By his own art, and toil, and sweat.
Seek not to over-reach your neighbour,
Nor reap the fruit of other's labour.
Keep within compass, act the square,
And rule your lines out full and fair.
Remember for what end you're made,
And never get above your trade.
Be not the drone, nor act the sloven;
But lay a hearth, or mend an oven;
Do small jobs well—and then you'll rise,
In art and knowledge grow more wise;
And thus in time you'll build a tow'r,
Which storm or earthquake can't devour;
Which shall not like proud Babel fall,
But pyramid-like firm, and tall,
Shall lift its head above the spheres,
And stand its ground to endless years.
   GRAND MASTER.
   BRETH'REN, our worthy friend has ended,
The noble task that he intended.
Now let us push the liquor round,
And wash the learned lecture down;
For every true masonic foul,
Dilutes his knowledge in the bowl.

SONG, BY THE WHOLE BROTHERHOOD.

LET Apollo here preside,
Jolly Bacchus by his side;
Sermons, charges, and orations,
Preface all our computations.
Let's be merry while we're wise,
Banish dulness from our eyes,
Fill your hearts with knowledge fine,
And our skins with rosy wine;
Thus we learn the mystic art,
Grace the head, and warm the heart.

Index

Symbols

1845 Baltimore, Maryland Convention xi

A

Ab 71, 72, 79, 81, 82
ADHD 131
Adinkra 126
Afa 84
Afikpo 52
African Grand Lodge viii, x, xi, xii, 96, 196, 198
African Grand Lodge of Boston viii
African Lodge #1 2, vii, xiii, xvi, xvii, xix, 21, 38, 40, 69, 76, 96, 157
African Lodge No. 459 ix, x, xi, xii
   African Lodge No. 459 of Philadelphia x
African Shaman 64
Ain 67, 70
Ain Soph 67, 70
Ain Soph Ur 67
Akan 57
Akom 57
Amani 85
A.M.E. Church xvi
Amen 55, 67, 69, 70, 71, 78, 84, 85, 86, 182, 183
Amen, Ra Un Nefer 55, 69, 71, 86
Amun. *See* Amen
An Afrocentric Guide To A Spiritual Union 55
Anansi the Spider 28
anxieties 118
archetypes 23
Armed Forces 129
Asclepius. *See* Imhotep
astrology 130
atoms
   electrons 67
   neutrons 67
   protons 67
Auditing. *See* Scientology
Ausar 57, 70, 73, 76, 77
Ausar Auset Society 57
Auset 57, 76, 77, 104, 107

B

Ba 71, 72, 83
baby Albert 124
Bah'ai services 57
Bakhtiar, Lahleh
  Spiritual Chivalry, God's Will Be Done 117
balance 61, 95, 117, 118, 119, 126, 201
Banneker, Benjamin xviii
Banneker City. *See* Washington, DC
Bantu 66, 70
Baptist viii, 58, 64, 159, 169, 185, 198
baptized 63
Batt, Sergeant John vii
Bellman, Beryl
  The Language of Secrecy 74
Benin 126
Best, Peter vii
Bhagavad Gita 23
bioluminescence 36
births 50, 52
Blue Lodge 63
Book of Coming Into the Light. *See* Pert Em Heru
Book of Genesis 154
Book of Matthew 29
Boston, Massachusetts vii, viii, 196
Boukman, Dutty 61
Brotherly Love Lodge No. 55 ix
Bufform, Duff vii
Bureau of Engraving xiv
Burkino Faso 75
Busama 74

C

Canton, John vii
Carver, George Washington xvii, 22, 31, 139
Castle William vii
Catholicism 23, 64
Catholic Mass 57
cedis 147, 148
Celestial Lodge No. 4 xii
Center for Substance Abuse Prevention (CSAP) 97
Chinese 40, 133
Christianity 64, 74, 179, 183
church 21, 47, 57, 58, 164, 169, 172, 192

Index

Church Mothers 58
collective unconscious 23
Continental Congress xiv
cosmogony 68, 69, 79
cosmology 68, 69, 70
Council of Sir Knights xi
cowrie shells 130

D

Dagbara 75
dalasi 147
Dalton, Thomas xi
Declaration of Independence ix, x, xi
de Hoyos, Arturo
   The Scottish Rite Ritual Monitor and Guide 62
Delany, Martin R. 185
Deredomie, C.A. xi
Dervish 65
Dilogun 84
din 72, 73
Diop, Cheikh Ante 69
divination 28, 64, 130, 149
Divine 23, 40, 72, 76, 77
DNA 68
Dogon 35
Dominican Republic 64
dowry 56, 57
DuHart, Past Master Rufus 95
Dummo Breathing 80, 136

E

East Africa 66
East Indians 133
Egbe 57
Egypt xvi, 23, 68, 76, 95, 101, 130, 141, 172, 175, 176, 188, 189, 202, 203, 204
Egyptian xvi, 21, 34, 71, 78, 95, 101, 105, 188, 191, 202, 204
Egyptian Room 95, 101
Ellicott, Andrew xviii
Emanuel (God with Us) 148
empathic 132, 133, 136
enemy of Ra 133
energy healers 125
Enkhamit, Hehi Metu Ra
   African Names 53

enslavement xvii, 36, 64, 90, 129
Eshaka 149
esoteric 23
ESP 44, 45
  extra-sensory perception 44
Ethiopia 39, 76, 168, 172, 188, 189, 203, 204, 205
etiology 126
European xi, xiii, xvii, xix, 27, 52, 56, 64, 74
Ewe 63, 75, 143, 149

F

fetish 66
Fisk University 140, 153
flooding techniques 118
Fort Independence. *See* Castle William
fortuna 116
Founding Fifteen 38, 39, 96
Frederic, Henry - Duke of Cumberland ix
Freeman, Peter vii
French Jesuit 75
French military 61
Freud, Sigmund xvi, xvii, 23, 133
funerals 50

G

Gambia 57, 63, 64, 75, 143, 147, 149
Gaul, George xi
Geb 70
geometry xiii, 68, 205
Ghana 63, 75, 126, 143, 147, 148, 152
  Kumasi 149
  Pokuase 149
Gordy, Berry
  The Last Dragon 128
gradual desensitization 118
Grand Lodge of England vii, viii, ix, x, xii, xix, 38, 96, 185, 186, 196, 199, 200
Grand Lodge of Massachusetts viii, xi, xii, 195
Grand Lodge of Pennsylvania 95, 101, 197, 198, 199, 201
Grand Lodge of Scotland ix, 65
  Year Book of 1967 65
Greek 39, 40, 113, 119, 122, 189
Greek letter organizations 40

Index

H

Haiti 61, 64
Hajj 63
Hall, Prince 3, vii, viii, ix, x, xi, xii, xv, xvi, xvii, 22, 38, 39, 40, 43, 64, 88, 96, 98, 156, 157, 159, 167, 169, 185
Hancock, John ix
harmonics 46
Hebrew xvi, xvii, 23, 39, 70, 93
hekau 84
hematite 142
Her Bak 34, 79, 141
herbal remedies 64
Her-Em-Akhet 104, 105
Hermetic 30
Heru 21, 23, 76, 77, 78, 101, 102, 107, 150
Heru Bedhet 101, 102, 107
High Priest 61, 202
Hilton, John T. viii, xi, 196
hip hop 47, 143
Hippocratic Oath 120, 122
Hiram Abiff 40
Hiram Lodge No. 3 x
Holy Bible 23, 202
Holy Quran 23
Holy Spirit 58
House of the Temple 104, 106, 107
Howard, Fortin vii
Howe, James H. xi
human eye
  cornea 24
  iris 24
  lens 24, 92, 94, 156
  retina 24
  sclera 24
Hurricane Katrina 26

I

I Ching 61, 84
Ifa 23, 28, 57, 63, 70, 75, 84
Imam 58
Imhotep 120
indiscriminate imitation 78, 79
indwelling intelligence 84, 85
initiation 3, 21, 25, 27, 28, 30, 32, 37, 40, 41, 44, 63, 65, 70, 71, 73, 74, 75, 76, 77,

78, 79, 80, 81, 82, 83, 84, 85, 86, 91, 95, 111, 112, 116, 119, 120, 124, 125, 127, 128, 133, 134, 136, 138, 141, 143, 148, 149, 150, 152, 154, 155
interdependency 82
Isis. *See* Auset
Islamic Jumu'ah 57
ISLIP Airport 153
Ivory Coast 147

J

James, George G. M.
  Stolen Legacy 111
  ten virtues 119, 151
Japanese 133
Jesus 22, 29, 31, 141, 150, 170, 178, 181
Joker 134
Jolla 61, 63, 75, 149
Jonbus, Cyrus vii
Jordan River 63
Juggernaut 136
juju 61, 64
Jung, Carl G. xvii, 23

K

Kabbalah 23, 70
Kemet 23, 67, 68, 70, 71, 76, 119
Kemetic Priest 63
Kenya 76
Kether 70
King James Bible 29
Ki-Swahili 66
Knights of Malta xi
Knights of St. John of Jerusalem xi
Kundalini 80
Kunjufu, Jawanza 74

L

Lago Niassa 66. *See* Lake Nyasa
Lake Malawi 66. *See* Lake Nyasa
Lake Nyasa 66
Laurel Lodge No. 4 x
Law of Analogy 30, 36
Law of Complements 33
L' enfant, Pierre Charles xviii
Lewis, Walker xi

Index

Lew, Peter xi
life force 67, 80, 102, 118
   Chi 133, 142
   Prana 133
   Qi 80, 133, 136, 142
locus of control 94, 95, 96
Lodge No. 441 vii
Long Island, NYC 153
Lord Howard, Earl of Effingham ix
L'Ouverture, Toussaint 61
love 54, 55, 76, 137, 140, 159, 160, 162, 165, 167, 169, 170, 171, 174, 178, 181, 182
lucidity 46
Lwa 23

M

Maafa 90, 93
Maat 25, 30, 73, 119
MacPherson, J. Harvey
   Antient Landmarks and Daily Advance 65
Malawi 66
Malkuth 70
Mama Zandi 153
MamiWata 149
mantra 84, 148
Marrant, John 159, 169
Marriage 53
Master Mason 139, 194
Matrix, The 33, 90, 91
meditation 31, 80, 85, 162
method of loci 30
Metu Neter (oracle) 84
Metu Neter Vol. 1 (book) 69, 71
Middleton, George xi
minister 58
miracles 58
Moody, Sampton H. xi
Moody, William - Worshipful Master ix
moor xv
Morris, Robert xiv, xv, 100
Moses xvi, 23, 172, 176, 188, 193, 202, 203, 204, 205
mosque 58
Most Worshipful Grand Lodge of Scotland ix
Mozambique 66
Mt. Kilimanjaro 66

Mud Masons of Mali 108
music xii, 46, 47, 49, 134
Muslim 63, 149
Mystery Schools 23, 69
mystical 51, 62, 74, 149, 154

N

Naddi Madi Shudi 80
Narby, Jeremy
   The Cosmic Serpent (book) 68
Neter 34, 35, 69, 71, 84, 86, 96, 105, 118, 119
Neter-t 118
Neuroanatomy 28
New Guinea 74
New York African Band xii
Ngonde 66
Nigeria 28, 64
Nilotic 66
Nkonde 66
nous 113, 114
NTR 23, 70
Ntu 70
Nu 70
Nubian 66
Nyanseba 66

O

Obatala 70
Obelisk. *See* Tekhen
Objective realm 69, 70
occult 23, 31
ODD 131
Odu Ifa 23, 28
Olokun 63, 75
Omnipotent 71, 194
Omnipresent 67, 71
omniscience 30
Omniscient 71
operative xv, xvi
oppression 96, 151, 167
oracle systems 52, 84
Order of the Eastern Star xvi
organ systems
   circulatory system 24

digestive system 24
nervous system 24, 123
reproductive system 24
skeletal system 24
Orisha 23, 64
Osiris. *See* Ausar
Ottenberg, Simon
   Boyhood Rituals in an African Society, An Interpretation 51

P

Palestine 65
paradigm xv, 91, 98, 151, 156
Pare Mountains 66
past-life regression 125
Pentecostal 57
permanent witness 84
Pert Em Heru 23, 78, 102
phobias 118
photographic memory xviii
Pike, Albert
   Morals and Dogma 62
plantation 64
Plumb line 109
Poro society 73
Pranic Healing 142
preacher 58, 72
Prince Hall Freemasonry vii, ix, xii, xv, 88, 98, 156
Prince Hall Grand Lodge xii
Prince, Nero xi
profane 28, 31, 33, 37, 43, 74, 203
Protestant 64
psychoanalysts 125
Puat Neteru 23
Puerto Rico 64
pyramids xiii, 44, 102
Pyramid Texts 76

Q

Qi Gong 80, 136, 142

R

Ra 53, 55, 69, 71, 80, 86, 95, 103, 118, 133
racism xvii, 38, 96
Rastafarian 142

Rayden, Prince vii
Redemption Lodge No. 24 xii
Rees, Prince vii
Reiki 80
Revolutionary War vii, viii, x, xiv
Rhode Island American Newspaper xi
Rising Sons of St. Johns Lodge No. 3 xii
rites of passage 51, 54, 73, 74, 76, 77, 78, 86, 87, 88, 89, 91, 92, 93, 94, 95, 96, 97, 98
ritual xvi, 21, 35, 36, 37, 40, 41, 43, 44, 45, 46, 47, 48, 49, 50, 51, 52, 53, 55, 57, 58, 59, 60, 61, 62, 63, 64, 93
romance 54
Roundtree, Alton G. xii
Rowe, John vii

S

sages 68, 72, 116
Sahu 71, 72, 79, 81
St. John's #3 (Cincinnati) 3, 95
St. John's African Lodge xi
St. John's Day vii
St. John's Royal Arch Chapter xi
Saints 23, 64
Sakhmet 118
Sanderson, Thomas vii, viii
Sanders, Past Master Jerome 95
Sande society 74
Sankofa 126
Santeria 64
Scales of Maat 118
Schwaller de Lubicz, Isha 34, 79, 84, 141
scientific method, the 44
Scientology 124
Scota, Queen of the Scots xvi
Scotland ix, xvi, 199
Scott, Captain James ix
Scottish Rite 62, 63
Scranton, Laird 69
secret societies 23, 27
self-knowledge xvi
Senegal 147
  Dakar 147
Sephiroth 70, 131
Set 76, 77

Index

Shaolin Master Killer. *See* The 36 Chambers of Shaolin
Shu 34
sign language 35
Sirius 35
Skinner, B. F.
  Beyond Freedom and Dignity (book) 151
slavery vii, 167, 168, 180, 193
Slinger, Bueston vii
smart phones 47
Smith, Boston vii, viii
Smithsonian Museum of Natural History 108
Some', Malidoma 64, 75, 112
  Of Water and the Spirit (book) 75, 112, 149
  Ritual (book) 64
sonogram 130
Speain, Cato vii
speculative xv, 108
Sphinx. *See* Her-Em-Akhet
spiritual cultivation 3, 40, 74, 80, 119, 120
spirituality 38, 40, 67
Spiritual Midwifery (book) 53
Steiner, Rudolf 31
step-pyramid 106
subatomic particles 68
Subjective realm 69, 70
Sudan 76
Supreme Being 21, 24, 36, 67, 159, 192
symbolist xv
synthesis 82
Syrian 65

T

Tai Chi 142
Tantric 80, 142
Tanzania 66
Taoist 112
Tefnut 34
Tehuti 118, 119
Tekhen 110
temperament 130, 136
temple 47, 58, 60, 141, 164, 176, 177, 188, 190, 191, 192, 193
temples xiii, 76, 177, 178
Temples, Placid
  Bantu Philosophy 74

Tesla, Nikola xvii
The 36 Chambers of Shaolin 85
The Creators 116
The Farm 52
The Gods Must Be Crazy (movie) 126
The Intelligences 113
The Matrix 33, 90, 91
The Mortals 111
The Secret Life of Plants 31
The Sons of Light 116
thurible 58
Tiber, Benjamin vii
Tilley, Richard vii
Ting 61
Tinga Tinga 29
Torah 23
trance 57, 61, 62, 78, 80, 85, 112
tree of life 41, 70
trotro 148
Trowel 109
T'Shaka, Oba 69
Tupac 146
two dollar bill xiv, 100

U

Uganda 68, 76
Union Lodge No. 2 xii
Union Lodge No. 3 x
Union Station 106
United States 2, 5, xi, 31, 38, 54, 61, 75, 97, 149, 185, 194, 195, 196, 197, 201, 202
Universal Men and Women 156
U.S. Senator xiv

V

Van Sertima, Ivan 69
vegetarian 142
veil xv, xvii, 27, 28, 182
Vibe Magazine 146
vibration 46
visualization 79, 89, 116
Vodoun 23
von Sebottendorff, Baron Rudolf
   Secret Practices of the Sufi Freemasons: The Islamic teachings at the heart of Alchemy 65

W

Waldorf education 31
Wanyakyusa 66
Washington, DC xviii
Washington Monument 110
Washington, President George xvii
weddings 50, 54
Will 24, 36, 67, 73, 80, 118, 149, 202
Winbush, Dr. Raymond A.
  The Warrior Method (book) 73
winged sundisk. *See* Heru Bedhet
wisdom xiii, 22, 23, 25, 26, 28, 29, 30, 31, 32, 40, 53, 62, 63, 68, 84, 92, 116, 119, 122, 125, 139, 150, 174, 176, 177, 179, 181, 182, 188, 189, 190, 191, 194, 202, 203, 204
worldview
  axiology 39, 41, 90, 156
  epistemology 39, 41, 90, 156
  ontology 39, 40, 41, 90, 156
Worshipful Master vii, ix, xi, 101, 103, 201

Y

yoga xiii
Yoga 80, 142
Yoruba 28, 70

Z

zodiac 137
Zuesse, Evan
  Ritual Cosmos 43

Symbolically Speaking: African Lodge #1

Index

Other Mind on the Matter Publications

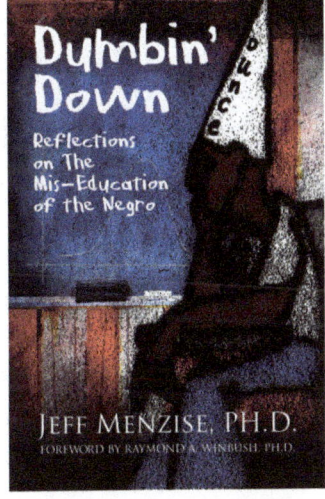

Coming Soon...
African Heritage Playing Card
Series: Dogon De-Lights
and
Kemetic Kulture

www.ingramcontent.com/pod-product-compliance
Lightning Source LLC
Chambersburg PA
CBHW051916160426
43198CB00012B/1915